Loving them FROM A Distance

DARLEEN TURNER

Quantum Discovery
A LITERARY AGENCY

ISBN
978-1-960197-24-5 (Paperback)
978-1-960197-25-2 (eBook)
978-1-960197-23-8 (Hardcover)

LOVING THEM FROM A DISTANCE

Kate and her mother were inseparable. Kate and Emma were the best of friends, and Kate had always hoped that one day she would have a daughter and they too would have that kind of friendship.

From the time they laid her daughter Angel in her arms, Kate was love struck and no one took first priority in her life from then on. As Emma and Kate were, so were Kate and Angel, inseparable.

Kate and Angel face terrible traumas in their life with the death of Angel's father, Ben, and her baby brother and then Grandma, but they got through them because of their love for each other.

Angel dating older men came between her and her mother. The unspeakable moment happens and Angel moves out leaving with harsh words that tore her mother's world and heart apart. Kate mourns for her daughter who has had no contact with her mother since he took her away.

Kate feels like she has died from the day her daughter left. It takes its toll on Kate's new marriage.

After years of no communication from Angel, Kate decides that she has mourned her daughter long enough and she was going to go find her and mend their broken hearts. It is a tough road she goes down, and she finds her daughter. She also finds out that her daughter is very ill and is in need of her help, but they get reunited in the end just to say good-bye.

ACKNOWLEDGMENTS

Thank you to my husband for sharing in this dream and in helping make it come one step closer.

Thank you to all my family who continue to provide me with stories to write. Every day each one of you help put life into my stories in some small way. The tears and the laughter and the heartaches that we have shared through the years make our memories and life worthwhile.

Thank you to *you* my fans; without you, there would not be the third. I hope you all read and enjoy the story as much as I have enjoyed writing it.

Sincerely, Darleen Turner

turnerdarleen1@gmail.com

ONE

It is plus-thirty day today, and I'm out walking in the park. Not seeing too much of what is going on around me as my mind is so consumed with thinking of ways of getting closer. To be able to get almost close enough to touch her. Just so I could smell her perfume. Every time I smell her perfume on someone else, it makes me look around for her. My heart quickens with the thought that just maybe she is close by. Then it is always the same letdown when you know all the searching for her has come to the end and you no longer can smell her perfume it has been carried away into the breeze.

There are so many women out there with her build and hair color that I'm constantly looking and double looking. I spend most of my days watching and praying that just maybe one of them will be her.

It has been three years since I've seen the face of my Angel or heard the sweet melody of her voice. With each day that passes, a little more of me dies. Every day I make a trip to the post office in hopes that perhaps she has dropped me a line. The post office has always been one place I would stay away from—I have always dreaded going there—and now each morning, I can't wait to get there. Whenever the phone rings, I stand and stare at it to see whose number it might be. Most of the time, I don't answer it because I'm so disappointed when I see that it's not her calling.

Up until now, I have walked around in limbo since that awful day she left.

It was Mother's Day weekend. There was no "happy Mother's Day" from her or even a good-bye. She was just gone.

This hasn't stopped me from buying her a Christmas present each year that I put under the tree just in case she comes home Christmas Eve.

I would never want her to think for one minute that I have forgotten her or quit loving her. I also buy her a special card and birthday present. Her birthday is the third of January. This makes for a double letdown when both occasions go by and I haven't heard from her. The only good thing about both of them being so close together is that the severe pain is all over at one time. The dull ache returns and takes over my life.

I always felt that we had a very special relationship and knew each other inside and out. All the dreams of the future that we had talked about over and over have all since gone with her. Not being able to share in any of them until now has been tearing the heart right out of me.

For me to go on, I am going to have to find her so I can put my mind at ease and mend a broken heart.

What changes have come into her life? What has she become? These are all unanswered questions that I want answers to.

When you really think about it, time has gone by fast. For my heart, it has come to a standstill, and I know now that I must push on and do what I can to find her.

I have known of the last place she was working, and I always stayed away. I did not want to cause a scene, nor did I want to embarrass her or myself.

Until now I have left it in God's hands, and every night, I prayed that he would help her find her way back to me. I really hoped it would be while I was still in good health and still had my mind. Going this way, I won't have my mind much longer and no one can stay in good health when you are consumed with so much grief, so I have decided to take action. I have been thinking about this for some time now and making some plans on how I was going to go about this. With her living out of town, it will be easier to put my plans into action.

I have wondered if she ever looks for me. While she is walking down the street or even in her place of work. Does she ever see someone who might make her think of me? Does she pass by someone who wears the same perfume as I do? Does it make it hard for her to breathe? Does it choke her up to the point she thinks she's going to pass out right there on the spot? Does she get the terrible pain in the chest that comes after the disappointment of not spotting me in the crowd? Does she even think about those last words she spoke to me as she went out the door that

Mother's Day? I think of them often and wonder how anyone could say such a cruel thing to someone who loves her unconditionally.

At this time, I'm walking down Main Street, and I've decided to go ahead with my plans. First on my list is to find a hair shop that has an opening. I'm afraid that if I wait and make an appointment, I would end up backing out. This way I will just walk in, and before I know it, it would be done.

It was beginning to look like it was going to be a no-go today. Every shop I went into, they were booked up for days. They tell me it's because of all the weddings. I guess it is that time of year. The last shop that I entered, they had room for me.

"Good morning, dear."

"Good morning. May I help you?"

"Yes, dear, I would like to have a makeover done. Do you do that here?"

"Just what were you thinking of, madam?"

"I want you to do something that will make me feel younger and look it."

"Oh! It's that time, is it?"

I wondered what she meant at first.

"You need a little lift in your life, do you?"

"Yes! I sure do. I've gotten myself in a slump, and it's time to get out."

"Then come with me, and I will see what all we can do for you."

"Thank you." Following her to the back, I saw several women in there doing Lord-only-knows-what to themselves. But probably not one of them was doing it for the same reason as I was. Once the girl had shampooed my hair, I got seated so the real chore could begin.

"Now do you have any plans? Do you need a book to look at?"

I took a couple of minutes and thought about it. "You know what? I am giving you the reins. This will be your chance to do whatever you think I need. After all, if it doesn't work, I can always have it changed to something I would want. How does that sound to you?"

"Let me get this straight! You want me to make the choices?"

"Yes, I do. You have taken training in this, and I know you are taught to look at people and be able to put the right cut and color together to get what you want." I wasn't going to tell her that I am also a hairdresser, but I just haven't had to work for years.

"Oh, but your hair is so long and is a beautiful white. Do you know what people pay to get their hair this color?"

"Yes, dear, I do. Like I said, I need a big change in my life. I don't want to wear it up in a bun anymore. I would also love to have some color for a change."

"Are you really sure about this, madam?"

"YES, dear, I am! Now if you don't want to do it, maybe one of your coworkers will."

"OH! Madam, I will, and I know just what I will give you."

"Then what are we waiting for? Let's do it."

"You will be here for a while."

"That's fine with me. I have nothing but time."

My husband was used to me just coming and going. I'm darn sure he knew that I left as soon as he had left for work. I didn't always get home before him. He would come and find me sitting in the mall or a park watching people. He never asked. He didn't have to; he knew why I would be there. He would just come along and sit down beside me and wrap his arms around me and say, "Are you ready to come home yet?" He used to ask me if I thought this was healthy for me. I would just tell him, "Why? I'm just on an outing." He nods his head and, taking my hand, says to me, "Come on, babe, I will buy you a coffee." So we go for our coffee before we go to our home of silence.

Our marriage has paid the price. She consumes my every thought. I go about and do what has to be done on a daily basis as far as housekeeping goes. My husband is on the back burner, and I have tried so many times to change how I am, but something will always take me back to thinking of her. When she first left, I spent most of my days crying and talking with my husband, but it got to where it was all negative talk and it started to make me feel worse. I didn't need to hear any more negative talk. I needed to see her. I need to be able to wrap my arms around her and tell her how special she is to me and how much I love her.

I don't think my husband felt the same as she is his stepdaughter. He has been a very good stepfather to her. He always went the extra mile for her no questions asked.

The morning she left our house, the way she did and the things she said also hurt him. He also knows that as a mother, I would put my life on the line for her.

The young girl working with me didn't seem to know what she was doing; at first, she made me a little nervous. I was thinking maybe I don't want her cutting my hair. When she took the first, cut our eyes met in the mirror. I just smiled.

"See, that wasn't so hard now, was it?"

"No, madam." She carried on until I had a cut that was shorter in the back then the front. Yet it was full of body.

"I want to put a perm in it, and it will be very easy for you to do every day."

"I don't want an old fuzzy perm."

"No, madam, it will be tighter in the back, but the front and sides will only give you a very loose curl."

"What about a color?"

"Oʜ yes, madam. But not until after I have permed it. The perm would strip some of your color out, and we don't want that."

"Yes, madam." Jessie was her name, and she did as she said and done the perm. I looked at what she was mixing up.

"That's really red."

"Yes, madam, but I want to also do foiling as well which will bring this color to more of a strawberry blonde when I'm finished."

"Oʜ, all right, that sounds very delightful."

"It won't be such a drastic change if we do it this way seeing how your hair is so white. This will also go with your skin color better than one solid color."

Sitting there watching her put the foil on my hair, I got to thinking about how old she was. She was small and very dark. I could tell by her language she wasn't from here.

"Jessie, how old are you?"

"I'm twenty-three, madam."

"Were you born here in Canada?"

"No, madam." That is where she left it. I figured if she wanted me to know where she was from, she would have offered the information without me having to ask. Seeing how she didn't, I wouldn't push it. She did seem to be a very private person. I could hear the other girls talking away to the women they were working on, but not Jessie; she hardly said anything at all.

I wonder if my daughter is like Jessie. Does she keep all her life a secret, or has she told anyone how she left that dreadful morning?

"Well, madam. What do you think?"

I hadn't realized that I had been off on some trip and hadn't noticed that Jessie was done. When I did finally focus on myself in the mirror, I didn't know who I was looking at.

"Wow! Wow!" was all that would come out. I knew when people had makeovers, it really changed their appearance. Which I understood for people who never did anything as far as doing their hair or putting on makeup. I always do both and always thought I had done a good job of taking care of myself. This girl has done a miracle. I'll be surprised if my husband doesn't turn around and walk out of the house thinking he's got the wrong place.

"You don't like, madam?"

"Oh no! On the contrary, Jessie, you have done a fantastic job. The cut and color are beautiful. I like the way you work it all in. I would not have asked for this because I wouldn't begin to have dreamt of it. I think I must have been out of touch with the up-to- date hairdos now for some time. Thank you so very much."

"You're welcome, madam. I sure hope this helps you with the change you needed."

"Oh, it sure will. I'm glad I found you." Thinking that my daughter won't know me. If I had picked something, she would have been able to pick me out of a crowd because she knows me. But this she would never think I would do something so hip. It has taken ten years plus off my face.

After I paid the young girl, by the look on her face, she was very happy with her tip. I really felt she deserved it. It was really a job well done. I couldn't believe how this made me feel almost like a new person. I think I will stop one more time on the way home.

TWO

I pulled into the dress boutique where I always shop. I wanted to buy a wide brim hat and some white sunglasses. When I entered, no one came to me as always. I leave a pile of money behind when I come in here so the salesgirls are usually right there to see what they can help me with. It's like they haven't even noticed me.

I did, however, notice some of the new arrivals hanging by the window. Yes, I think I like these very much and there sure will go with the new me.

"May I help you, madam?"

"Yes, you may," I answered, turning around to greet the owner of the shop.

"My god, it's you! I did not recognize you at all. You look great, when and where?"

"I just now got it done, and it was at the small shop down at the end of Main Street. You know what, I don't even know the name I had just walked in after going to all the rest and no one had an opening. But believe me, I know where to find it. I just hope the girl who worked with me is still there when I have to go back."

"I can't believe it. I almost want to touch you to make sure it is really you."

"Thank you, April. You don't know how happy you just made me. Now you can make me happier by getting me some of these outfits together."

"All right, you are going somewhere?"

"I think I am." So we went ahead and put some of these outfits that she had hanging there together in my size so I could try them on. The long sweater dresses were in style this year with legging which I also bought. I had picked out a black-and-white striped one, a gray one, a white one, as well as a plaid one in black and white. The fifth one was in tan and off-white with metallic gold thread in it that was very dressy.

"Is there anything else I can get for you, Kate?"

"Yes, I would also like two of those wraps, one in black and one in red please."

"You got it."

"While you're getting them for me, I will go have a look at your hats and boots."

"The Peter Pan ones would go great with these."

"Thank you, April. Great minds think alike." I had found a couple of wide brim hats for the hotter days, and I got a couple of tams for the cooler days coming. My boots were both black, but one pair had silver studding on them, and the other pair had a large buckle on them. They would set the outfits off right to a tee. I wasn't going to worry about sunglasses because I know my daughter won't be expecting me in any of these. After all, they are something most younger girls wear. That's only because we think we are too old for these. But we are not. When I tried them on, they also made me feel young. Even young at heart and that is something I haven't felt for a long time. Happy with everything I have picked out, I had told April that I had best get home and get my husband's supper made.

"I hope you have a bottle of wine because that man of yours will think he died and went to heaven."

"I sure hope so." I'm glad she thinks I did this to get my husband's attention.

No one knows that I haven't seen or heard from my daughter in three years. I just led them to believe that she left town once she had finished high school to carry on her schooling. When anyone would ask, I would always have an answer. So no one knew the truth. Sometimes I had faux going away on weekends. Saying I was going to spend the weekend with her. But sometimes I just stayed at home and wouldn't answer the phone or go out all weekend. These were the weekends my husband would have to be away at work, so it would all fall into place. I could always dream up some kind of good time that my daughter and I had. I could even make myself sound so excited about it.

This was starting to worry me. To be in this pretend world when it wasn't doing a damn bit of good. It wasn't replacing my daughter, nor was it bringing her back. I know now is the time to go find her.

I hope my husband will understand because I have no way of knowing how long this will take me. But I do know it is something I must do, and I can only hope he will understand me. He will have to let me do this on my own. For one thing, there is no way he would let me change his looks so drastic to where people wouldn't recognize him as I have done to myself. I can't see this being any harder on him than the last three years have been. I pray that I still have a marriage after this. It is a lonely world without my daughter. I know it will also be lonely without my husband, but I feel I have to be the parent and try to fix what my daughter has broken. This is if she will let me in to her heart once again. I hope she hasn't lost what we had. I pray that this is what has been getting her by as it has me. Just maybe she doesn't know what steps to take to turn this around. I feel like I have given her plenty of time to figure out how she wanted to handle this and to figure out just how she was going to undo the damage that she has done.

Arriving home, I see that my husband has made it home before me.

Damn. I didn't want this to happen today. I was excited to go into the house just wondering what his reaction was going to be when he saw me. Just thinking this way had my heart beating so fast. It was from excitement, not fear, and I hadn't felt this way for a very long time. I actually feel sexy. I should have taken April's advice and bought some wine. Although knowing my husband, the wine would be more for me than him. He doesn't have a problem when it comes to sex or telling me how sexy I look to him. I just have felt dead inside and out. There have been times when I want to tell him he is free to go find someone who will love him the way he deserves. I love him with all my heart. But my heart hasn't healed, and it won't let me give like I used to. I have talked to myself so many times because I don't like what I have become. I have a lot of living to do yet, but that just isn't happening.

I listened to my husband at first while he would tell me. Don't worry, she will need you before you need her. She isn't gone forever. I'm telling you, it feels like forever now after three years. At first, when he would come home, he would say to me, "Any word?" The answer was always the same sad *no*. He doesn't ask anymore, and I know it isn't because he doesn't care;

it's because he can't stand the pain that shows in my eyes because I haven't seen her today. Nor the pain in my voice when I say no I haven't heard from her. I know he is trying so hard to be there for me. He also deserves more from me than his meals and laundry done. I pray the good Lord will give us the strength that we are going to need to see us through this next journey I am about to embark on.

Getting into the house, I notice how quiet it is. Now is my husband lying down, or is he just in the bathroom? I walk down the hall to see where he might be. Then I hear him on the phone, and I listen for a bit. I've heard some of this language from him, so I know he's ordering chemicals for work, so I just turn around and go back to the kitchen. I might as well start supper. He could be a while as he knows all the men in these places very well and they do like to bullshit a lot. They talk about women.

I had taken chicken out for supper, so I will carry on making the chicken cordon blue that I was planning on. While I had that in the oven, I made us a fresh salad. Both of us have gotten into liking our salads. Getting down on my knees to get another bag of croutons, I saw in the back a bottle, so I reached in and pulled out, to my surprise, a bottle of wine. Yes! I even had a smile. This was a bottle that we had received from a friend at Christmas time, but we weren't in the mood to open it, so it was just put away and ended up way at the back. I hurried up and put it into a pail of ice. By the time supper was ready, it would be chilled; I can only hope it is a good-tasting wine, for I don't like those dry bitter ones. I have enough bitterness in my life I sure the hell don't need my wine tasting that way as well.

Everything was going along smoothly, and supper would be on time like it used to be, when I actually cared.

"Excuse me." I turned around to see my husband staring at me like he was scared to move. I raise an eyebrow up and cock my head to see what else he had to say.

"Lady, are you in the right house? Has my wife hired a housekeeper that I didn't know about?"

"Oh, I'm in the right house, all right?"

"Kate? Kate?" he says as he takes a step closer as if he thought I was just going to go puff and disappear.

"Yes, dear! May I pour you a glass of wine?"

"Aww, yea!" he says as he comes over and wraps his arms around me. He starts to pull me closer and then says to me.

"May I kiss you?"

"Do you have to ask?" It was a kiss like none we had shared for an awfully long time. I felt warm all over, and I hadn't even had any wine yet. So what will the rest of the evening bring if things are this hot already?

"Why did you do this to your beautiful white hair?"

"Are you telling me you don't like it?"

"Not at all, I love it. But I loved your white hair as well. But this is like having a stranger in my arms."

"I really hope you don't greet all strangers this way."

"Only the one I love. Oh, sweetheart, you look fantastic. People are going to think you and I have separated. That I have found myself very young woman."

"Does that bother you?"

"Yes, and no. Yes because I would never do that to you, and no because I know who it is that is in my arms." He kisses me as if our lives depended on it.

"Um, I better get our supper on the table."

"Do we have to?"

"Yes, dear, we have to eat."

"I'll eat you for supper."

I slap him and pulled away. "Come on now, we have all night, I'm not going anywhere."

"Me either," he says as he takes the wine to open and pour. While he pops the cork, he's looking at me.

"May I ask you why the big change?" Oh, this could be a tough question to answer, and it could spoil the night.

"Well, dear. I really need a lift, and I couldn't think of a better way to do it. I have to say I haven't felt this way about myself for a long time. I also went shopping and got some neat upbeat clothes to wear. I'm sure you will love them."

"I'm sure I will. But then I love everything about what you wear. You always look good to me."

"Do I look good to you now?"

"Are you shitting me?" he says as he comes around the counter and takes me in his arms.

"You are so damn sexy at this moment I could make love to you right here, right now."

"See, then there is a big difference between me this morning and now. I went from being a good-looking old woman to a sexy lady in your eyes. So I take what I have done to myself was well worth it."

"Yea, and I'll prove it after supper."

"I'll hold you to that." Once our supper was on the table, we sat and ate and talked about a lot of things that we hadn't talked about for a long time. I had noticed my husband looking at me more than he was eating. I also noticed how my husband was looking tired. Have I done this to him? He seems to have lines on his face where there were none before. Has his worrying about me turned him older than his time? Or is it because so much time has passed us by and I hadn't been noticing my husband? Oh, I knew he was here but not really. We were just coming and going and sort of doing what we wanted to do without each other. Spending so much time alone was so out of context for us. We had always done things together and enjoyed doing so. Then out of the blue, he asked, "Sweetheart, can I ask you something?"

"Sure you can."

"What are you really up to?"

"What makes you think I'm up to anything?"

"I think there's more to this than you're telling me. Please don't get me wrong. I do love what you have had done. In fact, I'm having a hard time eating because I feel like you might just disappear if I'm not careful. Please be honest with me. Is there someone else you're seeing?"

"Someone else I'm seeing?" I almost choke on my food. Not only did my mouth hit the floor, but so did my fork. I never thought for one moment he would think I had done this for another man. Putting my napkin on the table as I got up to go around to his side, I felt the tears coming and the end of a perfect evening.

"Oh no! Dear. There is no one else. I love you with all my heart and soul, and I always will. Who else would have put up with me these last three years like you have?"

He pulls me on to his lap and says, "Are you sure? 'Cause I would lose my mind if I lost you."

"I promise there is no one else who has my heart or part of it." I kiss him and hold him tight. When I pull back and look into his eyes, I could see the tears that were sitting there waiting to spill over. Oh god, what have I done to this man? I have to tell him what I have planned.

THREE

"I guess saying there isn't anyone else who has a part of my heart is wrong." I saw the blood drain from his face. I thought he was going to be sick right then and there.

"My daughter still holds a large part of my heart. It feels dead right now, but I plan to change that right away."

"Thank God."

"You mean that?"

"Yes, of course I mean that."

Hugging him ever so tightly, I say to him, "Honey, I knew you would understand.

I don't know how long it will take, so I'm not sure how long I'll be gone for."

"Gone? Gone where? What are you talking about, sweetheart?"

"To find my daughter of course. I don't know how long it will take because I'm not coming home until I have talked to her like we used to. This is killing me, and I have decided to put an end to all this pain and craziness. Don't you think it's about time?"

He is sitting there looking like I have just dropped a bomb on him.

"Honey, are you all right?"

"I do not quite understand this. Are you telling me you are leaving me?"

"No, I'm not really leaving you. I thought you said you were happy about this?"

"No! Well, yes. No! I mean I was happy to hear that it wasn't another man who had a part of your heart. The rest I don't know if I'm crazy about it at all."

"I'm sorry to hear that." I went to get up off his knee.

"No! Stay right here and tell me about what you think you're going to do."

"Not if you're going to be pissed about it."

"I'm not pissed about anything. Maybe a little taken aback and shook-up because my wife is leaving me and I don't understand why. Has our love gotten so old that it doesn't mean anything to you anymore?"

"True love never grows old, honey."

"Then please tell me what is going on."

"All right. A big part of me is dead inside. It died the day my daughter told me that she was sorry that I was her mother and walked out of my life. Maybe for you it has been easy to go on day after day without talking to her or weeks and years without seeing her, but it is killing me. It is killing us. Every day she consumes my every thought. I want to see her, I want to know where she is, what she is doing. For Christ's sake I want to hold her in my arms again and tell her how much I love her. I miss my baby, hon, and I can't go on without her. I can't be whole again until I have her back in my life like it used to be." Now the tears are falling, and I'm blubbering like a fool.

"Shush, shush now, sweetheart, calm down. I didn't mean to upset you so much. But I do think we should talk about what you think you have to do. I didn't say you couldn't find your daughter. I just don't want to lose you while you're doing so."

"You have already lost a big part of me, the day she left."

"No, I still have the same loving, caring, beautiful woman I fell in love with twenty years ago. Perhaps you have quit living to some extent since she left. But my wife is still here with me, and I would hope this is where she's going to stay."

"Please you have to understand I'm not leaving you. I'm just going to go find my daughter while I can still do it on my own."

"So you don't want me to come with you? Is that what you are saying?"

"I have to fix or try to fix whatever is wrong. You can't do that. When she left here, she was mad at me. I just didn't think she would drag it on for so long. This really worries me. Seeing how it has been so long, we don't know if that guy is still with her, and if he isn't, why she hasn't called me. Seeing how it all started over him wanting to take her away. What if he isn't with her anymore and he has done something to hurt her.

"I don't understand why she would have stayed away so long without being in touch over something as insignificant as me not talking to the guy. Guys like this scare me. He has had her all to himself for so long now maybe she is scared to try to come home."

"But why? What would he be gaining by keeping her away from us or you?"

"I don't have the answer, but I'm going to find out."

"All right, I get that you are bound and determined to find her and there is no way I can stop you. But can we finish our wine and supper and perhaps carry on from where we left off before supper? Even with the tearstains on your cheeks, you're still the sexiest lady I have had the pleasure of kissing and holding all day. I would love to end our evening on the note we started on."

"But—"

"Shush," he says as he lays his finger across my lips.

"I'm not trying to say your daughter isn't important, but we will start fresh tomorrow on your plans of finding her." He kisses me so gentle it was like he wasn't even there.

He gets up and, grabbing what was left of the wine, carries me up to our room.

I don't know where he came from, but he was not being the man I had been with a couple of weeks ago. I don't remember him ever been so gentle and caring in his lovemaking. He was always the rough-cowboy type, which, when we were younger, was great; but as we get older or as I get older, I guess I'm in need of the slower hand and the easy touch. He woke up feelings that, for the last three years, have been sleeping. I know some of this is because right at this moment, I feel very good about myself.

I have been to my doctor and have talked to him about my lack of interest in sex these days, and I wanted to know why. I had told him that for my husband, it must be like making love to dead women because things just didn't happen for me anymore. He told me that most of it was my mental state. He suggested that I book a hotel room for us on a regular basis and get away from what was bothering me. He told me it would make a big difference. Unless it was my husband that was my problem. Or that it was I who wanted out of the marriage. I had told him that it was neither one of those problems, and I don't think he really believed me.

I never went into detail to tell him what was bothering me wasn't something I could just leave behind. I take that sweet child of mine with me wherever I go.

At this very moment, she has been put on a shelf. She is safe there. I will pick her up again later, but right now, I really want to give all I have to my husband. I don't know when things will be this hot between us again especially with me going away for however long it was going to take. So for now I was going to take whatever he was willing to give me, and I will give back whatever was possible.

Our night went on the slow loving mode, for half the night, neither one of us thought we had that in us anymore. We were both pleasantly surprised. So I guess, I would have to say my doctor was totally right. Your mental state plays a big roll in what kind of sex you are going to have, if any.

It would be great if it could be like this for us always. I know right at this time in my life, that is not possible. Until I find my daughter and get to hold her in my arms again, these tender moments that my husband and I are sharing right now will be far and few between.

Perhaps he knows this, and that's why tonight has been a very special night. It is one that I will remember for a long time to come. It has almost been like we've been reborn.

With me going away, tonight will have to carry me through my tough days without my husband. One thing about it, we have our cell phones and we do call each other a lot. For a long time now, this has been our communication line. We seem to be able to talk better to each other over the damn cell phones than we have been able to do face-to-face. I don't know why, sounds stupid, but this is how it has been for a good year now.

Sometimes I think I should go see a shrink, but then I think for what. I know what my problem is, and I would be paying them a hundred dollars an hour to tell me to go find my daughter and talk to her. After all I am the parent. I have been her age, but she's never been fifty, so it is up to me to make the first step and show her the way. Someday she may have kids and find herself in the same boat we are in. Only she'll be able to think back to how her mother handled it, and she'll be fine.

I hope we can get to the point in our lives where we will sit and laugh about this. I know that is years down the road. We were both so relaxed we finally fell asleep in each other's arms, something we haven't done in years.

Most of the time, I would end up on the sofa. So I could be alone with my thoughts of my daughter without pissing my husband off. This has become a routine way of sleeping. It hasn't been good for our marriage as well as for me mentally. When I woke in the morning, my husband was lying there looking at me and still holding me.

"Good morning, sweetheart."

"Good morning, dear."

"Did you sleep well?"

"Yea, I did. I think it is the best sleep I have had for the last couple of years for sure. What about you, dear? Did you sleep well?"

"With this new lady I have in my arms, how could I do anything but sleep well. I have to say I'm glad to see her still in my arms this morning. I was afraid I had dreamt of this and I would wake up alone again."

"I'm sorry for that, dear."

"Don't be sorry for something you feel you have to do. I know you don't sleep, and I also know that you move out at night so I can sleep. I do appreciate the consideration that you show me." He touches the tip of my nose with his lips. He didn't stop there, and things got warmed up quite fast. It was almost as good as the night before.

"I wish we could stay here today, but my job calls."

"I know, dear, but you have been great, and I will remember this time for some time to come."

"I was hoping there was going to be more of this now that we remember what it is we are supposed to be doing." We both laugh as he climbs out of bed to go have his shower and I head for my bathtub.

"By the way," he says from the shower, "we are having our talk over coffee this morning. You are going to tell me your plans."

"All right. I'll get the coffee going as soon as I'm out of the tub. I won't be long." I was even feeling good about this. We were going to talk over coffee; it has been a while since we did this at home.

So I rushed my bath and had gotten dressed. I even had time to make made muffins to go along with our coffee by the time my husband came downstairs.

"Hey, it smells good in here," he says as he comes up and plants a kiss on the top of my head before he takes a seat beside me.

"Now, my dear, I want you to tell me all about your plans. I don't want to rush you, but I do have to go to work, and I'm pretty sure you already have a plan, so spill it."

"Well, first, I will find out if she still works. I know she worked at the Sports and More on Main Street there in the city. So I plan on going there first."

"How are you going to find out if she is still there?"

"You didn't know me, neither will she."

"I don't know, I think your daughter knows you pretty damn good."

"Maybe. It has been three years, so she won't be expecting me to show up."

"If she is there, then what?"

"I'm getting a hotel room, and I will watch for a while. I hope I will be able to get close enough to hear her talking. Maybe then I can find out where she is living. If not then, I will try to follow her so I can see where she lives. I'm glad I have a new car because even this will throw her off."

"You think you can really do this?"

"I don't know, but I have to try."

"Aww, babe, I don't want you hurting yourself anymore."

"I can't hurt anymore than I already do now."

"Okay, promise to call me. Please! Maybe on the weekend, I can come and see you. What do you think?"

"Let's wait and see how things go. I will call every night."

"You be sure to do that, Kate." Kissing me on the top of the head, he turns to leave. "I love you, please remember that always. Thank you for last night."

"I Love you too." I put my hand up on my chest over my heart. Watching him walk away made me mad at myself because I knew I was hurting him. Except I felt deep down inside this was something I just had to do and I had do it without him.

FOUR

After he had left for work, I quickly packed my bags and watered all my plants. The ones that have survived the neglect over the last three years.

I knew that our cat was a survivor as well, but she is also loyal. Perhaps by the time I get back, her loyalty will have changed. Can't say I would blame her. Just at that moment, like she knew I was thinking of her, she came along rubbing herself around my legs and lightly purring. Scooping her up and sitting on the side of the bed, I started to pet her. "It's all right, Missy. I hope I won't be gone long. As a mother, you know I have to do this, right?" Missy just snuggles in that much closer. "Oh, you poor thing, I'm sorry we can't do this any longer. I must go." I put her down, and she took off back to her babies. She gave me the distinct feeling that she was not upset with me. I don't care what anyone says; they understand everything.

Pulling out of our driveway, slowly taking a good look at our home. The one that used to hold so much happiness seems to wear a black veil now as if it were in mourning. To me, even the shutters drooped. Oh, I hope you will shine again soon.

Speeding up before I changed my mind, I did not see how many of our neighbors would have seen me packing up the car.

The tongues would get wagging once again. I no longer spent time with any of the group that I used to coffee with. Many had called to see why I wasn't meeting with them anymore. Some of them would bring their daughters along just like I used to. I could not take that; my heart ached so bad I wanted to scream at them, "CAN'T YOU LEAVE HER AT HOME?" I had started to take it personally as if they were rubbing it into my noise. See, my daughter is here. Where is yours? That wasn't right when I really thought about it. I never told anyone what had happened. I was so embarrassed that this happened to me. Many, many times people would say to me, "You are so lucky to have such a friend in your daughter." I would always put my arm through hers and say, "Yes, I am." So I found it very difficult to tell them how and what she had said to me. Now it has been three years. I wouldn't even know how to start. It seems like a terrible nightmare that I just can't wake up from. I know everyone has one of them in a lifetime and they are the bad ones that keep coming back to mind time and again.

My sister lives not more than five miles away. I have never told her anything about what had happened. They never saw much of my daughter, so to them, these last three years have meant nothing. When and if they ask about her, I can always tell some fantastic story. She is another one that brings her daughter with her every time we were to meet. So it is another outing that I don't go out on anymore. She thinks I work at the old folks home. The shift work there is crazy hours, so she never calls me. I bump into her now and again downtown. Rarely do we go for coffee. The days she doesn't have her daughter, I will go and I try to stay away from those topics that would involve the girls. I talk a lot about the old people that I never see. I know she doesn't like it, and that is why I don't see much of her anymore. I know they just won't understand. They would say the same thing as my husband did. "Oh, she will need you before you need her." But it is quite obvious that is not true. I needed my daughter right after she left.

I'm hoping I can come back a new woman who has had a second chance at life. One who not just sees the sunshine but can feel it as well. Returning a genuine smile to all those who smile and greet me as they pass. Speaking the truth again instead of living a life of fantasy. Being able to embrace life again as though you know you only have one kick at the kitty, so enjoying it all to the fullest while you can. Sharing it with all the ones that you love more than life itself, my daughter.

Driving along gave me so much time to think about my life and where I have been and where I want to go. I knew there was no place I wanted to be without my daughter.

I remember when she wasn't quite two years old, she tipped her riding duck over and had broken her wrist. There was no swelling or bruising and very little crying from her. After she started to walk and she would fall down from time to time like they all do while learning how to walk,

I would always tell her, "Get up, you're tougher than that. Come on, Mommy's big girl." She would smile and get up and keep on going. I had done the same when she fell off her duck, hitting her arm on the coffee table. The week following her fall, she would fuss if she laid on her arm or bump it, so I decided to take her in to see a doctor. The x-rays showed that she had broken her arm. I was so sick to my stomach. Thinking I had let my daughter down. I let her go around all week in pain with a broken arm. What kind of mother did that make me? So the nurse ended up consoling me instead of my daughter who kept saying, "You okay, Mommy? You okay?"

I remember looking into those big beautiful brown eyes and saying, "Oh, Mommy loves her little girl as big as the sky." Taking her in my arms and wanting her to know how sorry I was for what had happened. As always, she just hopped off the table when the casting was done, saying, "Can we go show Daddy!" She was so excited about the cast she never complained about any more pain. "What a little trooper," her Daddy would say to her whenever she bounced back from something.

The following year, she was stumbling all the time, and it got progressively worse over a short period. When we took her to the doctor, they told us they thought our daughter had a brain tumor. She was put into the hospital and was being put through a series of tests. This time, it was like the floor had been pulled out from under my feet. A brain tumor is not a little thing, and this is my baby we are talking about. Doctors back then couldn't tell you too much about them until they got inside to see where the tumor had grown into. After a week of testing, they couldn't really tell us too much more than when we came in.

Sitting and holding my baby every day, not knowing how much longer I would have her made each day more special than the next. My husband would come up after work and bring me supper, and we would lie on the bed together and cuddle our sweet Angel, read her stories, and hold each other. He would leave in the wee hours to go home and shower for work. Our Angel felt him every time he moved. She would say to him, "Please take me home, Daddy." He would always tell her, "I will, Angel, but you be a good girl for Mommy." While he was kissing the top of her head, his eyes would meet mine, and there were always tears ready to fall. I knew he was as scared as I was.

We got our answer one day when my sister had called and wanted to talk to my daughter. We gave her the phone, and after a minute, she had hung up on her auntie, saying, "No one there, Mommy." My sister called back, and we tried it again, same thing. My sister told me that she thinks my daughter is deaf. That morning, when the doctor came in, I told him what had happened, and that it was her right side.

"Well, there are tests we can do for that, but I don't think this has anything to do with the other problem." That afternoon, they took her away for a hearing test and Lord only knows what else. When they brought her back to me, it was the first time I had ever seen her look so down.

"What is it, Angel? Why are you so sad?"

"The doctor said I has a broken ear, Mommy. Do I has to have a cast on it too?"

"Come here, Angel." I pull her close and look up at the doctor.

"What did you find?"

"Your daughter has a terrible ear infection in the middle ear. Her pain tolerance is so high I can't believe she isn't crying with this. She also needs to have her tonsils out, and we hope that once this is done and the infection is cleared up that she will get her hearing back and she will be able to walk without falling."

"You mean you think that is all it is?"

"Yes, we do, so we have booked her for surgery tomorrow morning at eight thirty. We hope that the damage is not gone beyond repair."

"You're sure about this? Our daughter doesn't have a brain tumor."

"Yea, I'm positively sure." I knew the tears were flowing, and I didn't care who saw. I picked up my baby and cried and cried.

"Mommy, you hurting me."

"I'm sorry, Angel."

"Mommy, you okay?"

"Yes, Angel, Mommy is just happy."

"Then why you crying, Mommy?" How could I tell her that we thought we were losing her to God. We have always told her that God takes care of the sick that the doctors can't fix.

"Shush, Angel, Mommy is fine." I was bursting at the seams when my husband showed up at supper time. Our Angel was having surgery in the morning and coming home the next day.

Our chicken take-out supper was a celebration supper. I don't think either one of us wanted to voice what we had been feeling especially not now. We were just happy to know our baby was going to be fine and back home with us in two days. The three of us sleeping in that small bed was great last night. There were no complaints of kinked necks or sore backs. Everything was going to be great.

Our Angel had her surgery the next day, and even after a month of healing, she did not get her hearing back. She had to learn to walk all over again and to ride her bike. It was sad yet fun to spend that quality of time with her again.

We had noticed that she didn't take to her falls so good anymore, and we did not brush them off as though she wasn't hurt. Instead of saying, "Get up, you're tougher than that," we would run over and help her up, kissing her better and say, "Let's try again." She was always up to trying again, but she had gotten to be more cautious with everything she did. In a short time, our Angel was walking, biking, and swimming and doing all the things a normal little girl would do.

Being deaf on the left side wasn't something we could just forget about. Angel had been sent to many specialists, and they all came up with the same answers.

She would not get her hearing back, and nor would a hearing aid do her any good. The doctors had told us that we should all learn sign language. Seeing how Angel had lost her hearing to an ear infection, there was nothing saying it couldn't happen again. They gave us a pile of small books, and we had learned a lot on sign language. We had turned it into a game and told Angel that was our special way of talking. She could tell me secrets anywhere, and no one else would know. It was a blast for us, but as time went on and Angel got older, she never got any more infection and we just learned that we had to talk to her on her good side. If she missed what people had said to her, then they would say, "Are you deaf?" Angel would always answer with a big grin, "Yes, I am." We had always kept up on the sign language just in case, and of course, we used it when we were being smart about someone who was with us or close by. That was not right, and we knew it, but it was our special code and kept us close. My husband wasn't as good at it as we were, so we could make fun of him too. Of course he would just laugh and shake his head, asking, "What are my angels up to now?"

"Nothing, Daddy," Angel would say and giggle. This went on for a few years. When Angel started school, she had some trouble at first with a few boys who like to tease her about being deaf. They tried to make it out to be something a whole lot worse than it was. They were trying to turn her into a freak show, but it backfired on them in a very short time. When Angel made friends with these two little girls and taught them sign language, they got the better of the boys, and the boys finally backed off.

At first, when the two little girls would come over, you could hear them giggling away whenever they had made a mistake and Angel would tell them what they had said. I heard the smaller one—Liz was her name—say to Angel, "I wish I were deaf like you."

"No, you don't."

"Yes, I do."

So I stepped into Angel's room and sat on her bed with them.

"I heard what you said, Liz, and that is a good thing to want to be like your friend. Please don't ever wish for something bad to happen to yourself or anyone else."

"But Angel is special, she can only hear a little, and she can talk with her hands."

"You're right, Angel is special," I say as I pull Angel close and hug her. "You are special now too, Liz. Angel has taught you to talk with your hands even through you can hear really well with both your ears."

"Do you think my mommy will think I'm special now that I can talk with my hands?"

"Aww, sweetheart, I bet you are very special to your Mommy already."

"No, not no more." I saw the look in my daughter's eyes. I knew I had best find a way to fix this uneasy feeling that had come over all of us.

"Why do you say that, Liz? All little girls are very special to their mommies."

"My mommy has a baby boy now. She and Daddy, they don't need me. I heard them say that."

"No, sweetheart, you must be mistaken. Your mommy and daddy love you very much, and they do need you."

"When they brought my baby brother home, I heard them say, "Now that they had Jimmy, they didn't need anymore." I couldn't help but laugh and the look on those little faces when I stopped and saw that they could not figure out what I found so funny. Thank God for simple things and easy fixes.

"Sweetheart, all they meant was that they already have you, their darling beautiful little girl, now they have their sweet little boy, so they don't need any more babies. The two of you were all they needed to make them happy."

"Do you really think so? 'Cause it made me real sad when I heard them say that."

Taking Liz up on my knee and rocking her back and forth, I said, "I know that is exactly what they meant. All mommies and daddies want to have one girl and one boy. It makes the family even, whole, happy, and complete."

FIVE

"Mommy."

"Yes, Angel."

"You and Daddy not happy."

"Why, of course we are, why do you ask, Angel?"

"'Cause you only have me, we don't have a baby brother to make us whole."

"You're right, Angel, we don't. But that doesn't mean we are not happy. You make us very happy, Angel, and if the good Lord sees his way, maybe he will give us a son soon."

"You mean that, Mommy? I will have a baby brother just like Liz? Oh, Mommy, I would be so happy."

"Yes, my sweet Angel, we will have a baby brother just like Liz."

"Oh, thank you, Mommy, thank you." She wraps her arms around my neck so tight, but it felt so good to be so loved.

"Now, girls, I must go put my buns in the oven. If we want a snack this afternoon. Is everyone okay in here now?" I ask as I give them all a hug on my way out.

"Yes," they all answered at once.

The sounds of those little girls giggling would always bring a smile to my face and make me wish they would stay that age. They were so carefree and easygoing, and Mommy knew everything. Well, almost everything. I did not know that Angel was wanting a sibling so bad. I guess it is something her daddy and I should talk about. We have been happy the way we are, with just the three of us. At least, that's what I always thought. But then I never have asked Ben if he wanted another baby. With everything happening with Angel, I guess she just kept us occupied, so we didn't miss not having another little one.

Another little one, aww, that would be great, all right, I thought as I rubbed my stomach. To have another child as sweet as Angel, hell, why not? Yea, definitely something to talk about tonight and maybe something to start on. I was feeling a little giddy while putting my buns in the oven. It wasn't because sex between us had died 'cause it was great, but we just never thought about a baby, or at least I haven't, but just the thought of a baby was making me excited. Hope it has the same effect on Ben.

The girls and I were just finishing up our hot buns and jam for our snack when Ben came through the door.

"Daddy, Daddy," Angel calls to him as she jumps down from the table and runs for her daddy. Scooping her up with no effort at all, tucking her under his arm like a football, and she starts to giggle all over again. He takes her in and dumps her on the sofa and says, "Touchdown."

"Daddy, I'm not a football."

"Oh, what are you then?"

"I'm Angel."

"No!"

"Yes, I am, Daddy."

"Yea, you are my Angel, and don't you ever forget that," he says as he pulls her close and gives her a bear hug. Now he has her up on his shoulders and their coming back to the kitchen when I hear her say, "Daddy, you know I'm getting a baby brother just like Liz. I'm so happy, Daddy." The look on Ben's face was all I needed to see. He was just as happy as Angel.

"Well, Angel, I did not know that," he says as he comes and wraps his arm very tightly around my waist.

"I guess that must be something Mommy forgot to tell me. Right, Mommy?" Oh, he was going to be disappointed to find out it hasn't happened yet. It was just a wish of Angel's.

"No, sweetheart, it is not something I have forgotten to tell you." Now he looks confused.

"Come, have a coffee and a hot bun with jam. The girls are going home, and we will talk."

"Talk? Oh, this sounds too serious. Angel, should I have a coffee and bun and talk with Mommy?"

"Yep, Daddy, I'm going to walk my friends halfway." She wiggles to get down.

"All right, then you be careful and stay on the sidewalk."

"I will, Daddy."

"Now tell me what is this all about us having a son," Ben pulls me down on his lap and kisses my neck just below my ear.

"Angel was saying today she would love to have a baby brother like Liz. I told her if the good Lord saw his way, maybe we could have one."

"Are you serious, Kate? Do you really want to have another baby?"

"Sure, I mean why not? I think it would be great, don't you?"

"Oh, absolutely, I just didn't think you wanted anymore, You seem to be so content with Angel. I figured having another baby was not something you were up to. After all, we have been through with Angel."

"That is all behind us now. Having another baby isn't something I was against, just that we were always so preoccupied with Angel I never really gave it much thought until the girls brought it up today."

"The girls brought it up?"

"Well, in a roundabout way. Liz was sad, thinking that now that her parents have had their son, they didn't need her anymore."

"Why would she think that?"

"She overheard her parents talking after they brought the baby home, how now that they had him, they didn't need anymore. So Liz took that to mean they didn't want her anymore."

"Aww, poor little thing, did you straighten her out?"

"I sure hope so. That's when I told her it only meant that now they have both a daughter and a son they didn't need anymore they were very happy to have one of each. That was when Angel got involved and thought that we were not happy because all we had was her. I told her it was not true that we were very happy with her. She was quick to inform me that she would be happier if she could have a baby brother like Liz. So I told her that if the good Lord saw his way, maybe we could.

"You're sure about this, Kate? After all, Angel will be in school full time next year, and you would be freed up again."

"See, I would have so much time on my hands I have more than enough love to give to another baby, and all the time it would need."

"Kate, what if the baby is a sick baby or?"

"Shush now," I tell him as I bend down and give him a kiss.

"We will not think that way. Only good thoughts can go through our minds. We have to be positive and think positive. Otherwise, we will jinx our baby." "So you are serious about another baby, Kate, for sure?"

"Yes, Ben, more than you know."

"All right then." He pulls me down and starts to kiss my neck where he knows he gets to me every time.

"Now, now, let's not get too carried away. Angel will be back right away."

"Just getting warmed up for later. Oh, Kate, you have made me a happy man."

"Ben, you're not happy?"

"Aww, Kate, of course I'm happy, but what man doesn't want a son. I just thought Angel was all we would have. Not that she's not great and enough. If you had not brought this up, I would not have ever mentioned it."

"Ben, this marriage is two of us. That is something you had a right to bring up or ask. We might have had another baby by now if you had."

"I think now is the perfect time. Everything with Angel is settled down, and we could just enjoy a baby. It will be fun watching Angel play mommy."

"Yea, that should be cute. I only hope she won't regret it after as the baby will take some of our time from her. She may not like it in the end."

"Kate, you won't let that happen. We won't let that happen. Angel will always be our special little girl."

"Hope she will be our only little girl. You and her will be so disappointed if we have another girl."

"Maybe I would be for a short time at first, but, Kate, I know we don't have control of these things, and it is like you said. If the good Lord sees it his way, maybe he will give us a son."

"See, Daddy, I told you we were having a baby brother."

"Angel, where did you come from?" Ben says as he picks her up.

"Outside, Daddy, silly. So when do I get my baby brother?"

"I guess we will have to start working on that later." He pats my behind when I get off his knee.

"How come you have to work on it, Daddy? Mommy said the good Lord will give us one."

I chuckle and wink at him. "Yea, Daddy, why do you have to work at it?" I ask.

"Well, for the good Lord to give us a baby brother for you and Daddy and Mommy. We have to be extra good and eat all our meals and bathe on time every night, and we must remember to go to bed on time and get lots of rest."

"Why do we have to get lots of rest, Daddy?"

"Yea, why, Daddy?" I say with a smirk. I want to see what kind of answer he could come up with for that one.

"Well, if the good Lord puts a baby in Mommy's tummy to grow for us. We have to make sure Mommy gets lots of rest, and so our baby can grow to be strong and healthy for you to play with."

"Okay, Daddy, we can do that, right, Mommy?"

"Yea, we sure can do that. Now let Mommy get supper on the table."

"Daddy, we have to make supper now so Mommy can get lots of rest."

"You're right, Angel, so what should we make?"

"Pancakes, Daddy."

"All right then pancakes it is. Mommy, you just take a seat and see how well you have taught the two of us to fend for ourselves."

"Okay, that should be scary."

"Mommy, would you like a cup of tea while Daddy and I make you supper?"

"That would be very thoughtful, Angel, thank you."

"See, Daddy, this won't be hard. God will give us a baby brother soon."

"You could be right, Angel, but what if he has run out of brothers and gives us another Angel."

"No, he can't, Daddy. I'm your Angel. Remember, Daddy, you said I would always be your Angel."

"I said that?"

"Yes, Daddy, you did, and I don't want no more Angels."

"You're right, I did say that and know what Daddy doesn't want any more Angels either 'cause you are all the Angel one Daddy needs." Ben picks her up and gives her another bear hug.

"Okay. Daddy, you can put me down now. We have to make Mommy supper."

"You're right, we do, so why are you stopping me from all this hard work?"

"Daddy, you are so funny, making pancakes, not hard work. I watched Mommy do it lots of times."

"Okay, little miss, you make the pancakes. I will watch this time."

Angel got the box of mix out and the milk, and before we knew it, she had the batter made up. It was a little on the runnier side but nothing a little more mix wouldn't fix. She was so proud of herself I'm sure the smile was still spread across her face when we tucked her into bed.

"Daddy, Mommy," she says in her sleepy voice.

"Yes, Angel, what is it?"

"Do you think God is proud of me too."

"Oh yes, he is."

"Then will I have a baby brother tomorrow?"

"How about you go to sleep now. Mommy and I will go see what we can do about that. Good night, Angel, sleep tight and remember we love you as big as the sky."

She was asleep before we had left her room.

"Now, my dear Kate, we have some work to do so the good Lord can fulfill Angel's wishes."

"Work."

"Yes, this is serious business, and we must put everything we have into it. Angel may have to eat all her meals and go to bed on time and be a good girl to get her baby brother. But you and I, well, we have our work cut out for us."

"How do you figure it's going to be so much work?"

"Well, Kate, we have an extra part to put on this one. Angel was an easy pattern to follow." Ben was trying to be so serious that I burst out laughing.

"Well then, my dear husband. If it is going to be so much more work to add that one small detail, maybe we shouldn't just be talking about it. Maybe we should really be working on it. What do you think?"

"I think you have a very good idea." Scooping me up and carrying me to our bedroom the same way he did on our wedding night made me giggle the same as I did that most glorious night.

"I love you, Ben."

"I love you, and I want to show you just how much I do." He starts kissing me on my neck where he knows it gets to me every time.

"That's cheating, Ben."

"Hey, whatever works." We fall on the bed together laughing.

SIX

It took us longer to get pregnant this time. With Angel, it happened right away. We weren't even expecting on getting pregnant for the first couple of years. We thought we had it all planned out. Except Angel wasn't waiting. We don't regret having her when we did. Now we couldn't think of our lives without her.

Angel would ask morning and night if she was having a baby brother yet. She was getting very discouraged, and we did not know what to tell her. I had gone to a couple of doctors, and they assure me that we would conceive but it was just going to take more time because I had been on the pill for so long. The doctors had told us to quit trying so hard and just relax and let it happen. One night, lying in Ben's arms, I had said to him, "Ben, can you believe that there is such a thing about trying too hard to have a baby?"

"Well, sweetheart, we do trust our doctor, right?"

"Yes, we do."

"Then we have to believe in what he is telling us. So don't fret it so it will happen."

"I know you're right, but Angel is wearing on me. She asks every day about her baby brother."

"I know, sweetheart, I think it might be time to tell her a little more about the making of babies."

"No, Ben, she is too young to hear about sex."

"I'm not talking about that part. But the fact that it takes time for a baby to grow even. Maybe we can use the calendar to show her what kind of time is involved. Maybe tell her about the egg somehow so she can understand that the baby just isn't there over night. Well, it can be but not really."

"We have to figure something out to tell her. I will talk to my doctor next time and see if they can help us on this."

"I think that would be a very good idea, Kate."

In the end, we ended up forgetting about having another baby. We took it that the good Lord didn't see us with any more than Angel. I had gone out and bought Angel a doll dressed in blue that did everything a real baby would do. I could not believe they made such dolls today. I'm telling you this doll also has all *his* parts. We know it not the same as having her own baby brother, but it did help her accept that we were not having one of our own.

"Mommy."

"Yes, Angel."

"Am I a bad girl?"

"No, not at all, you are a very good girl."

"God doesn't think so."

"Oh yes, he knows how good of a girl you are."

"Then why won't he give me a baby brother?"

"Oh, Angel, it has nothing to do with you."

"Then why, Mommy?" Now the truth had to be told, somehow.

"Come here, Angel, and let Mommy try to make you understand. Every baby needs an egg to grow from, and it doesn't look like Mommy's has any eggs."

Angel jumps off my knee and runs for the fridge. "Look, Mommy, we have eggs, lots of eggs, now we can grow a baby."

I couldn't help but laugh, getting up and going over to the fridge, saying to her, "You're right, Angel, we do have many eggs, but the one Mommy needs has to be in here." I put my hand on my tummy.

"You want me to cook it for you, Mommy, so you can eat it, then it will be in your tummy?" Oh, this is not going so well. Angel is just too smart for this lady.

"Come here, Angel."

"But the egg, Mommy."

"Just leave the eggs for now, Angel, we are going to the library."

"What is a library, Mommy?"

"A big place that has many, many books."

"Books for what, Mommy?"

"Well, they have all kinds of books on all kinds of babies."

"Okay, Mommy, even on baby brothers. Yes, I think so."

"Yippee, Mommy, I get to see my baby brother."

"Let's go see what we can find, then Mommy will take you for an ice cream, how about it?"

"Okay, Mommy, can we bring home a picture of my baby brother so I can show Daddy?"

"We sure will try, Angel. We sure will try." All the way to the library, Angel sang a little song she had made up about going to see her baby brother. It was a good thing we only lived three blocks from the library because it was starting to drive me crazy. I found this upsetting because nothing Angel ever did I find annoying. She was very bright for her age and always asking questions which we never minded, so why is this getting to me so bad? I was about to snap when I saw Ben's car pulling up. I felt the tears coming.

"Hey, what are my girls doing here?"

"We come to see a picture of my baby brother, Daddy."

"Oh, it looks like we all think alike." He wraps his arm around my waist and sees that I'm near tears.

"Come here, you." He pulls me in tight and whispers in my ear, "It's going to be okay, sweetheart, I promise." I start to sob into his shoulder, and he just holds me still for a minute.

"Mommy, you okay?"

"Yes, Angel, Mommy is fine."

"Why you crying, Mommy?"

"Oh, Mommy is just so happy to see me, Angel." He scoops her up as I wipe my face.

"Come now let's go inside and see what we can find." We all go into the library, and Angel is just so busy talking to everyone about her baby brother, we kept getting these sideway glances from people and a smile. A smile that says, "What are you telling this child? You don't get babies from a library."

"May I help you people find something?" the librarian asks.

"Oh yes, please, can you find my baby brother?"

"Excuse me?"

"Can." I cut her off.

"Angel, please let Mommy and Daddy do this."

She had no idea what she had done wrong. I was not about to go into great details right now.

"We are looking for books on preparing a young child about birthing of a sibling," Ben had asked the librarian.

"Of course we have some for her age group on the second shelf, row 5. They are very simple, but your daughter will get the idea."

"Thank you so very much."

"You're welcome, madam, and congratulations."

"Oh, we—"

Ben grabs my hand, saying, "Come, Kate, no need to explain." The books were just what she said but were to the point, and Angel seemed to take it all in and even about the egg and sperm. She asked very few questions but was totally taken by the pictures.

"Mommy."

"Yes, Angel."

"Babies are very ugly."

"They are not ugly when they are born, sweetheart."

"Are you sure 'cause I don't want one like this. Can we pick another one please, Mommy?"

"Angel, we don't get to pick. We have to take whatever the Lord gives to us. That includes whether it is a boy or a girl. All we can do is pray that we get what we want. But if we don't, we will still love the baby with all our hearts."

"Okay, Mommy."

"Do you understand, Angel?"

"Yes, Daddy, I will love a boy or a girl with all our hearts."

"Good girl, now let's go home. Mommy is tired."

"Mommy said we would go for ice cream, Daddy."

Ben looks across at me, and I just nod my head.

"It is what I said, and I'm fine now."

"Are you sure, Kate? We can always pick up ice cream and take it home."

"Trust me, I'm fine, we can talk later."

"All right then, Angel, looks like we are going to Mr. Softies."

"Yippee." Angel was quiet for the rest of the evening. She never said anymore about the baby which I was so pleased about. I have begun to hate the subject of babies. So I only hope she will put it to rest now. I want the Angel that we had back. The sweet simple little girl that gave me all the joy I needed. Who said a baby was what we needed to be happy just the thought has brought me so much distress that I don't want to get up in the morning just to start all over with Angel and her baby brother. Once Angel had her bath and we were tucking her in, I was so sure she would say something more. But not a peep. Hugging us as always and saying, "Good night, Mommy, good night, Daddy, I love you."

"Good night, Angel, Mommy and Daddy love you as big as the sky."

"So what do you make of that?"

"I hope that we didn't go overboard with those books, Ben."

"The librarian said they were her age group."

"I know, but she has been so very quiet ever since."

"Let's see what tomorrow brings, and if she is the same, we will ask her what she is thinking so hard about."

"I hope it wasn't too much information for her, now she is on overload."

"Kate, don't worry, Angel is a bright little thing she can take a lot in that little brain of hers."

"Maybe we just think she can, and we treat her too old for her own good."

"Now don't you go thinking that we are raising our daughter wrong. I think we keep things down to her level when we are talking to her. We have never had any troubles with her. Nor have our parents said that we tell her too much. You know my mother would be right down my throat if we were doing that. All Mother ever says is, 'She is so grown up for her age.'"

"That's my point, Ben. Maybe we tell and show her too much."

"Oh please, Kate, let's not do this."

"Do what?"

"Second-guess ourselves as far as being parents. I think we have done a wonderful job until now, and I don't think we have caused any distress in Angel's life."

"I hope you are right. I think there was too much in those books for her to take in all at once."

"Now that you could be right about. Let's just let it play out and answer her question the best and as simple as we can when she asks."

"Oh, Ben, I'm so tired of answering baby questions."

"Is that what you were so upset about when I met the two of you at the library?"

"I tried to talk to her about the egg and that maybe I didn't have any. Well, you know what she did?"

"What?"

"Angel went to the fridge and informed me that we had lots of eggs and she would even cook me one so I could eat it and put it into my tummy." I never saw Ben laugh so hard and for so long. He was rolling on our bedroom floor. Every time it seemed like he was going to be quiet, he would look at me and start all over.

"Ben, please!"

"Come here." He pulls me down on to the floor with him and wraps his arms around me.

"When I saw how upset you were, Kate, I thought something horrible had happened, and I was dreading coming home to hear about it. To be honest, I thought you were going to tell me that you had been pregnant and had lost the baby. I couldn't imagine what else would have upset you so much. Now I hear it is all over the eggs in the fridge." He starts to laugh again, but this time, I was laughing with him. It did sound hilarious now that I had heard myself say it to Ben. We laugh so hard that my laughing had turned to crying.

"Aww, Kate, don't worry so much. Please quit doing this to yourself. You are going to make yourself sick. Just be the happy Kate that you always are."

"Ben, Angel is getting to me with all the baby talk all the time."

"We will have to figure out a way to get her off the topic. Get her into something else that she might like to do that will fill her head so she can't think of anything else. Her dolls are not doing it."

"I know, skating. Figure skating starts next week."

"Good idea, Kate, she will love that look how she dances around the house all the time."

"Yea, you're right, maybe this will be just what the doctor ordered."

In the morning, I had told Angel about putting her in figure skating. It was just as we had thought; she was delighted.

"Angel, we have to talk about something before we put you into skating."

"Okay, Mommy."

"If you are going to do a good job skating, you have to promise Mommy not to worry about a baby brother."

"Why, Mommy?"

"You cannot skate your best if you don't think only about your skating, and we will have to practice a lot so your time will all be used up and you will be very tired."

"Does that mean I don't get a baby brother anymore, Mommy?"

"No, it just means that you are going to do your very, very best at skating, and you will have to keep your mind on your skating, that's all."

"Okay, Mommy, I can do that."

"Promise me."

"I promise, Mommy."

"That's my good girl. Now run off and play with your friends. Mommy will call you for lunch."

"Okay, Mommy."

Oh, my sweet Angel, I hope this works.

SEVEN

The following week, I kept Angel and myself so busy getting her set up for figure skating. We had a blast buying outfits, and Angel was in seventh heaven as she loves her clothes and to dance around. I let her wear the skating outfits all day, and she had changed several times trying to decide which one she would wear to show Ben when he came home.

"Oh, Mommy, this is too hard."

"What is, Angel?"

"I don't know which one to wear for Daddy."

Bending down to be eye level with her so she would feel like a big girl, I said, "Tell you what, Angel, why don't we have a fashion show for Daddy. You can dance and twirl around and show Daddy how good you are going to be, and he can see all of your new clothes."

"Can we, Mommy? Can we?"

"I don't see why not. Now you go pick out which one of your music CDs you want to dance to, maybe even practice until Daddy comes home. He should be along anytime now."

"Okay, Mommy." She was gone like lightning. Then it was just a matter of minutes before I heard her music blasting. Looking over my shoulder from the kitchen, I could see her doing her stuff. Oh, Angel likes to perform so she should do very well in figure skating. Taking side glances at her and not hearing much when Ben put his hand on my shoulder, I damn near wet myself.

"Sorry," he says as he points to his ears.

"Our figure skater."

"I hear and see, she looks happy."

"I'm glad we thought of this, she will be so preoccupied."

"And we will be deaf." We both laugh and walk toward our living room where Angel was dancing up a storm.

"It should be interesting watching her on skates unless she is like me on them, then that won't be funny at all."

"Why, Ben, don't you know how to skate?"

"Can't say I do, Kate, I have been on them a couple of times but never stayed on my feet, or I should say off my butt."

"Then I think we should spend more time at the pond this year, Ben, seeing how Angel will be out dancing both of us."

"Dancing, good Lord, Kate, I can't stand up on them."

"Daddy, Daddy, look what I can do." She twirls around and around, then tumbles to the floor giggling.

"I see what Daddy's Angel can do, very good for a beginner."

"Daddy, I'm not a beginner, I dance all the time."

"Sorry, you're right, and you do a mighty fine job."

"Mommy, can we do the fashion show now for Daddy?"

"Don't see why not, put on your other outfits and restart your music. I will get Daddy his coffee so he can sit right here in his chair and watch you."

"I get a fashion show?"

"Oh yes, Daddy, wait and see what Mommy bought me. I will be right back." Off she ran to her room.

"Did someone get a little spoiled today?" he asked as I'm setting his coffee down on the table.

"Yea, guess we did, but what is new?"

"It doesn't matter, Kate, so long as you and her are happy, that is all that I care about. Angel seems like she is happy with her new endeavor."

"I sure hope it last 'cause I wouldn't know what to do next?"

"Oh, Kate, you would find something for our Angel to do."

"I might just help with the skating program if they need me."

"That would be good because then you can dance with Angel on the pond while I watch."

"Oh no, you're not getting out of skating that easy, mister."

"Okay, Mommy, I'm ready for the music," Angel called from the hall.

"All right, Angel, here goes, and Daddy is ready." I put on her music and went to get our supper on the table. It took Angel an hour to go through her clothes and to give Daddy a show of a lifetime. Once we were all sitting at the table, Angel got so quiet. I thought, *Oh no, here we go again.*

"Daddy"

"Yes, Angel."

"The lady said today that my practices are all before supper."

"Yes, that's okay."

"Then you won't see me, Daddy."

"I will sneak away just in time to watch you. Maybe I won't get to all your practices, but when your big day comes, Daddy will be there. Sound like a deal?"

"Okay, Daddy." Angel was happy with that, and there was no problem or big stories or many questions when it came bedtime. She climbed into bed like a big girl and went off to sleep quite fast. One thing about Angel, she never woke up from a bad dream. Sleep came easy to her, and she always slept well.

Ben was true to his word and came to see her at her practices, and there was so much excitement over the big winter carnival that they were putting on. Angel had problems when it came to skating in order with the other children. For her to hear the instructor, she had to skate in the opposite direction than the other children. This upset the instructor, and she had asked me to take Angel out because it was distracting the other children. I tried to make them see how important it was for Angel to be in the skating club without going into our personal life. There was no way of making them understand. I told them I would talk to Ben first. She told me we had a week. I thought how inconsiderate she was; after all, we had spent a lot of money so Angel was happy and she looked good and she had everything she needed and then some. Guess that was no concern of hers nor was it fair for me to think just because it was Angel that she should let her do her own thing. With Angel not being able to hear her properly, she would end up doing her own thing because the instructor just ignored her in the end anyway.

Foremost was that Angel loved it. How were we going to tell her that because of her hearing, she wasn't going to be able to continue? This was going to be devastating to her. She will feel like she is being punished because she cannot hear on one side. I was totally upset by the time Angel got off the ice. She knew something was wrong. I could tell the way she was looking at me, but she never asked any questions. We drove home in silence, and that was so out of the usual that it made me uncomfortable.

Once at home, Angel changed her clothes and spent most of her time in her room.

"Hi there, sweetheart," Ben says as he comes in and plants a kiss on the side of my cheek.

"Hi yourself, how was your day?"

"Good, where is Angel, at a friend's?"

"No, in her room."

"Oh, why?" He caulks his head to look at me.

"Not sure, she has been very quiet since her skating and went right to her room when we got home."

"That's not like her, I will go get her."

"Okay." I know Ben won't be happy when I tell him they want us to pull her out of skating. He has been so proud of her. I will wait and tell him after Angel has gone to bed.

"No Angel."

"No, she is asleep."

"What! At this time?"

"Guess they must have played her out today."

"Well, she does skate hard when she is there and never stops."

"That's my girl, she not a quitter I will say that much."

"No, she's not a quitter, you're right about that." Should I tell Ben now seeing how Angel is already asleep?

"How is the winter carnival coming along?"

"They have it fairly well worked out, and those children are so amazing when they work together and on time."

"Is Angel skating with them? Has she finally been able to figure it out?"

I get us some coffee and sit down with Ben. "No, Ben, she hasn't been able to skate with the children. She is still going the opposite direction than the rest."

"Kate, there isn't much time before the carnival. Why haven't they gotten her strengthened out yet?"

I felt the tears coming.

Ben frowns and says, "What is it, Kate?"

"The instructor has given up on Angel. Furthermore, they want us to pull her."

"What? Why, Kate?"

"She tells me she is too distracting to the other children and they don't want her in the carnival."

"Aww, Kate, no way. Does Angel know this?"

"No, I haven't told her yet."

"Are you sure? Maybe that's why she went to her room. Could she have overheard you talking?"

"I don't think so, but possible. I never thought about that. She has been so quiet since we left there. She just hasn't been Angel at all. Ben, I'm so scared of what this is going to do to her. She has been so happy."

"Not only her, Kate, you have been happy too."

"You're right, it has been fun. I don't know what I will do with her now."

"Let's just take it one step at a time and see how she will react to the news. When are we going to tell her?"

"The instructor gave us a week. I told her I wanted to talk to you first."

"Wasn't that kind of her?"

"Now, Ben, I know how you are feeling. Believe I was some upset at first, then I got to thinking. It's not their problem if our daughter can't hear, so she can skate to the program. I believe it is their responsibility to see that all the other children get the most out of it."

"Sorry, Kate, you're right of course. Just that Angel is going to be some upset."

"Yes, she is. We will all get over it, and she has to learn that life is not easy, and for her, it may never be easy."

"Who would have thought by losing your hearing on one side could cause so much."

"She is still better off than being totally deaf."

"Yes, Kate, she is, and we have to be thankful for that right now. Although I can't see her thinking so."

"I just hope she doesn't take it as some kind of punishment 'cause she is different from the other children."

"Why couldn't they switch which way they were skating so Angel would have been able to skate with them?"

"At one point or another, she would have to turn to her bad side, and that's when she would get lost. The other children laughed at first, then they started to get upset with her because she was causing them to fall and to get all mixed up. That's when the instructor got upset as well."

"I guess I should have tried harder to be at more practices."

"It wouldn't have mattered, Ben. She still couldn't do it."

"I thought she was doing great. You never said anything."

"Angel was enjoying herself, and I didn't want you to be disappointed in her."

"Kate, she is still a little girl. How could I get disappointed in her? Now when she is a teen and does something stupid, then maybe and only maybe."

"Ben, she will always have you wrapped around her little finger."

"Hell, her and Mommy have me wrapped around their entire hand, never mind little finger." He takes my hand and pulls me over to his knee. He starts to nibble on my neck.

"Supper won't get made this way."

"I have supper right here."

"Not very filling."

"It fills my heart, Kate, and that is so much nicer than a full stomach."

"Oh, you mean I don't have to cook anymore?"

"We still have to feed Angel."

"You're right."

"I will eat then."

"Thought you said." He shuts me up with a kiss.

"Do you know you talk too much."

"Think you have told me that a time or two." We both laugh, and before we knew it, we were in our bedroom.

"Angel might wake up."

"So we have a lock, she will knock." Time went by fast, and we had fallen asleep. Angel never did get up and come see us. I had gone to check on her, and she was still sleeping, so I just left her door open a little and went back and climbed in with Ben.

"I sure hope Angel is okay. This isn't like her at all."

"Now, Kate, don't go getting worried because Angel has played herself out. She will be fine in the morning with more energy than you could wish for."

"I know, I know. I just can't believe she is still sleeping. Not waking up for supper and all. She has been skating so hard and thinking she is doing so good. She is so excited about the carnival. I don't know how I will tell her she's not going to be in it."

"You would think that the instructor would have found something for her to be able to do instead of just giving her the boot."

"How do I tell her, Ben? The carnival is in two weeks."

"Why didn't they say something right away? Instead of waiting until she thinks she is doing so good. It seems to be a mean way of dealing with a child."

"Yea, you're right."

"No matter what we think, we still have to break her heart."

"Oh god, I don't want to have to do that."

"You are not doing it alone. We will tell her tomorrow after supper." Ben pulls me in close, and we lie in silence, each thinking their own thought on the matter. Knowing tomorrow is just another day and no matter what, life goes on. Some things we have control of and others we don't. The ones you don't you have to learn to live with whether you like it or not. But we all know when it comes to a child, no one wants to bring any kind of pain or disappointment to them. We all want to be their heroes. Their knight in shining armor. This will be harder on Ben than myself because he never says no to Angel. Angel is his life; our life and tomorrow will be a horrible day for all of us.

"Mommy, Mommy."

"What is it, Angel?" I sat up in bed so fast I got a head rush.

"I don't feel good, Mommy."

"Come here, Angel, and snuggle with Daddy and me." Pulling her into bed, I realize she has a high fever.

"Oh, baby, you are so hot. Mommy better get you some medicine. Mommy will be right back. You stay here with Daddy."

"Okay."

"What is the matter, Kate?"

"Angel is running a high fever. I will go get her something for it."

"All right, come here, Angel, and snuggle Daddy."

She slides over to snuggle with Ben, and when he feels how hot she really is, he gets a little scare.

"Kate, she is so hot."

"I know she is, she must have a flu bug."

"I have a bug, Daddy?"

"Sort of, honey, that is why you are hot."

"Here, take this, and Mommy is going to run you a bath."

"What can I do, Kate?"

"Maybe you could get her some soup."

"You got it." Ben goes to make the soup, and I take Angel in to give her a cool bath. I don't like fever in children; it is too hard on the brain. I have always been afraid of fevers. I kept Angel in the water until Ben called to tell us the soup was ready. Angel now was shivering, so we took her from one state to another. Having the shakes is no nicer than having a fever. Her head was cooling down, so that made us happy. She did eat her soup and was content enough to just sit on Ben's lap for a while. He sat there and rocked her back and forth; she would doze off and on while we chatted about different things.

"Daddy, she cried." Only it was too late; she was bringing up her soup all over him and the floor.

The look on his face made me want to laugh. I knew if I didn't do something fast, he was going to be throwing up with her. Taking Angel from him and heading to the bathroom so I could clean her up.

"I will get the rest in a moment," I call to Ben over my shoulder as I walk away with Angel.

"It's okay, Kate, I can get this."

"You sure, you're all right with that mess?"

"Yea, I will be, it is the act of that can get me going."

"Me too sometimes. Thank you." I bathe Angel again and put her into clean pj's. I gave her another small shot of medicine for her fever. I didn't think she would have too much left in her body to do much good.

Ben was busy out in the kitchen, cleaning up the floor and whatever else Angel might have hit. I could smell the bleach, so I was thankful for that. Vomit is a very hard smell to get rid of if you just wipe. So I was happy that he had paid attention on the cleaning end of these mishaps that we've had before.

"Why do I have a bug, Mommy?"

"It is that time of year, Angel, and many people will get this. One thing about it, it won't last long."

"I really don't feel very good, Mommy."

EIGHT

"I know, Angel, but try to sleep now. Tomorrow you will feel better, I promise. Mommy will put some apple juice beside your bed, and you drink as much as you can, okay?"

"But what if I foow it up, Mommy?"

"Don't worry about that. Every time you throw up, you get rid of more bugs out of your tummy."

For the next two weeks, Angel was so sick I had to take her to the doctor. What I thought was just a simple flu was influenza. Our poor baby lost weight, she lost energy, and she even scared us when her fever would hit 104 and stayed there for three days. It did not matter what we did; her fever didn't seem to come down. At one point, she got delirious, and that was very hard on Ben and myself to see our little girl go through such a hard time.

"One thing about this, Kate, we didn't have to tell Angel she couldn't skate in the carnival."

"Oh my god, Ben, I forgot all about that."

"It's okay, Kate, it was taken out of our hands."

"Yea, but she will want to go back skating when she feels better."

"Then we will deal with it then. Kate, you look terrible. You should take a nap while she is sleeping. You have a touch of the bug too, don't you?"

"Why do you say that?"

"I heard you throwing up a few times, Kate, and you are so pale. Have you got a fever too?"

"I don't think so, but I am tired. Maybe you're right, and I will lie down for a while."

"That's good, when you wake up, I will make you some chicken noodle soup."

"Sounds good, thanks, Ben."

He kisses me and tucks me in. I did not realize until now how drained I really was. Sitting up with Angel has worn me right out. I sure hope Ben doesn't get it as well.

He can't afford to lose any days in work as we had just bought a house and are getting back on our feet from the big down payment. Furthermore, Ben wants to have it paid for in ten years instead of thirty-five. He says he's not paying more than we have to. So he puts in as much time as he can without jeopardizing the family time. Most of the time, he does really well. If he gets too worn down, he could get sick for a long time. It has been over three weeks now for Angel, and she is just starting to keep food down. By food, I mean soup broths, Jell-O, some ice cream. Nothing heavy yet and her appetite just is not back yet. I was worried about it, and the doctor said not to be as it will take her body time to come back to itself.

The days turned into weeks for me, and it seemed like I just was not going to shake it. I spent most of time sleeping, and I kept very little down. Ben did not come down with influenza as I had. For some reason, he had managed to stay healthy. Angel and I kept him busy. We were able to take care of each other while he was at work. It was so great when he got home and I didn't have to worry about Angel. I could just sleep. Angel got well enough to go back to school. She would go to bed very early when she got home but was always excited about getting up for school. She wasn't even sad that she had missed the carnival. I think being sick for so long, she has forgot about her skating. Going to school kept her busy, and I wasn't sure if we really needed to put her into any other activity. It took Angel over a month to get back to her old self. She was small to start with, but with the weight loss, she had dropped in clothes size. I bought only a few new things to get by because I know it won't take long for her to gain it back now that she is eating good again.

"Mommy, you still have the bug?"

"Afraid so, Angel."

"How come, Mommy?"

"'Cause Mommy has a bigger body and it can hold more of those bugs, so it will take Mommy longer to get better." I had lost weight as well, but

I didn't mind. I had too much in some places anyway and not enough in others. "You need to eat more chicken soup."

"I know, sweetheart, and Mommy will." If I eat one more bowl of chicken soup, I will scream. The fat in the soup turns my stomach. There's a lot of things turning my stomach.

"Daddy's home, I will tell him to make some soup, Mommy."

"Thank you, Angel, Mommy is getting up." When I reached the kitchen, Ben was already making, you guessed it, chicken noodle soup.

"Hi, sweetheart," he says as I came into the kitchen.

"Hi, hon, how is it going?"

"Good, how about with you? Your soup will be ready right away, and I put on a pot of tea."

"You are a good man, Ben. Don't know what I would do if I didn't have you."

"That's what I like to hear, now eat up." He set the bowl in front of me, and the first whiff had me running to the bathroom. God, how can I still throw up so much? Is there no end to this?

"Sweetheart, you all right?" Ben asked as he came into the bathroom.

"Yea, I will be just fine."

"I want you to go see the doctor, Kate. This is going on way too long."

"I will be fine, Ben. I don't need a doctor. Angel is fine, and I will be fine."

"Please, Kate, you have lost so much weight, and you are still throwing up. You can't even eat chicken noodle soup."

"Oh, please, don't mention it." I cover my mouth and gag.

"See, Kate, please, for me, go see a doctor. You aren't able to really take care of Angel."

"That's what I have you for."

"Kate!"

"Okay, okay. I will make an appointment tomorrow."

"Thank you."

"You're welcome, now can we go chat somewhere besides the bathroom?"

"Oh sure, Angel is still at the table." Going out to the kitchen, we find Angel has gone. Glancing outside, we could see her talking to a friend on the sidewalk.

"So much for still being at the table."

"It is good to see her back playing with her friends. I was worried when she was so sick."

"Makes two of us."

"Now I'm worried about you, Kate."

"Oh, Ben, no need to be worried about me. I'm not as sick as I was, so I'm on the road to good health as well. Just taking longer because I got run-down taking care of Angel. I will be up and running soon."

"Not soon enough to suit me."

"Oh, Ben, don't you like playing nursemaid?"

"For a short time it is fine, but enough is enough, Kate."

"I know what you mean, and I'm sure I will be as good as new next week."

"You are still going to the doctor right?"

"Yes, Ben, I will go and waste our health care just so you can relax."

"That's my girl, now sit and have tea while we watch our Angel have fun."

"I like watching her play."

"I think she can be a little bossy towards the other kids."

"I think you're right, but she is so much older acting than most of them. I think she has spent too much time with just me. I should have put her into play school or something where she would have had to deal with more kids her own age. She is too old for her own good."

"Maybe so, Kate, but she is still a little girl and has many years to grow and change. We can only hope that when she is old enough to be on her own, this will all come back into play."

"What do you mean, Ben?"

"That she will be older than her peers and hopefully wiser. We won't have to worry so much about our little girl making wrong choices because she wasn't ready to leave home."

"Yea, well, maybe that could backfire on us, Ben."

"Why do you say that?"

"She may think she's old enough to do things she shouldn't be doing. Then what?"

"Oh, I never thought of that. Like guys thinking she is older than she really is because of her mentality."

"That is right, so we might not have been all that smart in letting our little girl get old so fast."

"Well! It's not like we did it on purpose. It just happened."

"We should have been waiting to talk about some things after she had gone to bed."

"It's not like she was in on the conversations."

"No, but their little ears are always open, and they hear more than we think they do. They seem to have such a large memory card in their little heads. I think as we get older, it must shrink. No, Kate, we have to delete some things to make room for the future."

"That's how it works?"

"Afraid so, can you imagine the overload we would be running on if we didn't delete."

"Do you know how crazy you sound using the phrase *delete*, Ben?"

"Sorry, but it is true. Working with computers all day my whole day runs on delete."

"Well, please make me a promise."

"Sure, Kate, what is it?"

"That you won't delete Angel or myself from your life."

"Oh, Kate, that is the easiest promise to make." He reaches for my hand across the table and squeezes it softly.

"I could not imagine my life without you and Angel in it. In fact life would not be worth living, Kate, if it weren't for you and Angel. At the end of every day, I'm so happy when the clock chimes four bells 'cause I know I'm coming home where there is nothing but love and happiness."

"You're really that happy with your life, Ben?"

"Of course I am, why would you ask? Aren't you happy, Kate?"

"Yes, I'm happy, Ben, and I would hope that I'm just as happy as you are."

"Why do you have so much hesitation in your voice?"

"I know you wanted another baby so bad, Ben."

"Shush, Kate, don't do this to yourself."

"It's true, so how can you say you're so happy."

"Kate, I'm very happy with what I have. Sure another child would be nice, but so what! Things happen for a reason, and I wouldn't want to give up anyone I have. Maybe the good Lord is telling us that Angel is all we need. Maybe that is why she got so sick. He was reminding us of just that. The three of us are one, Kate, and I'm happy this way. I want you to be happy that we have each other, and that is all that matters to me." He lifts my face up and says, "Look me in the eye, Kate, and tell me that Angel and I are all you need. Please!"

"You are, Ben. I feel like I have let you down."

"No, you haven't now you get that ridiculous idea right out of that pretty head of yours. Remember, Kate, it takes two, so maybe it's not you. Maybe it is me. You are a loving, trusting wife, and you are a fantastic mother. I cannot ask for more."

"How did I get so lucky to find you?"

"Well, for starters, you didn't find me. We ran into each other, remember? Literally."

"Yea, we sure did, didn't we? That was the best tumble I had ever had."

"Me too. So far as the rest of this goes and us not being able to have another baby means nothing, Kate, but we could tear ourselves apart. We could destroy our marriage because of it, and please, I don't want us to do that. So I'm happy being us, just the way we are. Let's enjoy Angel to the fullest. Watch her grow up and then enjoy being grandparents.

"In the meantime, let's enjoy each other and all we have to give. We have much more living to do, Kate. Angel is old enough now to enjoy traveling. We can enjoy traveling with her. She will learn a lot, and we can learn a lot from her."

"You're right, Ben, you have made me feel better already."

"Good, I will get us more tea."

"That would be great, it's even staying down."

"Perhaps I should make you some more soup now that your tea is staying down."

"Ben, I swear, I will throw it at you."

"There, see my Kate is back."

We sat for a while in silence and just watch our little girl play with her friends and enjoyed each other. One thing about Ben and me, we could spend quiet time together, and it was always very relaxing. Sometimes we read, and sometimes I did knitting while he read. We talked about the odd thing that would come up, but it wasn't nothing stressful or urgent. Just plain simple conversation.

Ben was on the ball, and while I had dozed off, sitting there in the late afternoon sun. He got busy in the kitchen and made some fried egg sandwiches with french fries.

"Mommy, Mommy," Angel calls as she is shaking my arm.

"Yes, Angel, what is it?"

"Daddy made supper, you pose to come eat."

"Okay, sweetheart, Mommy has to go to the bathroom first, then I will be right there."

"You sick again, Mommy?"

"No, honey, Mommy has to pee."

"Oh sorry, Mommy."

"That's okay, honey, we have all been sick too long, but everyone will be fine soon."

"I'm glad, Mommy, 'cause I miss you."

"Honey, Mommy has been here all the time."

"No, Mommy, sometimes you not."

"Listen, Angel, Mommy really, really has to pee. I will talk to you when I come for supper, okay?"

"Okay. Mommy." Angel skips away, and that made my heart skip with happiness 'cause I knew my little girl was back. But what did she mean by I wasn't here all the time? I haven't gone anywhere for a month and a half now. God, with us both being sick, we didn't dare go far from the washroom. I wonder how Ben managed to miss all the sickness. Not that I'm not glad because I don't know what I would have done without him. I could hear them laughing and talking like they did before we got sick.

"Mommy, Daddy made french fries."

"That sounds great to me."

"Here is a fried egg sandwich too, Kate."

"Oh, Ben, this is great, and it smells so good. It is so pleasant to have real food again. I was beginning to think you had bought all the chicken soup the stores had."

"I don't think I did, but I could go back and check to see if I forgot some."

"Don't you even think about it, Ben!"

"Mommy, you said chicken noodle soup is the best when we are sick."

"Yes, Angel, I did, but not when you are sick for a long time. Mommy is full right up to here with chicken soup." I pass my hand over my head, and Angel starts to laugh.

"What can't you see it coming out of Mommy's ears, I'm so full."

"No, Mommy, I can't see nuffing." She leans over to look in my ears. Now Ben is laughing too.

"Now I would say both my girls are back."

"We didn't go nowhere, Daddy."

"No, you're right, you didn't. Daddy is just so happy that you and Mommy are not sick no more. I was getting lonely you and Mommy sleeping all the time. I had no one to talk to."

"Daddy, you can always talk to me. My little ears, they hear everything."

Ben raises his eyebrows as he looks over to me.

"See I told you." We broke down with laughter.

"What is so funny, Mommy?"

"You are Angel. You are." The egg sandwich and french fries were so good. I hope they stay down. It feels like a lifetime since we sat and ate a real meal. Although I don't think this qualifies as a real meal, but it sure the hell beats chicken noodle soup. I'm sure I will never buy another can as long as I live. Whoever said that chicken noodle soup was the best thing to eat when you are sick, must be out of their mind 'cause if you're not sick, it is going to make you sick.

"Mommy, can I do bowling like Jenny does?"

"Bowling?" Ben asks and looks at me.

"What do you think, Kate? Could she join bowling?"

"Well, I don't see why not."

"Goodie, goodie, Jenny needs one more on her team."

"Then we will have to go down and see about getting you on to her team."

"I don't want to skate no more."

"Oh, and why not? Daddy thought you like to skate."

"I do, Daddy, but the kids laugh at me 'cause I have to skate backwards. I don't like them anymore." Ben was looking over at me as if I had the answers.

"Well, Angel, if you don't want to skate anymore, that is fine. Mommy won't take you anymore."

"I want to bowl with Jenny. Jenny has a bad ear too, but she said she doesn't have to bowl backwards." Ben and I cracked up, and Ben went over and picked Angel up off the chair.

"Oh, Angel, we love you so much even if you did bowl backwards. That wouldn't matter to Mommy and me, would it, Mommy?"

"No. It would not, remember, we love you as big as the sky. I stretched my arms out as wide as I could to show her how much we loved her.

NINE

The next day I left earlier than need be on the way to the doctor so I could stop at the bowling alley. Angel was right; there was a team that was in need of one more person. I questioned them first about Angel's hearing problem to see if that was going to make any difference. Again Angel was right; she would not have to worry about being teased or bowling backward, so I signed her up. I knew she would be a happy camper once again. I thought about what she went through at skating and could not believe that I didn't see what was happening. I will have to make a point of really listening this time. Angel hasn't been out in community group activities, so this was all new to her and ourselves. I did not realize that small children could be so mean.

What surprises me the most is Angel never said a word to me or her dad. She always seems to be so happy out there on the ice and always so excited to go. It had to be while she was out on the ice. I was with her all the time while she was off the ice. While they were out there on the ice, I couldn't hear what was being said by the children or the instructor. The times I saw them laughing, I did not think for one minute that they were laughing at Angel, that she had been the point of their joke. I thought it was something in their program that they all find so funny. Here it was, our little girl that was the joke they were all laughing at. Inside she must have been so sad to know she was the joke on the ice. How could I not see it? Then that was our little trooper. She always held her head up high and kept on going. That was our fault because we always told her to be tough, that sure didn't mean for her to be bullied from the other children and we must remember to talk to her about that. I'm sure it will be one of our topics at the table tonight.

Ben could be upset at me for not seeing what was going on with our daughter and the other children. Hell I'm upset with me. I had a fifteen-minute wait once I was at the doctor's office, so leaving that early wasn't necessary. It was okay. I still had plenty of time before I had to pick Angel up from school.

"What brings you back to see me?" Dr. Adams asks.

"I can't seem to shake the flu. I'm still throwing up, not as much as I was, and I'm so tired."

"Influenza is a very harsh flu to get. It can take a very long time to get completely over it. It has killed more than one person over the years. I will send you for some blood work. Come lay down, and I will check your appendix as well. Sometimes those crazy things will act up just enough to keep us feeling ill, but not enough to make us want to do surgery." So I lie on the table, and Dr. Adams pushes down on my left, then my right, and he makes my tummy bounce up and down as much as he could. None of this bothered me.

"Well, Kate, I think it is still the flu, but the blood work will tell all, so go down to the lab and get it done. Come back at the end of the week. If there is anything to worry about, I will call you on it. In the meantime, stay resting and I want you drinking more fluids and eat chicken." At that word, I put my hand up and said, "Please don't even say the words. I'm so sick of that soup I will never buy another can."

He chuckles. "All right, have it your way. Eat whatever you can stand to keep down. I'm sure you are out of the worse. It just has to finish running its course. You are well past any danger, Kate, so just relax and you will get well. Before you know it, you will forget you've been so sick."

"I have never had the flu so bad and for so long."

"You were run-down taking care of Angel, so it got a real good hold on you. How is Angel now?"

"She great, you wouldn't know she had been so sick."

"That's what it will be like for you too, Kate."

"I can't wait. Thank you, Dr. Adams."

"Is there anything else, Kate, while you are here?"

I knew what he was getting at, but I just said, "No, Dr. Adams, that's all. I'm good."

"All right then, you go get your blood work done. I will talk to you when that comes back." He puts his hand on my shoulder and pats it as though I was a little girl in need of some consoling.

"Thank you for your time, Dr. Adams."

You're welcome anytime, Kate. Remember, I'm always available if you need to talk."

"I know and thank you." For some reason, when I left there, I got into the car and cried my eyes out. I had no idea what I was crying over. I almost couldn't see the road to the lab to get my blood work done. Wiping my eyes and blowing my noise, I felt like such a wimp. This is crazy. It is just the tail end of the flu. I will be okay. So why did I feel like something deep down inside of me was trying to tell me something. If you are tuned in to your body, you should be able to read the signs it sends you. My head has been in such a state for so long. I couldn't decipher what anything was trying to tell me. Other than it's time to throw up or it's time to sleep.

There was a line up waiting to have their blood work done. At first, I thought about just leaving. I reconsider knowing how Ben will be full of questions when I get home. If I were to tell him Dr. Adams ordered blood work and I didn't go, he would have my head. So I waited around for my turn and was pleasantly surprised that it didn't take long before I was in having my blood taken. After vile number 6, I was getting a little worried.

"Do I get a blood transfusion after this?"

"Dr. Adams is covering all bases, not to worry, just one more vile." I knew my arm was going to be black and blue halfway up my arm and halfway down. They never take blood from me without bruising me terribly. This will upset both Ben and Angel. This is something I have lived with all my life. When Ben had blood work done a couple of years ago. I couldn't believe that all you saw the next day was a pinhole. I will be changing color by the time I get home. This stays with me for up to two weeks easy.

I went in to the hospital with chest pains, thinking it was my heart they put small injections into my tummy with blood thinner in it. Now after a week, I was a solid rainbow of colors across my tummy. I look like I was sicker than I really was. That took a very long time to clear up. Ben just kept saying, "Are you sure you're not sore?" Every time he would touch my tummy, he never believed me when I would tell him no.

Angel will want to play nurse and will think I should have a bandage on it. Of course I will have to have one just to satisfy her. After all, it is just a bandage.

When I picked Angel up, she was so excited because she gets to go bowling after school today.

"Mommy, do you think I can bowl like the others?"

"Maybe not just like the others, but it won't take you long to catch up, Angel."

"Will they laugh at me, Mommy?"

"I don't know, Angel, maybe."

"Oh," she says and screws up the side of her face.

"Angel, Mommy is going to be right there beside you. I won't let them laugh at you."

"You won't, Mommy?"

"No, Angel, Mommy won't let anyone make fun of you."

"Okay. Mommy." She didn't look like she really believed me. Hell, I didn't know if I believed me. How do you stop children from laughing?

"Are you hungry, Angel? Would you like fries and nuggets before you go bowling?"

"No, Mommy, I'm not hungry. Thank you."

"You're welcome, but are you sure?"

"Yes, Mommy, I'm sure."

"Okay, you let me know if you change your mind."

"I will, Mommy."

"Promise."

She looks over at me then gets the biggest smile. "I promise, Mommy."

"Is your tummy a little scared?"

"It feels funny."

"Funny how? Throwing up funny?"

"No, Mommy, just funny."

"Oh, you have butterflies in your tummy."

Angel never answered me. I could see she was thinking really hard about something.

"What are you thinking about, Angel?"

"How they all get in there."

"What do you mean?"

"Well, I had that bug that made me sick all over, and now I have butterflies. Will they make me sick all over too?"

"No, you won't get sick, honey."

"How did they get in my tummy? I did not eat any."

I couldn't help but laugh. I wish Ben would have been here; that would have made his day.

"No, sweetheart, they call it butterflies 'cause if you hold a butterfly in your hand just lightly so it can flap its wings. It is the same feeling that you are having right now. It is caused by nerves that is all."

"So I don't have butterflies in my tummy?"

"No, honey, it is just a feeling."

"Oh, I'm glad, Mommy, 'cause I don't want to go to the doctor."

"Why would you go to a doctor?"

"So he could take the butterflies out."

"Of course, silly me." Once we were inside the bowling alley, the noise got to be so loud you could hardly hear yourself talk.

Angel's friend Jenny came running over right away to take Angel over to their seat. I got her shoes and paid for her bowling and bought her a shirt so she would look like the rest of the team.

"Angel, come with Mommy to the bathroom."

"I don't have to go to the bathroom, Mommy."

"Mommy bought you a shirt to put on so you look like your team, but you can't put it on out here. We have to take your sweater off."

"You did, Mommy? Thank you."

"Now come let's change before you miss your turn."

"Jenny told me I was last. That way I can see how it is done."

"I think that is a very good idea, now hurry up." It was great to see Angel so happy again. Little children should always be happy. They should not be allowed to be sad. There should be a rule for that.

It was a good thing that there were clear bumper boards they called them. Some of the children threw their ball high and hard. The bumper board stopped it from going into the lane next to them and causing a real chaos. When it came Angel's turn, she found the smallest ball but still found it to be heavy, and she dropped it instead of rolling it. No one laughed. I know she was waiting for that. The coach just said, "Take another ball, Angel, you have three tries." She turned around and saw me, and then she got a big smile.

"Go ahead, Angel, you can do it." She took her time. One of the three balls made it all the way down the alley. She was no worse than any of the other children, so there was no laughing at her and no teasing. They all chatted and had a good time. It was timeconsuming because more of the children were more like Angel than not. It was a long waiting process for the balls to get to the other end. Some of them didn't make it, and the coach would have to walk down the alley and take the balls off. There was no one really better than the next. They were all relaxed, and all listened to the coach very well. She had a knack with the children; she should have been a teacher.

When we got home, Angel had so much to tell Ben that I had forgotten to talk to her about letting herself being bullied by other children.

"So you really like bowling, Angel?"

"Oh yes, Daddy. Can you come see me?"

"I sure can, Angel."

"Did you make some new friends, Angel?"

"Yes, Daddy, I did. I had butterflies in my tummy, but they went away when I saw Jenny."

"I'm glad, Angel, that you like it and you have a friend there too."

"I thought you and I would take Angel bowling on the weekend. That way she would get more practice in."

"Oh, you did, did you?"

"Please, Daddy, you will like it, and you are tough."

"I have to be tough, do I?"

"Oh yea, Daddy, the balls are very heavy."

He reaches over and squeezes her upper arm. "Hum."

"What, Daddy?"

"I think you need to eat more so you can get bigger muscles then."

"I already can throw the ball, Daddy."

"I think your Daddy is right, Angel. Remember how your balls only went halfway down the alley. They didn't all make it down to the end and hit the pins. So if you eat more, you will get stronger in your arms and be able to hit more pins."

"Okay. Can I have a piece of pizza?"

"What?"

"Please, Daddy."

"How did you know I bought pizza?"

"I can smell it." She sniffs a couple of times.

"Mommy will get the plates."

"How about you, Kate? You having some pizza?"

"Real food, I sure am."

"I'm glad to hear that."

"Mommy, what is real food?"

"Mommy just means no soup, Angel."

"Mommy don't like soup no more, Daddy."

"I know, sweetheart."

"I will eat soup again, Angel, just not right now."

"I know, Mommy, 'cause you full of soup right up to here." She takes her hand and passes it over her head. We all break out with laughter. Eating our fair share of pizza while Angel went over all her new friends' names and told Ben what each one look like so Ben would know them when he came to the bowling alley. He would put on this frown and act like he was putting each child into his memory bank. The faces he was making had her giggling like she used to before she got so sick. It was heartwarming to see and to hear.

I had such a peaceful sleep that night; it was the first in a very long time. Getting up this morning didn't feel like such chore today. Getting Ben off to work and Angel off to school was always a delight. There was always so much chatter in the morning was as if we had stayed awake all night, thinking of things to talk about. Just as I was getting Angel into the car, my phone rang.

"Good morning, Kate, this is Jamie from Dr. Adams's office."

"Good morning, Jamie." My heart started to speed up with fear.

"Dr. Adams wants you to come see him today at 1:00 a.m. if possible."

"Oh sure, I can do that."

"All right, we will see you at one."

TEN

"Yes, thank you." My mind is racing while I take Angel to school. I know when the doctor is calling you back to his office, it can't be good.

"Mommy, Mommy." Angel is shaking my arm.

"Yes, Angel, what is it?"

"Why you not talking to me, Mommy?"

"Oh, I'm sorry, Angel, guess Mommy's brain is still sleeping."

"Oh." That was all Angel said for the rest of the trip to school. At least, I didn't hear anymore of what she had said. That doesn't mean she wasn't talking. It just meant my mind was somewhere else. The whole day went by so slowly. I had a hard time putting my mind into anything. All day I just thought of the worse. I feared that the doctor was going to tell me I had cancer. Why else was I still sick now that Angel is well, and why didn't Ben get sick. There was only one answer in my mind. Oh god, what will I do? Who will take care of Angel? Who will love her as her father and I do?

By the time twelve-thirty rolled around so I could head to the doctor's office, I was so sick I didn't dare eat lunch early. Now I wished I had told Ben about this appointment. I need him here with me. He is my rock. Why hadn't I told him about this appointment?

"Hi, Kate."

"Hi, Jamie."

"Have a seat, it will be a few minutes yet."

"That's fine, I know I'm a little early."

"Dr. Adams delivered a baby before coming, so it put him a little bit behind."

"Great" was all I could say. I picked up magazines and tried to read, but that wasn't happening. Tossing it aside, I started watching people. Wow, people really do come in all sizes and shapes. More on the large side than small or medium. Why do people do this to themselves! Do they not look in the mirror?

I know some of them are looking at me and wondering the same thing. I have lost so much weight that I look like I'm anorexic. I know I look terrible, and I hope today doesn't make me feel worse. I thought I was getting over the worse of it; the pizza we had for supper has stayed down. Mind you, it has been rolling around like it would like to be anywhere else but where it is at. I'm sure that by the time Dr. Adams is done with me, it will be in their toilet.

"Okay, Kate, Dr. Adams can see you now."

"Thank you."

She takes me back to his one office and puts my file up on the door. As she is closing the door, she says to me, "Have a good visit, Kate!"

"Thank you." I wanted to both scream at her and look at my own file that was hanging out there on the door. I know deep down that it wasn't long before Dr. Adams came in, but it sure felt like it. Will this day never end?

"Hello, Kate," Dr. Adams says as he comes in taking my file off the door.

"Hi, Dr. Adams."

"How have you been feeling since you were here last week?" he says this as he sits with his hands on my file. Don't they know how uptight people are when waiting for the bad news to come? Do they have to drag it on so?

"I think things are getting better. I had pizza for supper, and it stayed down."

"That is good to hear, Kate, 'cause you have lost way too much weight. We will have to see if we can get your weight back up to where it should be and then some because you will be needing your strength in the months to come." Now my heart is racing so fast I feel like I was going to pass out. I sit there nodding my head up and down, and nothing would come out.

"The first trimester is always harder on some people than others, and with you, having the flu on top of being pregnant has not helped the situation at all." Gasping for air and chocking and feeling faint. The room started to spin, and Dr. Adams was around his desk and catching me before I hit the floor.

He grabbed at the buzzer and rang for the nurse.

"Yes, Dr. Adams, how can I help."

I could tell by the look on her face, she was concerned about what had happened.

"Please bring Kate some orange juice."

"Yes, sir, right away." She left in a hurry, closing the door behind her. I started to cry totally out of control. Dr. Adams was rubbing his hand up and down on my back, saying, "Kate, just take some slow deep breaths. Come on now, you can do this. Slow and easy."

The nurse brings in the orange juice, and I sip it slowly so I don't choke myself.

"Kate, are you ready to talk about this now?"

"Yes," I say in a bare whisper.

"Now I want to know if this is a good thing or a bad thing to you, Kate."

"What do you mean, Dr. Adams?"

"No one has ever reacted that way to being told they're pregnant."

"I thought you and Ben were wanting another child?"

"Oh, Dr. Adams." I started to cry again and shaking my head from side to side.

"It's okay, Kate, you can talk to me. Have you changed your mind about a baby, or has Ben? You can put it up for adoption, but I think you really should think about this first. You and Ben were wanting a baby so bad a while ago, and you were so disappointed every month that went by and you weren't pregnant. What has happened since then to change your mind? Are you and Ben not getting along?"

"Oh, Dr. Adams, that's not it at all."

"Then tell me, Kate, I will see if I can help."

"Dr. Adams, you have already helped me."

Now he has that frown on his face that is saying, "What the hell is this woman talking about?"

"You want to explain please!"

"When your nurse called me in, I thought it was because I had something terribly wrong with me. All these horrible thoughts have been going through my head."

"Kate, you didn't know you were pregnant?"

"No, I never even thought that was why I have been sick. I was thinking I went from the flu to—"

"You were thinking you had cancer, Kate?"

"Yes, I couldn't think of what else it could be."

"Oh, my darling girl, I'm so sorry. It had to have been a rough morning on you?"

"Yes, it was, now that I have my breath and the room is not spinning, I'm so happy, Dr. Adams. I can't wait to tell Ben." I go to get off my chair, but he puts his hands up and says, "Just a few more minutes, Kate, I'm not done with you."

"Oh, what is it?"

"You are very run-down, Kate, so you are going to have to be very careful for a while until you have built your strength back."

"Oh, I will be, Dr. Adams!"

"No, Kate! You're not understanding me. You could lose this baby very easy right now. I am very worried about you and your baby, so please I want you to do little as possible and eat as much as you can that will help you put on weight as well as give you energy. The fetus has been starving with you being so sick. I am amazed that you have not miscarried by now. This could be a very good sign that this is going to be one very strong baby. But I want you to be careful for the next three weeks. You come back and see me then. If anything, and I mean anything, no matter how small it may seem to you, you get back here or the hospital. I will post a note both places, and you are to be put in to see me immediately upon arrival. Do you understand, Kate?"

"You're scaring me."

"Good, I mean to scare you. You do have to know how delicate you and this baby are right now. This is something you and Ben have wanted for a long time. I just want you to be prepared for everything."

"Like losing our baby?"

"Yes, Kate, I'm afraid so. Please do as I say to the *T*, and I want you to take these supplements and help rebuild your strength." Dr. Adams was writing out my prescription. I was bubbling over inside. We were having a baby. Finally, our dream and family will be complete.

Making another appointment in three weeks' time. Then I was out of there.

Getting out onto their steps, I stopped and looked up to the heavens, and all I could do was say "thank you, God" as the tears ran down my cheeks. People passing by looked at me in wonder, but no one stopped to see if I were okay. It has become a strange world we live in now. At one time, if anyone saw someone in tears, their first reaction was to stop and ask if they were all right. At this moment, I was more than all right, I was ecstatic, and I was hungry. Yea, I'm hungry. Putting my hand on my tummy and saying out loud, "Let's go eat something fattening, little one." I was off to the family restaurant. I wanted to call Ben and invite him for lunch, but it is way past his lunch break. Eating alone and enjoying it and anyone who had a smile got smiled back at no problem. Hell, even if they didn't smile, I had a smile for them from ear to ear. I was pregnant and damn proud of it. I couldn't be any happier. Once I had finished my lunch, I walk up Main Street a while. I had some time to kill before I picked Angel up from school, so there was no point in going home. Wondering into this one store that I never went into but now seemed appropriate. The store was called Baby's Galore. It took my breath away when I saw all the baby items that were out there these days. I had no idea that you could get such things. It has changed a lot since we had Angel. Ben and I had her before we were set up, and we didn't have the money to buy something that she would only use for the first couple of months. That seemed to be such a waste. I suppose if you buy it for the first one, then you would have it to use for the next. This is our last baby, so I'm hoping Ben and I will be very thrifty when it comes to shopping for this baby as well. I have always been what people consider a very practical person almost to the boring state. It has got me through some horribly rough times while I was single, so no harm done. In fact it made me much wiser than friends my age.

The time in the baby store went by fast, and before I knew it, it was time to go pick up Angel. I will have to bring her here, and there is no way Ben won't want to come here as well. If they have their way, I could see it becoming our second home.

Keeping the news to myself when I picked up Angel was one of the hardest things I have ever done.

"Mommy.

"Yes, Angel."

"Why do you look so happy?"

"I do?"

"Yes, Mommy, your teeth have been smiling all the time."

"I guess 'cause Mommy's not sick no more."

"You not, Mommy?"

"No, honey, I'm not."

"You didn't foow up the pizza?"

ELEVEN

"I sure did not. Mommy had lunch in town today, and I never threw it up either."

"I'm glad, Mommy, 'cause Jen's mommy said you were too skinny."

"She did? When did you talk to her?"

"Jenny forgot her lunch, and her mommy brought it to her. She asked me if you were sick. I told her you still had the bug like me. She said that's why you were skinny."

"Well, Mommy won't be skinny too long now. I feel a lot better, and Mommy can eat lots now. Besides, Dr. Adams gave Mommy some pills to help."

"He did?"

"Yes, he sure did, and he made Mommy feel very good today and happy."

"I like Dr. Adams, Mommy. He makes you smile all the time."

"That he has done, Angel, and Mommy is very happy. I can't wait until Daddy gets home, and we can tell him too."

Of course the minute Ben was through the door, Angel was up in his arms and was going on about the day she was at school.

"Well, now it sounds like you had a good day."

"I did, Daddy, and so did Mommy."

"Mommy?"

"Yes, Daddy, Dr. Adams made her better and happy today. See her teeth, they are there all the time."

"Oh, and just what did Dr. Adams do that made Mommy so happy, so her teeth show all the time?"

"He gave her some pills so Mommy won't be sick no more."

"Well, that is good news, Angel. Mommy has been sick for a long time."

"I know, Daddy, but Mommy is happy now. Right, Mommy?"

"You're right, Angel. Mommy is very, very happy." Ben reaches over and pulls me into his arms. Now he has both Angel and me wrapped in his arms. How safe and secure that made me feel. For a short moment, I go back to when I was in the doctor's office today when I needed him so badly.

"I'm glad you are well again, Kate. You had me very worried." He kisses the top of my head. I look up at him and saw nothing but love in his eyes. I knew he loved Angel and myself more than life, and this gave me a warm, fuzzy feeling all over.

"You know, Angel is right, sweetheart, you have a smile from ear to ear. Like you swallowed the cat. You want to tell me what's up?"

"Sure, but maybe you should sit down first."

"Oh, this is serious, did we win a lottery?"

"Oh much, much better than a lottery."

"What's a lottery, Daddy?"

"Lots and lots of money, baby."

"We have lots of that, Daddy, why do we need more?"

"You can never have too much money, Angel. So tell me what you did, Kate. Did you get a job?"

"A job?" I chuckle. "Well, in time I guess it will be."

"In time? What do you mean by that?" Ben says with a frown. So I go and sit on his lap. Wrapping my arms around his neck tightly and whispering in his ear, "Pitter, padder, Pitter, padder goes those little feet."

He pushes me back and says, "Are you joking?"

With a grin that felt like it was going to tear my face soon, I shake my head and say, "Nope, I'm not."

Ben starts to cry and is squeezing me so hard I could hardly breathe.

"What's the matter, Daddy, why you crying?"

"'Cause Daddy is so happy, Angel." He squeezes her too.

"You are?"

"Oh yea, Angel, more than you know."

"Then why are you crying?"

"Kate, you want to tell her?"

"Okay. We are having a baby, Angel."

"We are, Mommy?"

"Yes, Angel, we are."

"You got an egg in your tummy, Mommy?"

"I sure do, and it is growing us a baby."

"Yippie, yippie. I am getting a baby brother."

"Now, Angel, remember what we talked about before. We have to take whatever God gives to us." Ben tells her as he kisses my cheek.

"I also think this is a good reason to take you and Mommy out for supper."

"Mommy won't get sick no more, Daddy."

"That is good 'cause Mommy has to eat for two now so our baby can grow to be strong."

"You don't know how right you are, Ben."

"Hey, what does that mean? Everything all right?"

"Dr. Adams just said that I'm really underweight and it is important for me to get some weight on soon."

"Then what are we waiting for? Ladies, get your coats on and let's go feed our baby," Ben says this as he runs his hand across my tummy.

"Okay, Daddy." Angel jumps down off his knee and runs for her coat. Ben squeezes me a little tighter as I go to get off his knee.

"Is everything okay, Kate, with you and the baby?"

"So far, Ben, I just have to take it easy the next little while to make sure I get my strength back and put on weight. Dr. Adams says I'm in a delicate state right now from being sick and being so underweight."

"We could still lose the baby?"

"He says we could, but please let's not think that way, Ben."

"It will be hard not to, every time I look at you and see how thin you have become."

"I know, Ben, but look at it this way. I'm still pregnant after all I've being through. So I think we have a very strong and determined little fella growing in here, and I think we will be just fine. After all, I've started to feel better, and I'm able to keep food down. So there is no place to go but up from here."

"You are right about that, Kate, so let's go eat."

"I'm ready anytime you are."

"Mommy, Daddy, you coming? I'm hungry."

"We're hungry too, so let's go." The chatter all the way to the restaurant was light and giddy. Ben ordered enough food to feed an army. One thing about Chinese food is, it is good cold. But the one thing we found is that it does not fill you up for long periods at a time.

"Good night, Angel, Mommy loves you as big as the sky."

"I love you too, Mommy." I tucked her in, and we were waiting for Ben to come and say good night as well.

"Mommy."

"Yes, Angel."

"Thank you for the baby."

"You're welcome, sweetheart, now you have a good sleep."

"Our little Angel is already in bed?"

"Yes, she is."

"Daddy loves you, Angel, as big as the sky."

"I love you too, Daddy. Daddy?"

"Yes, Angel, what is it?"

"If you and Mommy love me as big as the sky, how can you love our baby?"

"Angel, that is a good question," Ben says as he sits on the side of her bed beside me. Looking like he is really thinking as he rubs his chin.

"Angel, do you see the sky?"

"In the morning I do, Daddy."

"The sky is very, very big."

"It is huge, Daddy."

"Okay, do you think you could move over and share the sky with your baby?"

Angel laid there for a few minutes before she answered him. Ben had looked at me and I at him, and I think we were thinking along the same page. Was Angel not going to be willing to share? This we had not thought about. She has wanted a sibling for so long, but now there might be one moving in to her territory, she may not want it after all. This has happened to many people who have their children this far apart. Some overcome it, and others never do. It follows the children through their childhood and into their adulthood. This is where sibling rivalry comes from. I have seen it destroy families. This is one thing I don't want to happen with Angel and her sibling, so we must get it under control right from the beginning.

"Do I have to share my bed? It is small."

"No, Angel, you do not have to share your bed, not if you don't want to."

"Okay, I will share the sky."

"That's our, Angel, thank you, sweetheart," Ben says as he bends over and kisses her good night. We leave her and go back to the kitchen to put away our leftovers. By the time we had finished picking, there was nothing worthwhile putting in the fridge, so we just sat down and finished what was left.

"Could I interest you in a glass of wine, Kate? I think we should celebrate."

"Oh, I don't know if I should."

"I don't think a small glass of wine will hurt you or our baby. It might help you sleep."

"I haven't needed any help in that area."

"That is so true, what do you say?" He holds up a small glass.

"Sure, why not? We haven't had a reason to celebrate for some time now."

"It was waiting for just the right time."

"Do you think this is a right time, Ben?"

"You bet it is, Kate. Anytime a baby is on the way is a good time."

"You're really happy about this, aren't you, Ben?"

"You have to ask me that, Kate?"

"Well, it has been a while since we wanted a baby, just thought that maybe you would have had a change of heart, that's all."

"Not on your life, whether it was now or ten years from now."

"Are you serious? You would want a baby ten years from now?"

"Why not if we can and our health is good and we still have money, what would be wrong with it?"

"Don't you think it will be great when it is just you and me again?"

"Oh, Kate, when we're in our sixties maybe. Let's take whatever is given to us as a gift and enjoy it to the fullest."

"Okay, I'm for that." We snuggled up on the sofa with our wine in front of our fireplace. We talk about what we thought the baby might be and how we thought Angel would really be with her baby as she calls it. A smaller version of Kate is what we saw. Sitting there and reminiscing about when Angel was born and all the things she had done gave us a good laugh. Wondering how much alike will the two of them be. We have seen it where the siblings are not even close to being the same. I have even seen twins that were as different as day and night. I know twins that have been born on separate days. One at 11:30 p.m., the other at 12:00 a.m. This was great for them as they grew older because they had their own birthday celebrations.

While they were little, their birthdays were celebrated on the same day.

Going to bed that night seemed to be a hard thing to do. It was as if we were afraid that when we got up, we would find that we had just been dreaming. Neither one of us wanted to let our dream slip away, so there we sat on the sofa until I feel asleep in Ben's arms. He went to sleep shortly after me.

We were woken up by Angel calling and shaking my arm. "Mommy, Mommy."

"Hum, Angel, what is it?"

"My school has already started."

"Oh my god, Ben, we slept in, you are late for work as well."

"No, sweetheart, I booked the day off, to be with you."

"You never said anything."

"No, but it's the best surprise I could come up with after what you gave me."

"Oh, that is so sweet of you, thank you." I lean up to kiss him.

"Mommy, I have to go to school."

"You're right, Angel, and Daddy will take you. We are going to leave Mommy sleeping, okay?"

"Our baby is sleeping too, right, Daddy?"

"Yes, it is and growing. Come now let's go."

"Bye, Mommy, see you after school."

"Bye, Angel, Mommy will see you after school." I could hear them bustling around out in the kitchen. Ben was making Angel's lunch while she ate her breakfast.

"Daddy, will my teacher be mad?"

"I'm sure, if you tell her why we all slept in, she will understand."

"Okay, Daddy." The house got very quiet when they left, and I had no trouble going back to sleep. I didn't wake until 10:00 a.m. Wondering where Ben had gotten to, I go looking for him and find him out in his shop.

"Good morning, sleepyhead," he says as he comes over to kiss me.

"Why didn't you wake me?"

"You need more rest. Remember what Dr. Adams told you?"

"I know, but you took the day off to be with me."

"Yes, I did, and we still have all day. Come now, and I will make us some coffee. Would you like a coffee?"

"I think that might be all right, thank you. I will go wash up and brush my teeth."

"Oh yuck, you mean I kissed you and you hadn't brushed your teeth?"

"That's right."

TWELVE

"What is this world coming to?" he says as he wraps his arms around my waist, and we walk back into the house. I go get cleaned up and throw on some clothes while Ben makes the coffee. In our house, you have to be quick as we bought one of those fast coffee pots. The one where your coffee is ready in three minutes. It has been a blessing on the mornings when everyone is running late; you can still get your coffee on the go. What would a morning without coffee be? Sluggish, that's what we would be.

"So what did you have in mind today?"

"Well, Kate, I think we waited long enough for this, so we are going baby shopping."

"Now, we have lots of time."

"Maybe we do, but we can go look. What harm can that be?"

"No harm, it will be fun. I know just the place to take you."

"Okay then, let's go."

"What about our coffee?"

"To go cups, Kate." He pulls two out of the cupboard and fills them up.

"Boy, you have thought of everything, haven't you, Ben?"

"Hope so, now get your coat, it is chilly this morning."

I took him to the Baby's Galore store, and we must have looked and played and felt with everything there. I don't know how many times we were asked if this was our first. That was starting to get to me; Ben found it funny.

"Kate, they could be asking if we are buying for a grandchild."

"What? Come on, were not that old looking." I punch him in the arm.

"Hey, now that is Daddy abuse."

"Could be worse if you don't watch it, mister."

Ben just laughs as he picks up another toy.

"You do know the baby needs more than toys? Right, Daddy?"

"That is yours and Angel's department. Mine will be the fun things. 'Cause Daddy knows what little boys want and like. Mommies do the other things. With the help of their little mommy." We both laugh.

"Ben, remember what we told Angel, the same goes for you."

"I know, I know, but it took so long. We must have got it right this time. Can't the mother tell what she is having? Don't you have eyes in there or something?"

"No, Ben. Mothers have eyes in the back of their heads."

"I knew it was something like that."

We spent hours in that store. Then we went for a late lunch, killing time until we could pick Angel up from school and take her to bowling. We had bought a few minor things for the baby. They would work for either boy or girl. I had told Ben we weren't spending a lot on the baby this soon. Anything could happen, and I don't want to jinx it. Let's just enjoy being pregnant and getting used to the whole idea I had asked him. He was okay with that.

Angel was excited to tell everyone at the bowling alley that we were having a baby. It also didn't take long for her to get into her bowling and forget about the baby. Angel was getting darn good at getting the balls to the other end, and she was becoming one of their top bowlers. The coach had asked us if they could enter into some bowling competitions. She thought it would do Angel the world of good. We were concerned about her not being good enough. The coach convinced us that she was most definitely good enough. So we let her join, and the traveling began.

Ben and I spent most of our weekends on the road with Angel. Our Angel took home many trophies. She and I also did the mother-daughter competition and took first place. Now I hadn't bowled in years, so either we were just lucky or Angel was very good. Either way she was so happy. Ben had bought her a bookshelf to put all her trophies on. Angel would polish them every day after school. She had her favorite one which was the mother-daughter one. She had taken it to school and used it for their show and shared to the class.

There was a daughter-father one coming up, and Angel was so excited. I knew that Ben was too, but he wasn't going to show me how much of a kid he really was at heart. He kept saying that he and Angel were going to beat our score. Now it had become a competition between our household. It brought many laughs to our table, and we enjoyed it to the fullest. It was surprising how something as simple as bowling brought so much enjoyment.

The whole next week, Ben and Angel went bowling every night. They were going to win and win big. Ben kept telling Angel, "If you are going to do this, then we are going to do it right. We are also going to have so much fun you won't want to stop."

I didn't go with them every night. Every second night was fine. It was snowing and a little cooler tonight, so I didn't mind staying home and sitting by the fire. This gave Angel and Ben the father-daughter time they needed. He hadn't been able to do much of this with Angel since his promotion. Now that he was all caught up, he was making good use of their time together. Every night they came home with some fantastic story to tell, laughing all the way through it. Sometimes I had no idea what they were talking about. I would just end up laughing along with them. Sometimes they would have to wake me up because I would doze off after a bit of reading. Tonight was no exception; after reading for a short time, I had dozed off only to be awakened by the doorbell. At first, I couldn't make out what woke me up. Sitting up and looking at my watch, then thinking this can't be right, Ben and Angel would be home by now. It was after ten, and they are never gone later than seven thirty because of Angel's bath time. They must have thought I needed my sleep, so I was getting up to go get ready for bed when the doorbell rang again. It dawned on me then, that was what woke me up.

Who would be at our door this time of night? First, I thought about going and waking Ben up. Then thinking, *Na, I can do this*. Ben didn't like me opening the door at night if he weren't home or up. The bell was ringing the third time by the time I got there and opened the door.

"Mrs. Parker?"

"Yes."

"Mrs. Ben Parker?"

"Yes, can I help you?" At this point, I was starting to feel a little faint, and the room was starting to spin around.

"I'm Officer Blues, and this is my partner, Maryann. May we come in?"

"I will have to wake my husband, just give me a minute please." I turn around, but Maryann takes me by the arm and follows me in to our kitchen. She sits me down on the first chair she found while Officer Blues closes the door. Then he starts in saying, "I'm so sorry to have to tell you this, Mrs. Parker. There has been a real bad accident, and we need to take you to the hospital."

"Ben, I need to go wake Ben." Trying to get up off the chair, but it was like I had gained one hundred pounds in two minutes.

"Please Mrs. Parker, where is your coat?" Maryann asked.

"My coat?"

"Yes, Mrs. Parker, we need to put your coat on you. We have to take you to the hospital."

"Ben, Angel."

"Yes, Mrs. Parker, we will take you to see them. Now come get your coat on so we can go." Maryann lifts me up off the chair, and I walk like I have just learned to do a new step. My feet are so heavy, and everything they say is like they are talking into a barrel. I'm in another world; I know I am. Where is Ben? Where is Angel? No one is answering me. Am I talking to myself? Why is no one answering me? I can hear them talking, but I can't make out what they are saying. The two officers get me dressed and put me into the backseat of their cruiser. The women officer gets in with me.

"Ben, Angel. Ben, Angel," I call for them the whole time I'm in the car, but no one answers me. I start to cry.

"Where's my family?"

"We are almost there, Mrs. Parker. Then you can see your family. They are waiting for you."

"Ben, Angel, please talk to me! Where are you? It is snowing and cold outside. Ben, please."

The officers are getting me out of the car, and I see all kinds of color lights flashing.

"OH my god! Are Ben and Angel in there?"

"No, madam, they are inside already." At this point, I found the strength I needed to get my feet moving. I was almost on a full run.

"Please be careful, Mrs. Parker, it is very slippery." That would explain why I didn't seem to be moving very fast. Everything seemed to be in slow motion.

"Mrs. Parker, please slow down, the freezing rain has made it very treacherous out here."

"I need to find Ben and Angel." I was on a mission, and no one was going to stop me.

"Ben and Angel are here, and I presume they are hurt. Otherwise, you officers would not have brought me to the hospital."

"We will help you find them," Maryann says as we go through the hospital doors.

"I don't need your help. I can find my husband and baby."

"Please, slow down."

Just as I saw Dr. Adams, he calls out to me and comes running. "KATE, KATE. Oh, my dear girl, I'm so sorry."

"Where is Ben and Angel?"

"Kate, I'm so sorry!" I could see a tear fall from his eye.

"Please, Dr. Adams, I want to see Ben and Angel."

"Please, Kate, sit down first."

"No! I want to see Ben and Angel."

"Kate, you have to understand I done everything I could for Ben, but he just wasn't able to hang on."

Shaking my head back and forth and starting to run down the hallway, calling, "BEN, BEN, where are you?" The tears were flowing by now, and Officer Blues caught me by the arm and pulled me around to face him.

"Mrs. Parker, you have to listen to Dr. Adams, please!" At that moment, Dr. Adams came around to face me.

"Kate, I don't have an easy way to tell you this. Ben is dead."

"No!" Screaming as loud as I could.

"No, NO, he's not, he is with Angel."

"No, my sweet girl. He is dead!"

With that, I fell to my knees, screaming.

"Please help me get her up into the wheelchair. Be careful with her. She is pregnant and in a very delicate state." A nurse was there and gave Kate a needle. It did not take much time to calm her down.

"Mrs. Parker is pregnant?" Maryann asked.

"Yes, and she has been very sick. She was just starting to come around and getting back on her feet."

"Now this! Which won't be good for her or the baby!"

"No, it could be the end to the baby. They wanted this baby so bad, and it took them a long time to get pregnant."

"I don't understand why things like this happen, Dr. Adams." Maryann had tears falling as well as Dr. Adams.

"They are called horrible accidents. With weather like this that changes so fast, people aren't prepared for it."

"Mr. Parker didn't have a chance, Dr. Adams, when that big rig hit the ice and jackknife. There was no way around it, and the driver of the big truck could do nothing. How is he doing, Dr. Adams?"

"He is in shock. We are watching him very closely."

"How about the little girl?"

"Angel is lucky. She has a broken leg and a concussion. She will be okay in time."

"Her daddy was smart to have her in the middle of the backseat. That was all that saved her."

"I have to get to Kate. She will be groggy, but I can still talk to her."

"You didn't knock her right out?"

"Oh no, Angel needs to see her, and she needs to see and talk to Angel. With her being pregnant, I have to be very careful of what I give her."

"Will it be okay if I come back after my shift to see Mrs. Parker? I'm off in half hour."

"I think Kate will need all the support she can find right now. You can come anytime. I don't imagine Kate will be going anywhere until Angel is able to go home. I must go see her now."

Entering the room where they put Kate, I found her lying and sobbing so hard she didn't know I was there. Sitting on the side of the bed and putting my hand on her shoulder, calling her name softly, "Kate, Kate, it's Dr. Adams, please look at me." I wanted to know if she was capably of understanding what I would be talking to her about. Kate turns her head into the pillow more and continues to sob.

"Come now, Kate, I need to talk to you. Angel needs to see you, and so I have to help you pull yourself together before I take you to see her."

"Angel?" she asked in a whisper.

"Yes, Kate, you need to come see her. She needs to see her mother. That little girl has been through hell in the past few hours, and she needs you desperately." Kate lifts her head off the pillow and looks at me. God, she looked like the girl from *The Exorcist*. I couldn't help but take her in my arms and rock her.

"I thought Angel was gone too?" she whispers in a croaky voice.

"No, Kate, and she needs to see you right away. Do you think you can do that?"

"See my baby?"

"Yes, Kate, go see Angel. Do you think you can?"

"See my baby," she says as she nods her head up and down.

"I'm going to wipe your face, Kate, then I'm taking you to see Angel."

"All right." She sits herself up on the bed, getting ready to get off.

THIRTEEN

"Just wait, Kate, I want you to ride on the wheelchair."

"All right." The life I had seen in Kate just days ago was gone; she had become a puppet in just over an hour.

"Kate, do you want me to call your mom?"

"NO."

"Who can I call?"

"Ben."

"No, Kate, Ben is dead. Kate!" Dr. Adams takes her by the shoulder and gives her a small shake. "Kate, please repeat what I tell you. Ben is dead."

"No, no, he can't be. We are having a baby. Angel and me, we need him."

"Yes, Kate. Ben is dead and Angel needs *you*. You don't have Ben anymore, and so you must be strong. For both Angel and the new baby."

"Baby," she says as she wraps her arm around her abdomen and starts to rock.

"Come, Kate, I will take you to see Angel now. Putting her into the wheelchair was a little unnerving. It was like dealing with a limp noodle. My heart broke more each time I looked at her. The way she looked was going to frighten Angel. You would almost think Kate had been in the wreck. Entering Angel's room was an experience I will never forget. I opened the door, and Angel was sitting up in bed. Her eyes were huge, and the look of calm that was on her face blew me away.

"Hi, Mommy."

"Hi, baby."

"Why is Mommy talking like that?"

"The nurse had to give your Mommy some medicine, Angel, but she will be okay."

"Mommy, I want to go see Daddy."

"Yes, Angel, we will."

"Now, Mommy. I want to see Daddy before the angels take him away."

Kate just starts screaming, and poor Angel didn't have a clue what to do.

"KATE, KATE, you stop that right now. You are scaring Angel. Angel needs you more now than ever, do you understand?"

I whip the wheelchair around so she has to look at me. "Stop it, Kate, or we will give you more drugs. You have to remember you have two children now that need you, so smarten up." I knew to Angel, I must have sounded like a real grump. In my profession, I have learned over the years that there are times when niceness doesn't cut it.

"Dr. Adams?" Angel says to me with such fear in her voice.

"Yes, child, what is it?"

"Is Mommy going to be okay?"

"Oh yes, sweetheart, she sure is. It is going to take Mommy time." I sit on the side of the bed and pull Angel into my arms. She begins to cry. This is breaking my heart. I know as a doctor, we are not supposed to get involved with our patients, but over the years of seeing them, they become our families. She has been like a granddaughter to me. I delivered her. I have watched her grow up, and she has always been a smart little girl. I would have been so proud to have a granddaughter like her.

"Can I go home with Mommy?"

"Not tonight, Angel, I want to keep you and watch you for a couple days, okay?" "Is it true that my Daddy is gone to heaven to be with the angels?"

"Why do you ask that?"

"I heard them talking when those men were bringing us in."

"Your daddy was still alive then, Angel."

"So why did he go? Why didn't he stay with Mommy and me?"

"Oh, Angel, your daddy was hurt so bad that I could not fix him, even with all the help I had."

"Why didn't the angels fix him? They shouldn't take my daddy. We need him. Mommy and me are sad now. I hurt in here." Angel puts her hand over her heart.

"I know you do, Angel. Over time that pain will go away."

"Dr. Adams."

"Yes, Angel."

"Will the angels take me to see my daddy?"

"Not for a very long time, Angel. At least I hope not."

"But I want to see my daddy."

"Your daddy is with his angels now. You and Mommy will have to be strong so you can take care of your new baby that is coming."

"No! I'm his Angel. Daddy told me I would always be his Angel."

"You're right, you are Daddy's little Angel. God's angels are taking care of him until you and your mommy can go see him."

"I want to go now. I want to see my daddy." She starts to cry all over again. This time it seemed to bring Kate out of the trance she had been sitting in.

"Angel, don't cry, Mommy is here." I watched her struggle to get out of the chair. Standing close by in case she loses her balance, not saying anything, I wanted to see how much she could do on her own at this moment. Angel needed her to be strong, so I don't want her to get more drugs. I want Kate to face this dead-on. Being drugged up just extends the inevitable. In the long run, it is harder for them to adjust. The pain is great, and it will be there for them for a long time. Angel will bring her out of it, and if she carries the baby after this week, it will also help her heal. More so if she has a son. One can only hope for the best. I believe everything happens for a reason. What goddamn reason there is for this at this moment I cannot fathom. A woman in her prime of life is left alone with two little ones to support, what good comes out of something like this?

"Come here, Angel." Kate gets up on the bed and tries to snuggle in with Angel and a broken leg. It is a straight cast right up to her butt, so there was no way Angel was just picking it up and moving it on her own. She was softly talking to Angel, and they would cry together. I moved as far back in the room as I could to give them room to grieve yet be there for them. Thinking this was a picture that I'm sure people will be seeing for some time to come at their home.

It was a sad thought to think about and knowing how happy they all were when they found out the news about the baby. Just for that happiness to be wiped out within minutes. I pray that God will see her carry this baby through. Kate and Angel will need this baby to survive. Hopefully, the next six months go by fast for them.

"Mommy, I want to go see Daddy."

"You do?"

"Yes, Mommy, I want to say good-bye before the angels take him away."

"Dr. Adams, can we see Ben?"

"You really think that is what you both would want to do right now?"

They look at each other and then turn and nod their heads at me.

"I will go see what I can do. I will be right back." Slipping out of their room, I couldn't imagine Ben being in any shape for either Kate or Angel to see. Now do I go and check him out for myself before I say yes to them? Is it really my call? He is their husband and father. Do I have the right to decide whether he looks okay for them to see before he is taken to the morgue? Where does the lines of duties as a family doctor end?

Finding the nurse that was there with me while I worked on Ben, I was able to find out he had been cleaned up. They thought that Kate would want to see him and took measure to make sure it would be as easy on her as possible. The nurse was shocked to know Angel was going to go see him as well. I explained to her that they were very close and Angel is very old for her age. Seeing her daddy like this is maybe something that will stick in her mind for a very long time. It will also help her see that Ben is not waking up. Daddy will not be playing with her anymore. It will show her that death is final; perhaps it will help Angel to heal faster, knowing these things by seeing for herself versus just being told. I think at this point, we are damned if we do and damned if we don't.

The crash won't be an easy thing for her to forget. I would think she will have nightmares for a long time, perhaps even years. Depending on what all she saw and heard taking place before and after.

I decided to go see Ben first. This was one of the hardest parts of being a doctor. Seeing someone so young lose their life while in your care. This happened to me shortly out of med school with a five-year-old child who had been hit by a car. I almost stopped my practice that day. Pushing the door open to where Ben had been left lying, I grew heavy in the chest. Walking over to him and laying my hand on top of his chest.

"Oh, Ben, I'm so sorry I have let you down. You are so young and had so much life still waiting to be lived. Kate and Angel are going to be lost and hurting for a long time. The baby you gave to Kate could not have come at a better time. Angel and this baby will see Kate through the rough days ahead. I promise you this, my friend, as I leave you here today. I will watch out over your family for you. I don't care if that is all I do for the rest of my life. They will not go without. Other than the lack of your presence and your love. I owe you that much." The tears are flowing freely now, and as the nurse comes in, Dr. Adams didn't care that she saw him crying.

"Are you all right, sir?"

"I will be fine."

"Is Mr. Parker suitable for his family to see?"

"Yes, we will bring them in now. The real bruising will start soon."

"All right." We go back to get Angel and Kate. They are quiet and are hanging on to each other's hands so tight we could see their fingers turning white. It was a good thing Kate had Angel's wheelchair to lean on as we went through the door. She buckled at the knees as soon as she saw Ben lying there.

"Oh, Ben." She goes over and lays her head on his chest, as if she were listing for a heartbeat. How I wished it would happen. The tears were silently flowing, and Angel was just watching her mother from the wheelchair. It was as if she had sensed that her mother needed this time with Ben. She was too old for her own good. I could see her taking in all the sights of Ben. She would remember him like this for some time to come. Although it is not a great thing for her, I'm sure it will help knowing that her daddy looked normal. Kate turns around to her and ask, "Are you ready, Angel?"

"Yes, Mommy."

Kate looked at me and nodded. So I go over and pick Angel up out of the wheelchair and take her over, and we stand beside Ben.

"Mommy."

"Yes, Angel."

"Daddy just looks like he is sleeping."

"That is right, Angel."

"So why can't we wake him up, Mommy? I want to wake Daddy up now."

"'Cause, Angel," Dr. Adams cuts in. "We all have a heart in here." He takes her hand and puts it on top of his heart. "Now tell me what you feel."

"I feel it going up and down."

"That is right, Angel. Daddy's heart is not doing that anymore. That is why he is sleeping."

"Why did Daddy's heart stop going up and down?"

"It got so scared from the big truck it caused him to have a heart attack. Sometimes these heart attacks are so big that they won't let the heart beat anymore."

"I want to lie down with my daddy."

I look at Kate, and she nods her head yes. I lay Angel down beside Ben, and she wraps her arms around his neck.

"Please, Daddy, take me with you when you go with the angels."

Poor Kate, I thought she was going to pass out right now. She turned so white and started to shake.

"Oh please, Angel, don't say that. Mommy needs you, and I would miss you so much. Remember, Mommy loves you as big as the sky."

"Mommy, you have the baby in there. You won't be lonely."

"Oh, you're wrong, Angel, Mommy would miss you so much."

"I miss Daddy, Mommy, and I'm his Angel. He doesn't have to go with those other angels, Mommy, please."

"I'm afraid it is too late, honey. Daddy does have to go with the angels. When it is time, we will go see Daddy and the angels. Now we must go, my Angel."

"I'm not your Angel. I'm Daddy's Angel. I don't want to go. I want to stay with Daddy."

"Sorry, honey, you can't stay with Daddy, we have to go." Kate went to take her hands from around Ben's neck, and Angel started screaming at her.

"I hate you, I hate you."

"Come, Angel, with Mommy." Kate got firm with her voice, but Angel wasn't buying it. I nodded to the nurse, and she left and came back in five minutes with a needle for Angel. She was so histrionic by now with Kate she didn't even know I had given her the needle.

"Did you have to do that?"

"Yes, Kate, she was getting out of hand. We will take her up and put her into her bed. She should sleep until tomorrow. Were you going home, Kate?"

"No, I will stay with Angel. If she wakes up, I want to be there."

"All right, we will have a cot brought into her room for you."

"There's no need to do that, the chair is fine."

"Kate, you are pregnant. You have to rest as well, or you could lose your baby. Ben's baby."

FOURTEEN

"Oh please, no, that is the last gift he gave me."

"Then you are going to rest, Kate."

"Okay, I will."

"Good, now that is settled, I will go let the nurses know you are our guest for the night."

Rest like that wasn't going to happen tonight. Dr. Adams is a great doctor, but does he not understand that without Ben, I really don't want to live? I know I have to. I have Angel and the baby. But I have no Ben. Climbing onto the bed beside Angel. Kate lay down and wept until she finally fell asleep. The nurses would check on them throughout the night.

Dr. Adams stayed in the room across from them and had his door open, so he would hear them if they need him. He was very concerned about Kate and the baby. It had to have been one of the worse nights he has had in a very long time.

Getting up, he thought he would just peek in on Kate and Angel before going to the doctors' lounge to shower and get ready to do rounds. Pushing the door open just a little, he could see that Kate was not in with Angel anymore. Looking at his watch. Thinking where would she be at five thirty in the morning. Thinking she must be in the washroom or has gone for coffee, God knows how I need one of them. He continues on his way to the lounge and has to go past the room where Ben had been kept. He noticed the door was jarred open. Looking inside, he saw Kate lying on the stretcher with Ben.

"Aww no, Kate." What was Ben still doing here? He should be at the morgue by now. He goes and finds the nurse that was on duty, and she tells him that Kate went in just before they came to pick him up. No one thought she would stay long, so they gave her the time they thought she needed. When they came back in to see her, she had fallen asleep there with him. The nurse said she was told that she cried for a long time before she finally fell asleep. No one wanted to be the one to wake her up and send away her husband.

"Guess you could say everyone found this too hard to deal with last night."

"That's fine, Kay, I will handle it from here, thank you." This is not how I wanted to start my day.

"Kate, Kate. It's time to wake up."

She stirred a little bit. You could tell she was still beat.

"Come, Kate, Angel will be waking up soon, and you should be there for her this morning. Everything will be like a bad dream to her."

"Dream, bad dream."

"Kate, I said a little louder. I didn't want to scare her, but God Almighty, she was lying next to a dead man. She had her arm over him and around him as if they were just sleeping on the sofa.

"KATE!" This time she jumped and almost fell off the bed.

"Dr. Adams?" She was so hoarse from crying I wouldn't have recognized her on the phone.

"Kate, you have to let Ben go. The men are here to take him to the morgue."

"I can't let him go, Dr. Adams, I just can't." She starts to weep again.

"Listen, Kate, this is not good for you nor the baby. Now you know Ben would want you to take the best care you can of this baby. Kate, it is your last gift from him, cherish it. Angel needs this baby as much as you do. Speaking of Angel, she also needs her mother, so please get up now, let these men do their job, and we will go see how Angel is."

"When can I see Ben again?"

"Kate, that is something you have to discuss with Bill. You can make whatever arrangements you want within reason. But first, they have to get Ben over there."

"Ben is so cold. I tried to warm him up, but I couldn't."

"No, Kate, once life is gone, so is the warmth, I'm sorry."

Taking Kate by the arm and walking with her back to Angel's room, we found Angel still asleep.

"Angel may sleep late, Kate, so don't worry about her. I would love to have a cup of coffee, how about you?"

"I think I would like that too."

"Good, I'm buying." I take her by the arm again and hold her close as though she were my daughter. I wanted her to pull strength from me. "The coffee is very tasty this morning. Usually our coffee sucks, but we drink it anyways."

She chuckles. "Thank you for being here for Angel and I, Dr. Adams. Your family is lucky to have you."

"You're welcome, Kate. Remember, it is my job."

"I know, I also know you didn't go home last night because of us."

"Like I said, it is my job."

"You must really like your job?"

"Sometimes it is hard to do."

"Like now."

"Yes, Kate, whenever I see this happen to someone I know as well as I've known you and Ben, it tears the heart out of me and makes me second-guess myself for being here. For being a doctor."

"You are a great doctor, we love you."

"Oh, Kate, I couldn't help Ben, and I'm so sorry for that."

"I know you are, and I also know you done whatever it took to try to save Ben. It just wasn't in his cards to stay with the children and I."

"Thank you, Kate. I promised Ben I would be here for you and the children. Whatever that is worth to you."

"That is worth more than you know."

I could tell she didn't want to talk anymore. She will do this for a while. Talk and then go blank as she thinks back to Ben. No one can take away her memories, and them alone in time will help her survive.

Angel was released four days after the accident. Kate never left her room during the day longer than to go get something to eat and drink. When Angel was asleep for the night, Kate would leave. Everyone thought she was going home to sleep.

In Kate's heart, she could not leave Ben lying alone at night as long as he was still above ground. Sitting and holding his hand and talking to him the whole time. Bill was concerned about her at first when she asked permission. He also had wondered if he should be calling Dr. Adams. She had told Bill that she and Ben had never spent a night apart from the time they were married. When Angel was born, Ben slept in the chair beside Kate all night. Now she feels she owes him the same consideration and respect.

When Kate had arranged to go to the morgue and sit with Ben at night, she knew if anyone else knew they would try to talk her out of it. So she kept to herself. When Dr. Adams would ask her in the morning how she was sleeping. Kate would always tell him she slept fine. He didn't believe her for one minute. He also could not believe that she would leave Angel alone at night. He was not going to question her although he had thought of following her one time. This was just not like Kate. It was just a gut feeling that he had, but he felt he knew where she was going and called Bill to see if he was right. Kate was always back by seven in the morning, coffee in hand but no food. Angel was awake by eight. She always tried sharing her breakfast with Kate. As always, Kate would decline and tell Angel she had to eat all her food if she wanted to be strong enough to come home.

Kate's mother was coming in the second day after the accident. Her flight was delayed because of the weather, so she wouldn't get there until the day before Ben's service. Everyone was in shock around town and tried to help Kate; she just kept putting people off. Everyone handles death in their own way. For Kate, so long as she could see Ben physically, he would still be with her, so she didn't need anyone, not until that awful day that just lies ahead of her. When they will put her beloved Ben deep down into the ground. From that day on, she will be needing all the support she can gather from every angle of life.

The day of Ben's service, the weather was mild and sunny. It was as if Ben was telling Kate. See, the sun will still shine again, and all will be beautiful.

Where all the people came from Kate had no idea. She didn't know so many people knew Ben and cared that much to come to his service. Living in a small place, everyone got to know everyone, but to all show up at a funeral service rocked her very soul. She spent most of time looking at people but not seeing a person she knew. Thinking of that day, there were many blank pages that had been turned that day, and she felt there would be many more blank pages to come.

Ben's casket was of deep red cherrywood. That was Ben's favorite color in furniture. It had the biggest brass handles on it Kate could get.

When her mother asked her why, she said it was so God would surely hear him knocking. He wouldn't be left out in the cold. Having Ben cold was bothering Kate, and the fact that she couldn't do anything about it made her struggle with the idea of putting him into the ground forever. She had even taken him a mink blanket to be wrapped in. Kate was going to take the one off their bed because she knew Ben loved it. When she picked it up, she could smell Ben on it, and she broke down crying. Keeping the blanket for herself and buying a new one for Ben. Kate had thought many times about having him cremated and, at one point, almost went through with it. If she would have had him cremated, then there would be an urn with his picture on it and her and Angel would have his face looking at them all day long. Kate would have put him on top of the fireplace where she knew he would be warm. Cremation was out of the question. Ben had said so many times he was afraid of being in a fire. He did not want to be cremated, so although she wanted him to be warm, she loved him enough to see his wishes were carried out.

"Here, Kate, you have to eat."

"I know, Mom, thank you, I'm not hungry."

"Kate, Dr. Adams says you are pregnant?"

"Yes, Mom, I know I am."

"Please eat then, honey. He says if you don't, he is going to put you into the hospital."

"No! I'm not going there. I have Angel."

"You're right, you do have Angel. What good are you doing her staying in bed all day every day? You don't eat enough for yourself, never mind the fact that you are carrying a baby."

"Please, Mom, just leave me alone.

"I will not just leave you alone. It has been two weeks now since we laid Ben to rest. God bless his soul. I also know he would be some pissed at you for not taking care of yourself and Angel. Now you had better decide if you are going to keep that baby and if you are going to be Angel's mother again. I know you lost the biggest part of your will to live when Ben died. But goddamn it, Kate, that little girl has lost her daddy and her mother. Just how the hell do you think she feels right now? Yes, I'm here to help. Kate, she's not talking to me, and if you haven't noticed, she doesn't come and see you. Angel spends most of her time sitting and staring outside at the sky. Kate, your daughter really needs you. I know you are hurting inside like hell. You feel like your heart has been ripped right out of your chest. We all know you have the right to feel like that. Ben was a great man. An awesome husband and father. But, Kate, he is gone now, and you have to fill in some of that emptiness for Angel. Please, Kate, I love you, and I hate what you have had to go through. It is time to try and move on, a little bit for Angel. It will hurt for a very long time. No one can make it shorter or tell you when it is time not to hurt. You have to think of Angel and the baby that is coming. Are you hearing me at all, Kate?"

Getting up and leaving her daughter in such a state was tearing her apart inside. There was nothing left to say.

"Thank you, Mom." Turning to look at her daughter, she saw that she hadn't even turned her face away from the wall to speak to her.

"You're welcome, I love you." Closing the door behind her and going out to find Angel. There was no guessing where she would be. She had taken up sitting in the big picture window and watching the sky.

"May Grandma sit beside you?"

Angel just nods her head. Sliding in beside her and taking her into my arms, I pull her into a hug. Waiting a few minutes before I try talking to her.

"What are you watching, Angel?"

Without answering, she just raises her shoulders.

"Are you watching those fluffy clouds?"

She nods her head in answer.

"You can see many things in those clouds if you watch them for a while."

She nods her head again.

"Have you seen anything, Angel?"

Nodding her head in answer.

"What have you seen, Angel?"

She doesn't say anything for a bit. Then all of a sudden. "I saw very pretty angel." All right, now we are getting somewhere.

"Yes, Angel, you could see a lot of angels in those clouds."

"Grandma?"

"Yes, sweetheart?"

"Will God let Daddy play with his angels?"

"I'm sure he will, Angel."

"When?"

"Now I don't know that, Angel, why?"

"I've been watching for Daddy to go play with the angels so I can wave at him. Grandma, he won't come out."

I'm so chocked at this moment. I'm not able to do anything but squeeze her tight.

"Why, Grandma, won't Daddy come and play?"

"It could be that God has things for him to do first."

"Like what, Grandma?"

FIFTEEN

"I don't know for sure. Maybe he has to clean his room and do more things to help people before God will give him his wings so he can go with the angels."

"Grandma, Daddy already had wings. That is how he went to heaven. Mommy told me."

"You're right, sweet child, he did have wings. He just doesn't know how to use them yet. We will have to give him a little more time to practice."

"Then will he play with the angels?"

"Oh, I'm sure he will."

"I'm mad at Daddy."

This sets me back, and I don't quite know what to say.

"Really? Why?"

"Daddy said I would always be his angel. Now he has all of them." She waves her hand up across the sky.

"Oh, Angel, don't be mad at Daddy. He didn't ask God to take him home yet."

"Grandma, this is Daddy's home."

"Yes, it was for a short time. God has a bigger home for all of us, and when he is ready, he takes us back. We don't have any choice. When God decides, that is when things happen."

"Just like for our baby?"

"What do you mean, Angel?"

"We had to wait a long time, for God to give us a baby in Mommy's tummy."

"Oh really?"

"Grandma, did you have to wait a long time for Mommy?"

"No, honey, I sure did not. Your mommy was in a hurry."

"Daddy said I was in a hurry too!"

"I believe you were. That was a very special day for all of us when you were born. We all loved you very much right the minute we saw you."

"Daddy said it took longer this time 'cause we order a boy. But I can't tell Mommy. Okay, Grandma?"

"Your secret is safe with me, Angel."

"What secret, Mom?"

"Kate! I'm glad to see you are up. May I make you some tea?"

"Yea, Mom, that would be great, thanks."

I get up off the bench, and Kate slides in beside Angel and wraps her arms around her tightly. I just took my time making the tea. Angel needed this time with her mother so badly, and Kate needed time with Angel more than she had realized.

Watching them for a while, I saw them crying and hugging each other like there would be no tomorrow. This was breaking my heart. How was I going to help my daughter and my granddaughter? There were no miracles for a loss that has created this much pain. I know that in time, the pain will ease and the healing will begin. At first, even their memories will bring them pain. Again, only time will turn that around, and their memories will be pleasant and bring them joy when they need it most. For now they have to turn to each other for the comfort that they will seek.

For the rest of us, we will be here to lend an ear or the shoulder, whichever one is needed at that moment. To offer more we cannot and for them to ask for more than we can give is not acceptable.

This was the turning point for Kate as far as spending time with Angel. She made sure Angel was taken care of. Kate still wasn't doing that great a job taking care of herself, and I worried so. If she loses the baby, I was afraid it would be more than Kate could handle. She was still so fragile; she didn't even look pregnant. Sometimes she made me feel like she wanted to lose the baby, as if she would be punishing Ben if she did.

Angel was back into school and her bowling. Even though Kate kept her very busy, Angel still cried often for her daddy. If they were out doing something and there were children there with their Daddy's Angel would always hang way to the back and not enjoy being there. She was always the first to want to go home. Her two little friends that used to be at our home most weekends never came anymore. Angel still spent all her spare time sitting and gazing at the sky. Sometimes she would talk to her father as if he were sitting right beside her. Kate never discouraged this; she felt it was good for Angel to talk to her daddy if only in her mind. Kate didn't want Angel to clam up and not let out her feelings. Some days she would be mad as hell at Ben, and she would cry while talking to him. Kate would just stay her distance but be ready to console her if needed. Most of the time, Angel handled it herself and later would tell Kate about the talk she had had with her daddy. This would unnerve Kate sometimes because Angel would actually have an answer that Ben had given her, or so she thought. When Kate would question her on the answers she supposedly got from Ben, Angel was very adamant that Daddy had answered her. So Kate never pushed the issue. She didn't see anything wrong with Angel loving her daddy from a distance. But thought she had best talk to Dr. Adams about it on her next visit. Which by the way she was way overdue. Not wanting to see Dr. Adams and have him tell her all the things she should be or shouldn't be doing wasn't something she was ready for. Although she also knew that for the safety of her unborn child, she better make that appointment.

Plus the fact that Angel seemed to be talking more to Ben than anyone else around her. Angel totally believed that she could hear Ben talking to her. Kate knew that there were people who could communicate with the dead. Was her daughter one of them? Who was she to deny Angel this pleasure of talking to the one person she loved so dearly, her daddy? She knew she would have to try and find out how much would be considered normal and how much before they would consider Angel crazy.

There is no way at this time did Kate see anything wrong with the way Angel was acting. When Kate talked to her mother about Angel. Her mother didn't seem to be too concerned either. Telling Kate, "When you were a young girl, you had imaginary friends, and no one ever thought you were crazy. You were lonely and found your own friends. Many children do this."

"So you are telling me the apple don't fall from this tree, Mom."

"That too, but mainly, you grew out of it, and so will she."

"Mom, this isn't just a made-up friend. It is Ben she is talking to. Seeing how it is her daddy, how long do I wait before I get worried?"

"Next time you go see your doctor, ask him. I'm no expert on child behavior. Especially when it comes to one who has lost her daddy so young and doesn't really understand why death happens."

"Oh god, Mom, I don't understand why death happens, especially to young healthy people."

"We might not understand why it happens? We do understand the concept. Angel doesn't understand about the body and how it all works yet. What is a heart? What does it do? What is a heart attack? Her seeing Ben lying there just looking like he was sleeping totally confused her. Because she doesn't know enough about how the body really works. This is something she will have to learn over time. Perhaps there are books at the library that would help you explain some things to her."

"The library has saved my ass before. Maybe you're right, and we will go see what they have to offer us. Thanks, Mom." Taking Angel to the library might be a very good thing. They should have medical books with good pictures and hopefully easy to read and understand. Like the ones about birthing were. Kate and Angel were there all afternoon, and by the time they left, Kate got the feeling that Angel understood more about death. By the question and answers, Kate was feeling sure that she had answered many of Angel's concerns and that her little demons would be put to rest.

Angel started to come around after our visit to the library. She started to talk more and was showing more interest in what was going on around us. Myself, I was feeling somewhat stronger although I missed Ben more than anyone knew. I didn't say much to Angel about it because it would set her back; she was just starting to move forward.

Saturday morning I had done up all that I needed to do in the house and made Angel and me a sandwich. It seemed like we ate sandwiches all the time. At least we ate.

"Angel, would you like to do something very special today?"

She looked at me for a few minutes.

"Well, would you?"

"Like what, Mommy?"

It was like, "Are you kidding me, Mom? What could we do that would be special? Daddy isn't here anymore."

"I thought we would go downtown and look for some baby things. You know it won't be long now before our baby is here?"

"I guess that would be okay."

"All right then, let's clean up our lunch mess and go. Maybe we can have supper downtown?"

Angel nods and helps me. Then she gets her boots on. I'm thinking boy is this going to be fun and so exciting. This little girl just has no pizzazz anymore. She does not enjoy life at all. When you look at her, you see empty hollow eyes where there used to be so much life and spark. Her loss of vigor has totally surprised me. It almost made me want to stay home. Except I felt this might be something she really needed. Maybe it was something we both really needed. I took her into the Baby's Galore place. We were in there a good hour, and she just wondered around. I tried to get her interest in different things, but she was one hard cookie to crack.

There was a young girl in there with a small baby boy. He looked to be about two months old. I saw Angel watching the girl and her baby, and I was wondering what she was thinking.

"How old is your baby?" I heard her ask.

"Two and a half months."

"My mommy is having a baby soon."

"Bet you're happy about that?"

"Yea, I am."

If it would have been me asking, I would have doubted her answer. But the young girl didn't seem to catch on to Angel's disappointment, which I was so glad for. The young girl was very bubbly, and she just kept asking Angel questions, and before I knew it, Angel was talking up a storm with the young woman so I just sat back and waited.

She had Angel checking things out and looking for certain items that she couldn't find; Angel was laughing. Oh god did that sound like beautiful music to my ears. I know I have been down as well but for a young child to be like this for so long. It was starting to wear me down even more than I was. As the mother, I knew I had to find something for Angel.

"Mommy, Mommy, come here, come here."

"Yes, Angel, what is it?"

"This baby has Daddy's name."

"Oh, that is a very nice name for such a cute little boy."

"Mommy, can we call our baby Ben too! Can we, Mommy? Can we? I really like that name, Mommy, really, really."

I hadn't seen that much sparkle in Angel's eyes now for the last three months. I didn't have the heart to say anything but "If we have a boy, Angel, we will call him Ben."

"Thank you, Mommy, thank you."

That wasn't a bad idea anyway. Ben's son should be named after him. Benjamin Allan Parker. I know this would also please his mother. Ben's father has been dead for some time. With Ben gone now, just maybe his son will be a good lift for all of us.

Angel really got into the baby shopping mode, and we went home with a whole new room for Benjamin.

"Mommy, can we put the teddy bear paper up after supper?"

"Well, now let's see if you and Mommy can eat all our hamburgers and fries. If we are good, then we can put up the paper."

"Deal, Mommy, I think I will beat you 'cause I'm really hungry."

I wanted to shout to the heavens, "OUR DAUGHTER IS HUNGRY. DO YOU HEAR THAT, BEN?" She hasn't said that since Ben died. Angel has been picking like a bird. I'm sure the only reason she isn't skin and bones is due to those meal replacement drinks I picked up. I know that they are all that have kept me going. Dr. Adams has not been very happy about all of this. He said he was trying to understand what Angel and I were going through. But I had to realize that both my children were depending on me to survive. He was absolutely right. My heart was a long way from being healed, and maybe it never will, but I had to step up to the plate and take charge of my daughter one more time. Her health was in danger, and it was up to me to see it turn around for the better. Dr. Adams said she could end up suffering from malnutrition, and it would be all my fault.

Angel could end up with bone disorder as well as so many other things if I didn't get her eating again soon. Well, it looks like we just turn that corner. The question will be "Are we going to be able to keep it up?" Once we get home and in around Ben's belongings, will Angel stay on the upside of things, or is she going to slide? I've been thinking about selling our home and moving. For both Angel and myself. It wasn't because I want us to forget Ben. No way in hell will that ever happen. The house is just so Ben. I find it hard to breathe, and I believe this could be Angel's problem as well. We need space. I will talk to her about this. Perhaps I'm wrong, and I wouldn't want to set her back. It is something we do need to talk about.

This is her home, and I want her to be happy with the choices. For her to be happy, she has to help make some decisions. It does seem silly to be thinking of either selling or doing the baby's room. We should be waiting to do the room after we sell. Then again if we don't sell, I will have all this paper sitting here going to waste. Oh, what the hell, it's just paper if it sells after we do the room; hopefully, it is to someone who has a baby.

SIXTEEN

This is going to make Angel happy and put life back into my little girl.

"I'm finished, Mommy."

"So you are. I'm just about done."

"How about your milkshake?"

"My tummy is really full, can I take it home?"

"We sure can. I think I will have to take mine home as well. My tummy is feeling full too."

"Remember, Mommy, you have to eat for Ben too."

"Oh why? He can eat for himself."

"No, Mommy, he is still to liddle."

"Oh, why do I have to do all the work?"

"'Cause you are mommy."

"I knew there was a good reason."

Angel started to laugh. I didn't want to see this moment end. That was twice today that my daughter had laughed.

"Mommy, can we paint too?"

"Paint what?"

"Ben's room."

"What color? Pink?"

"No, silly, we need to do it blue, blue like the sky."

"Why blue like the sky?"

"'Cause then maybe Daddy will come visit baby Ben. If he thinks it is the sky."

"Can Mommy think about that?"

"Yep."

She jumps down and takes her milkshake in one hand and comes over to help me up with the other hand.

"Thank you, Angel."

"Mommy, why can't you get up?"

"It is what happens when you have a baby in here. They make it harder to get up and down. Guess my bum is getting too heavy."

Angel giggles as she pulls on my hand.

"Come, Mommy, let's go home and put the teddy bears up."

"I think that is a very good idea." Grabbing the side of the table and pulling myself up with the help of Angel. She didn't let go of my hand until she was getting into the car.

"Mommy."

"What is it, Angel?"

"I'm going to help you more, okay?"

"You are? That would be really great, Angel."

"Yep, Daddy would want me to help you."

"You know, Angel, I think you are so right. Daddy would be so proud of you. Thank you."

"You welcome, Mommy." She climbs in and never stopped talking all the way home.

Once we were home and we had put away everything else but the paper we bought to do the baby's room in. I was going to get the things we would need to do the papering.

"Angel, Mommy has to go downstairs to get the paper tray and stepladder."

"Okay, Mommy, I will help."

"Thank you." We go downstairs and find my paper tray and our stepladder as I turn around to go back upstairs I saw two cans of unopened paint.

"What's this Angel?"

"I don't know Mommy?" Reading on it I see that it is a water base latex, no smell, one coat. I didn't ever remember buying this or knowing that Ben had bought any paint.

"Well, let's take it upstairs and open it and see what we have?"

"Can we paint too, Mommy?"

"First, we have to see what it is. I don't want red or purple."

"Me neither."

"Maybe it's yellow with blue polka dots."

"That would be funny, Mommy." She chuckles and is excited to see what color it is. I was eager to see it as well. Wiping the top of the cans off. The date caught my eye. I stood just staring at it, and the knot in my stomach was so tight I found it hard to breathe.

"What's wrong, Mommy? Why don't you open it?"

I nod my head up and down but can't say anything yet. I was about to open probably the last thing that Ben had gotten for our house. The date was only two days before the crash, so I knew Ben had bought it with the intention of repainting something. Opening the can would tell us what it was that he wanted to paint.

"Nothing is wrong, Angel. Mommy will get a screwdriver and take the lid off." Of course removing the lid didn't tell us much; it had to be stirred.

"Oh, that's not a nice color, Mommy?"

"Get Mommy the wooden spoon, would you, Angel? The paint needs to be stirred up."

"Stirred up, what does that mean?"

"I have to stir it around and around so it mixes and we can see what color it turns to then."

"Can I stir it too, Mommy?"

"You sure can, sweetheart. It needs lots of muscle, and Mommy's muscles are weak."

"You not weak, Mommy. Come on, you can do it," Angel says as I start to stir the first can. It took some stirring before it started to change color. Then the first swirl of blue came up to the top.

"Blue, Mommy, look it's blue."

I swallowed a lump and tried to be as jolly as she was. I wasn't going to tell her that her daddy bought this paint in hopes of having a boy. I just kept stirring, and we kept watching the color change that took place. Angel forgot that she wanted to stir. She was so fascinated by the color change. I was still stunned that Ben had bought this paint. I was going to use the paint he had bought. I didn't care whether I was having a boy or a girl. I will make it work. The paint was such a baby powder blue, perfect for a baby's room. I don't think it would matter which sex it turned out to be.

"Daddy would like this color, Mommy."

"Yes, Angel. I do believe he would. I think Daddy would have picked this exact color."

"You do, Mommy?"

"Oh yes, sweetheart. I do."

"We going to use it, Mommy?"

"What do you think, Angel? Should we?"

"She stops for a minute and closes her eyes, frowning and looking like she was really thinking hard."

"Yes! Daddy says yes."

"Daddy says yes?"

"Ha-ugh, he does."

I wasn't going to push that any further. She was not upset, and however she came up with that answer seemed to satisfy her.

"Okay then, it's a deal. I think it is a very nice blue."

"Me too, if there is some leftover, can we paint my room?"

"I don't see why not, even just one wall."

"Yippee, yippee."

"If we are painting, we have to do that before the paper goes on so Mommy has to go find a paint tray and my rollers. You go get old, old clothes on."

"Okay, Mommy, I will." She was down running for her room before I was headed for the basement. Finding what I needed wasn't hard. Ben and I were both good at cleaning up and putting things where they were supposed to be.

Angel and I worked steady, and we were pretty excited about how our baby's room was looking. I could picture it all done with the rocking chair and all the baby furniture. I always felt that a rocking chair is one of the main pieces of furniture anyone having a baby should own. It is a lifesaver as well as a place to nap when need be. Angel was allergic to milk, so she cried a lot, so I spent much of time in the rocking chair. I'm sure that after six months, I could rock and walk at the same time. I had this permeant sway to my walk.

After we finished the painting, we sat on the floor with our drinks and just looked at the room. Discussing where we would put everything. Angel had some good ideas, and we went with them. After all, it is just her and I now, and I like to include her into my plans as much as I can for her age.

"Do you think the baby will like the room, Mommy?"

"I'm sure the baby will love it. You have done such a good job."

"When can we paint my room?"

"We will start on it tomorrow. Right now you better have a bath and get ready for bed. You have school tomorrow. We are a little late tonight. Good thing you get out early tomorrow."

"I do?"

"Yes, so we will have lots of time to do your room. After I pick you up, we have to go to my doctor's appointment first, but that won't take long."

"Okay, Mommy, I will go have my bath."

"Thank you. I will tidy up here a bit more."

Angel leaves me alone, and I sat for a while wishing Ben could be here. I know I would not have been doing the painting; no way in hell would he have allowed it. That would have been fine by me.

Picking Angel up from school and going over to my doctor's appointment all seem to come quickly today. I wasn't sure if it was due to the nice weather or that I was just feeling so good that time just flew by.

"I want you to have an ultrasound done today, Kate."

"Today isn't it a little late to make an appointment?"

"I saw you were coming in, and I booked you one. Hope you don't mind?"

"No, I don't mind. Is there a problem?"

"I don't think so. I want to see the size of the baby. With you being so underweight for so long. I just want to see if the baby has suffered, that's all. Its heart sound steady and strong. I want to know size, that's all. Please don't worry about it."

"All right then. When?"

"Right now they are waiting for you."

"Then I will go. May I take Angel in?"

"I see no reason why this little lady can't be there with you." He lifts up her chin as he says that. He could see the sparkle that was back in her eyes, and that made his heart fill with joy. She had been a sad little girl for way too long. He knew it was all over the baby they were expecting, and he hoped that for them, things would just continue to get better.

Walking with his arm around Kate and holding on to Angel's hand on the way to the elevator made him feel more like Dad and Grandpa than their doctor.

"I will call you, Kate, when I get the results."

"All right, Dr. Adams, thank you."

"You're welcome, my dear, take care. You, little lady, take care of Mommy and this baby and of course yourself."

"I will." Angel reaches over to take Kate's hand that Dr. Adams had been hanging on to. "He is nice, Mommy."

"Yes, honey, he sure is. We were lucky when we got him for our doctor." They got onto the elevator and headed for the third floor. Elevators always make Kate's stomach come up to her throat. She didn't think she would ever get used to riding in them. Something like riding in an airplane.

Entering the office, the girls called her right in as they were waiting for her.

She lies up on the table, and Angel stands off to the side and listens while the nurse is talking to Kate and Kate to them. The nurse squeezes the cold gel on to Kate's tummy and starts to roll the wand around. Back and forth and from side to side. Once the nurse was done, some scanning and measuring and snapping pictures or whatever they call it. I decided to ask, "Is everything okay?"

"From what I see, it is. Would you like to have a look at your baby?"

"We sure would. Angel, come over here by Mommy." I pulled her up on to the table with me as we waited for the nurse to find the pictures she was going to show us.

"Does it matter to you whether you are having a girl or a boy?"

"We are having a boy," Angel says in a manner that suggests there was no other choice.

"Oh, you have had this done already?"

"No, I haven't. Why?"

"How would your daughter know you were having a boy?"

"We are?" Both Angel and Kate say together.

"Yes! You are, and here is his picture." She turns the screen so we could see this little baby wiggling around.

"Mommy, look, there's my baby brother."

"Yes, I see him, isn't he great?"

"Yes, Mommy, I'm so happy."

"Me too, Angel. Me too."

"Daddy is happy too, Mommy."

"I believe he would be very happy, Angel."

"Would you like me to print this off for you and you can show your husband?"

"My husband is—"

Angel cut me off, "Oh yes, please do, Daddy will want to see it."

"Angel, please."

"Oh, it's okay, we can do that. It will just take a second." She clicked a button, and before I knew it, I had a picture of our son in my hands. I hold it up close to my heart and say to myself, "Thank you, Ben."

"Here is an envelope to put it in so it doesn't get bent."

"Thank you," Angel says as she takes the envelope and puts the picture in. I finish getting dressed and look at her; she has a grin on her face that goes from ear to ear.

"Are you happy, Angel?"

"Oh yes! Mommy. I'm very happy, aren't you?"

"Yes, darling, more than you will ever know."

"The blue room was right, Mommy," she says as she takes my hand, and we leave the building.

"I think we should go celebrate. What do you think?"

"I think so too, Mommy. Can I have a cheeseburger?"

"Yes, you may. Would you like fries with it?"

"I think so, my tummy is empty."

SEVENTEEN

"All right then, I guess we better fill it up." While we were eating our early supper, Angel looked like she had something stirring around in that little head of hers.

"What are you thinking so hard about, Angel?"

"Well, Mommy, I was wondering if we could stop by and tell Daddy about the baby and show him the picture."

"I think Daddy already knows."

"Please, Mommy. I want to show Daddy the picture."

"All right, Angel, we can do that, but we won't stay long. We want to paint your room, remember?"

"Okay, Mommy. I will tell Daddy that too." Ben's grave site was not a place I went often. I could not bear to know he was down in the dark cold ground where I couldn't see or touch him. I always felt like I was letting him down whenever I left the cemetery. I knew I was always leaving my heart behind.

We finished up our meal and headed out to the grave site. Angel was very comfortable at Ben's grave. It was like it had been many years and she had just grown accustomed to this. Kneeling down over his headstone and talking away little, there was no time to waste. Showing him the picture and explaining how we have painted the baby's room blue.

"It was a very good choice, Daddy, thank you."

All I could do was raise my eyebrow to her in wonder. I thought I was keeping this big secret, and all the time she knew.

"Daddy, Mommy and I talked, and we are going to call our baby Benjamin Allan Parker. It is a lovely name, Daddy, and we will have you with us always. Mommy is very happy now, and she is doing good. I'm helping Mommy more now, Daddy, so you don't have to worry about her."

This brings a burning into my throat and takes my breath away. At the same time, I needed to squat because she was serious, and yet she is just a little girl. This is throwing me all off-kilter.

"Daddy, we will have to go now. Mommy and me are going to paint my room the same as Ben's. Thank you again, Daddy, I really, really like the color. I love you, Daddy, and miss you lots and lots." She lies down and hugs the top of his grave. Standing up and looking at me and waiting. I was still squatted down at the top of his headstone. I reached out and rub my hand across the top; even now I wanted so much to be with him it hurt.

"I will always love you, Ben, and I miss you with all my heart." Placing a kiss on my fingers and touching the top of the headstone, I stand up and take Angel's hand.

"Are we ready to leave now?"

"Yes, Mommy, we have to go home and paint my room."

"Yes, we do." This visit to Ben's grave didn't seem to fizz on her at all. I was dreading it, thinking she would be in tears and crying when it came time to leave, but once again, she was our little trooper. Ben would have been so proud of her. The only difference now is that she was my little trooper.

Angel talked nonstop all the way home. I believed that if she would have taken a breather, she would have broken down and cried for Ben. The only thing that stopped her was the fact that she had taken it upon herself to take care of me. So she had to be strong and help her mommy move on. I must say I was very grateful, but was this a good thing for Angel? I didn't really know. I would watch her and see how all this plays out, and I sure wouldn't let her take on more than she should. Just some things that would make her feel like she was needed by me. Simple little things will make a huge difference to Angel yet not put stress onto her. I know she will be a big help with the baby. She will be the world's smallest mother; I'm sure of that.

When we arrived home, Angel got right into her painting clothes.

"Mommy, you have to change your clothes."

I look down at myself. "Yes, I think you're right. I will be right back." Maybe she will be a little bossy. Oh well, so long as she is happy. I go off to change my clothes, and when I come back, Angel has got our paint tray full and paper stretched out over her carpet. I should have just took the carpet up and put down new after the painting was done.

"Mommy, can we paint two walls and paper two walls?"

"I think we could do that. Which walls do you want painted?"

She stands there and screws up her face and really thinks about it. "I think I want these two painted." She points to the wall with the door in it and the wall with the closet in it.

"That is a very good choice. It will make wallpapering it so easy."

"That is good, Mommy. I don't want it to be too hard on you."

"Thank you, that is very kind of you. It will also go quicker with the paper if we don't have to do lots of cutting."

"Okay." It didn't take long to paint Angel's room. She was getting pretty good with the roller. With very few oops. After a couple of hours, we were ready for a break. Taking a break on the floor with the iced tea we had left over from our meal. We talked about what kind of wallpaper Angel would want. After thinking about for a few minutes.

"I want angels on the walls, Mommy."

"Angels?"

"Yea, Mommy, they're pretty."

"They sure are. Just like you."

"Can I have angels, Mommy?"

"We will have to see what we can find when we go to the paper store tomorrow."

"Okay, I think that will be fun."

"I think so too. Seeing how it is Saturday, we will go in the morning so we will have plenty of time to look and pick. Then we will also have time to come home and get it up. We might even get your room all back together, so you can sleep in it tomorrow."

"That's okay, Mommy, if I can't. You have to be easy."

"I'm fine, Angel. This is light work, and it won't hurt me." We finished up the painting and cleaned everything up. Even without the wallpaper, it looked brighter. Angel was so happy with the color. Deep down I think it was because she knew Ben had bought the paint.

Maybe she will feel closer to Ben this way. I wonder if she will forget his face in time if the picture was all down. I hope not. I hope I never need a picture to be able to see his face. I really hope that our son looks like his daddy. I know he can't replace Ben, and I don't want that. But it will be easier to always remember him. By having our son, he would be staring us in the face every day. The same as Ben always said about Angel looking like me. He always told me if I weren't around and he was missing me, he just had to look at Angel. He often said it was like looking at pete and repeat. I would tell him, "Ben, I was just at the store for twenty minutes."

"I know, but twenty minutes is a long time." So to him, at that moment, Angel's face was my face. I sure hope it isn't like that with Ben Jr. Ben Jr.—now doesn't that sound strange? Yet it gives me goose bumps. Rubbing my abdomen and feeling the baby move as if he knew I was thinking about him. Perhaps maybe I just woke him up.

"It is time for your bath, Angel. We have done enough for today. I think Mommy has to have a rest now."

"Okay, Mommy, I'm going right now."

"That's my good girl."

Angel had her bath and her snack before she brushed her teeth. "Mommy." "Yes, Angel."

"Do you think Daddy will see baby Ben when he is born?"

"I think so. I'm told that the angels can see everything. They also know things before we do. If you are tuned into your body, they guide you through life."

"What does that mean, Mommy?"

"It's like having another person talking to you, letting you know what to do and what not to do. Sometimes choices are easy, then sometimes you have very hard ones to make. If you just let it happen, the answer will come to you. Your guardian angel will be helping you. They always want what is best for us. Never second-guess yourself. This is something you will find out in life as you get older."

"Mommy."

"Yes, Angel."

"When we see those old people in town talking and there is nobody around. Are they talking to their guardian angel?"

"I believe so."

"How come we don't see their angels?"

"When you have a guardian angel. That angel is just yours, nobody else's. So you are the only one who can see them."

"Are they like ghost then, Mommy?"

"No, honey, they are not. You know how pretty angels are. Ghosts are usually sad spirits that haven't turned into angels yet."

"Why are they sad, Mommy?"

"There can be so many different reasons, Angel. Once they are happy and have things settled, they become beautiful angels. Now it is time for this angel to go to sleep. We have a big day ahead of us tomorrow. So good night, my Angel, sweet dreams."

"You too, Mommy, good night."

I hadn't realized that I was so exhausted. I fell asleep almost immediately. Sleeping all night long and waking to the alarm on my cell phone was something I hadn't done for quite some time. I was up and had my coffee and toast by the time Angel had come wandering into the kitchen. One thing about it, I don't have much house cleaning to do. Not that Ben was a messy person, far from it. I think I just let things get behind so I could spend time with Ben while he would be at home. I'm so glad now that I didn't cheat myself out of that quality time with him. Who knew our time together was going to be so short. I don't have to live with regrets that I had put other things ahead of Ben.

"What do you want to eat, Angel?"

"Cheerios please, Mommy."

"You got it. Did you sleep well? Are you ready for a busy day?"

"Yes, I did. I can't wait to get my angel paper, Mommy."

"Now just remember we might not be able to find any. You should think of another one that you would like just in case."

"But, Mommy, you said I could get angel paper."

"Yes, sweetheart, I did. I don't know what the paper store has. If there is angel paper, I will buy it for you. We should think of something else in case they don't have it."

"I just want fluffy clouds then, Mommy."

"What?"

"Fluffy clouds. If they don't have angels, just fluffy clouds."

"We will have to see what they have." Boy, she wasn't going to make this easy. Fluffy clouds, what is up with that for a little girl's room? I'm not up to asking. I think I will just wait and see when we get to the paper store. Perhaps there will be something else that will catch her eye. Angels are probably down the list as far as popular wallpaper goes. This could turn out to be not such a great day after all. I sure hope someone is on my side today. I say to myself as I look up.

"Angel, have you finished your breakfast?"

"Yes, Mommy. All right, would you please get dressed now?"

"I'm already dressed."

"You are? That was quick."

"You sick again, Mommy?"

"No, why do you ask?"

"'Cause you were in the bathroom long time."

"I guess I'm just slower than I used to be. More weight to carry around." Rubbing my tummy.

"Is he heavy, Mommy?"

"They get heavier as they grow bigger, yes."

"Was I heavy, Mommy?"

"No, you were not, you were only six pounds when you were born. I hardly knew I was pregnant with you. It was great, I loved every minute of it."

"Do you like being pregnant with baby Ben, Mommy?"

"I sure do, Angel."

"Me too, Mommy."

"You do too?"

"Oh yes!"

I chuckle to myself as she takes my hand, and we head for town. I'm glad she is enjoying my pregnancy. This will make her love her little brother even more. She has felt like she has been a part of him right from the beginning. Too many people leave the siblings out of it all and, in the end, dump a new baby into their life and think everything should be kosher. Then they don't understand why the siblings are not accepting of the new one. Someone else has moved in to their place, and they have not been prepared for it to happen.

The snow is falling, but it is very warm out, and everything looks beautiful with its white winter coat. The sun puts the extra sparkle to everything. Making it look like glass. This would make the perfect winter pictures for those who have a good camera to be able to capture the melting droplets that are about to fall.

"Here we are, sweetie. Boy, it looks like everybody need wallpaper today. Guess we will have to walk."

"That's okay, Mommy, I like to walk."

"Me too. We haven't done too much walking in the last little while." We only had a block to walk, so I was fine with it.

The store was bustling with people, and there was a big sale on all paper in stock, so maybe today was our lucky day after all. We spent a lot of time looking at the papers. Surprisingly we did find two with just clouds. The girl had explained that they were more for baby rooms. Then you put up teddy bears stickers or pictures on the paper. The one wall they had done was so beautiful I was thinking of redoing our baby's room.

"Mommy! Look, here is angel paper."

"Oh yes, I see. And it is very pretty."

"Oh, but that's not."

I put my fingers to my lips to quiet her. I knew it was cherubs. Angel won't know the difference between angels and cherubs.

EIGHTEEN

They all have wings, and that made her happy.

"Look, Mommy, can we buy these angels too?"

"Oh, those are very nice, I think we can."

"There is a lamp over there with the same angels on it," the girl behind the counter said. So we went to look at it, and it was very nice as well.

"I will take the lamp too please."

"No problem." She got busy wrapping up the lamp while Angel and I looked around some more.

"Look, Angel, here are some book holders. Would you like them to put on your bookshelf?"

"I think so." She cocks her head off to the side as if to say, "Did you need to ask?" We found a few more that we could hang on her painted wall. Angel was tickled pink. We were lucky to find a window valance to go with everything. It was going to finish her room off beautifully.

"Okay, miss let's go home and get to work."

"Okay, Mommy." She was so happy.

"Thank you for your help, miss."

"You're welcome. When you have it done, would you take a picture and bring it in? We like to post things like this up on our help wall over there. It gives other people ideas. Some people don't know where to start when they are doing a room."

"Can we, Mommy, can we?"

"Sure, why not?"

"Yippee, yippee." She starts to skip out of the store.

"Thank you again for all your help."

"You're welcome, good luck." We wouldn't be stopping to eat in town. I know Angel is just as anxious as I am to get started. I could already see it done in my mind. This always made things easy for me, and I also loved doing it. I had been told so many times I should be an interior decorator. I always found people on the whole didn't want to pay for the work. They want the jobs done but for nothing. I wasn't going to give away my time and my expertise on things like this. They didn't want to pay, so they could do it themselves. I had lost a couple of friends because I refused to do their home for nothing. I guess they weren't much of a friend in the end. I had learned this after I had spent a lot of time and money on a place for someone I thought was a friend. She was always going to pay me, for the supplies I had charged on my account for her and my time. In the end, I got neither, and that was the end of a friendship. Or what I thought was a friendship. To her, I was just someone to use, and she cried a sad-enough story that I felt sorry for her and jumped in with both feet. It was an expensive lesson learned. I have never done anything like that for anyone again. When they ask, I just tell them. I did it, so can you.

I made Angel and myself a bowl of soup with a sandwich. This was perfect for this winter day. You can never go wrong with a bowl of soup. After cleanup, we went and got busy in her room. The wallpaper was a very good quality and went up easy. Angel did the rubbing on the bottom half. While I worked on the top half. This was so easy. All we had to do was straight cuts across the bottom. It was still early when we got done. The sun was still shining bright.

"Angel, would you like to go for a walk in the park. We can put the ladder and everything else away when we get back."

"Okay, Mommy, that would be fun. I can make snow angels."

"You sure can. Maybe I can too?"

"Mommy, you won't be able to get up."

"Hey, now I'm not that big? Am I?" I stick out my tummy and frown down at Angel.

"No, Mommy, you're not, I was just kidding." I could tell by her voice that she thought she had hurt my feelings. So I squat down in front of her and take her into my arms.

"You know what, Angel? I don't care if I get as big as an elephant?"

"You don't?"

"No, I don't. I love being pregnant, and I love my babies as"—she joins in—"big as the sky." We both laugh.

"Now let's get our boots on and go to the park." All the way along the walk, Angel made snow angels whenever she found fresh untouched snow. My daughter was obsessed with angels. She should have been my sister's child. My sister is also obsessed with angels. There is nothing else on her walls or in her curio cabinets but angels. She even has a large mirror, and on it is an engraved angel. It is beautiful and has a light that comes on in the evening.

I sat on the bench after we got there. The walk was good, but I can't say I didn't feel it. Angel was talking with other children, and then she was showing them how to make snow angels.

The park was full of angels, and the children were having a blast. The one little girl had her puppy with her. It was a shih tzu. What an adorable puppy. It was black and white and looked like a little Ewok. Angel has fallen in love with it. I knew she would be asking for one before we left. It might not be a bad idea for her to have a puppy. I do believe those stay small. It would give her a friend at home. I will have to check it out.

"Excuse me, I haven't seen you here before." I turned around to see where this voice was coming from, and this tall very nice looking man was standing just behind me.

"We haven't been to the park for a very long time."

"I come here every Saturday since I moved here three months ago. I love to watch the children, and I bring Molly here for her walk." He looks down at his dog as do I.

"That one looks like that one." I point to the puppy that the little girl had.

"Yes, this one is her mother. I was lucky to have five of those sweet little things running around. The house got quiet after they were all gone."

"I would imagine. They are cute. My daughter looks like she has fallen in love with that one."

"If you decide you want one Molly's here, will have another litter in the spring. I sell them for a hundred dollars."

"That's all? I thought they were more money than that?"

"They are, but I know I can sell mine fast if I keep it at a hundred. I have the male and the female, so it doesn't cost me for a stud."

"I see. I will have to think about it."

"My name is Jake by the way." He sticks out his hand for me to shake.

"I'm Kate." I reach up and take his hand. While we kept chatting, he held my hand. It was strange to have another man's hand in mind. I have never held another man's hand but Ben's. With that thought going through my head, I quickly pulled my hand away. You could tell by the look on his face that he wondered what he had done wrong.

"I'm sorry." I could not hear what he was saying as the blood was pounding in my ears.

"I was just saying that I'm here every Saturday. So if you decide you will know where to find me."

"I will and thank you. I must get my daughter home now." I went to stand up and was having a little trouble. Jake came around and says, "Here, let me help you." He takes my arm and gently lifts me up.

"I'm sorry, guess I sat too long."

"When is your baby due?"

"Within the month."

"That will be nice."

"Yes, it will be."

"How many do you have?"

"Just my daughter Angel and this one." Putting my hand upon my tummy.

"So this one better be a boy?"

"Yes, it is. We found out that we were having a boy."

"You and your husband must be so pleased?"

"My husband died shortly after we found out I was pregnant." I sure didn't mean for it to sound like it was his fault. I know I stunned the poor man.

"Oh, I'm so sorry, Kate. I did not know."

"No, I'm sorry. Of course you didn't know. I shouldn't have said it like that.

Please forgive me." I put my hand out for him to take this time. He hesitated for a bit, then with a big smile, he says, "Hi, Kate, I'm Jake, pleased to meet you, and this is one of my dogs, Molly."

I smile back, holding his hand a little longer. "Hi, Jake, it is very nice to meet you."

"Mommy, Mommy, can we get a puppy like this? I love this puppy."

Jake looks at me and raises an eyebrow.

"What did I say?"

"They say moms know everything." I see Angel looking at him with a protective look on her face, and she came between Jake and myself.

"Angel, I want you to meet Jake. Jake's puppy here is the mother to that one you are holding, so if we want one, we have to talk to Jake about it."

"We do?"

"Yes, we do. Now you say hi to Mr.—"

"I'm sorry. It is Jake Sanders."

"Hi, Mr. Sanders, I would like a puppy."

Jake squats down to be eye to eye with Angel. "Tell you what, Angel. Molly is going to have more puppies in the spring. When she does, how about if you and your mommy come over and you pick out the one you want. You will even be able to name it before it is big enough to come live with you."

"Can we do that, Mommy?" Now the ball was in my court, and what the hell was I to say, "If you want to, Angel, we could."

"Thank you, Mr. Sanders."

"You're welcome, Angel, and please call me Jake."

Angel looks at me, and so I nod my head. "Thank you, Jake." As she puts her little hand out to him.

He takes it so gently and says, "I'm so pleased to have met you, Angel."

"Me too." She squeezes the puppy she has into her face.

"Angel, you take the puppy back now. It is time for us to go home."

"Yes, Mommy. Excuse me." Way she goes to return the puppy.

"You have a very sweet little girl, and a very protective one as well."

"She seems to think that now that Ben is gone, she has to be the one to take care of me instead of me taking care of her."

"I can see that, she is quite grown-up for her age."

"Yes, she is." This man seemed to be lonely too. How could such a nice-looking man be lonely? He would be in his late thirty. I didn't notice a wedding band. Most men don't wear wedding bands so that didn't really tell me anything.

"Come, Angel, we must get walking."

"Coming, Mommy."

"You live that close by to walk, Kate?"

"Yes, we just live about four blocks that way, so it is a refreshing walk on a warm day."

"I live about the same distance that way on the left-hand side."

"I will have to get your address when we come to pick out a puppy."

"For sure. It has been great talking with you, Kate. I hope to see you and Angel again soon."

"I'm sure you will. Angel has had fun, and she will want to come back more often now."

"That would be nice. Maybe I will see you around soon."

"Maybe. It was nice meeting you, Jake, take care."

"You too, Kate. Bye, Angel, take care of your mommy."

"I will, I'm ready, Mommy." Then Angel takes my hand and starts to pull me away. I turn around to leave, and after a few steps, I glance back and see Jake still watching us with a smile on his face. He was a sweet man. He looked like he had skeletons in his closet. His eyes were sad. Yet he walked like a proud man. I had a feeling that his dogs were his life. I found myself hoping that we would meet again. It was good to talk to someone other than Angel, even if we didn't talk about much more than the dogs.

I know not having anyone to talk to has been of my doing. I just didn't like visiting with friends that had husbands to share things with. I felt like I was the third party all the time. I know it is just me, and I will have to get over it. In time I will, and I will be able to share more with them. Right now I don't feel like I have anything to share with them.

I think the walk did both Angel and myself a world of good. We made ourselves some hot chocolate and sat by the fire. Angel did a whole lot of talking about the puppy she would like to have, and I knew there wasn't any way around us not getting one. I'm sort of excited about having a puppy. Ben and I always talked about getting one; then we had Angel and guess we figured we didn't need a puppy after all. I think he would be pleased with Angel's choice of a puppy. That puppy seemed to be what Angel needed. Although spring is ways away yet.

Angel already had a name picked out. She wants to call her puppy Minnie.

"Why would you call it Minnie?"

"She will be so small, Mommy."

"You're right, they are small dogs. You can hurt them very easy."

"I won't hurt my puppy, Mommy, I promise."

"I know you won't, sweetheart. We just have to be careful not to step on her and things like that. Sometimes they get under our feet, and before we know it, we have stepped on her."

"I will watch her, Mommy, very close."

"I'm sure you will, Angel, and that will be a good girl."

"Mommy, will Minnie like baby Ben?"

"Oh, I think so. You will have to watch that Minnie doesn't hurt your little brother."

"She won't, Mommy. I know she will be good to him."

"You sure about this, Angel?"

"Oh yes, Mommy, I'm really, really sure."

"All right. You know that it will be your job to take her outside so she can go to the bathroom and to feed her."

"Yes, Mommy. Do I take her to school with me?"

"No, she will have to stay with a babysitter."

"A babysitter?"

"Yes, you need a babysitter. After all, your puppy will be your baby when you get her, and you can't go to school and just forget about her."

"Who do I get to babysit? Mommy."

"Well, I don't know. We will have to put on our thinking caps, won't we?"

Angel stewed on this for a long time. Then she came to me and said, "Mommy, will you be home when I get my puppy?"

"I don't know, Angel. Some of the time, why?"

"If you are home, why can't you watch my puppy?"

"Are you asking me to babysit your puppy?"

"Uh-huh."

"You know what, Angel. I think I could do that for you."

"You will, Mommy?" She comes over and gives me a hug. "Thank you, Mommy."

"Would you like to sit on my lap, Angel?"

"Can I, Mommy? Is there room for me?"

"Sure, there is room for you." I lift her up on to my lap, and she snuggles right into my breast. I started to rock back and forth in the rocking chair. We hadn't done this for a long time. I thought she would fall asleep seeing how we were outside for so long today.

"Mommy, why did you tell me I had to get a babysitter when you are here?

NINETEEN

"You can't take people for granted, Angel. It is like Mommy with baby Ben. I have to ask. I can't just expect someone to watch him or you. That is part of your responsibility. To make sure someone is available to watch your puppy when you're not home. Otherwise, there are people who will come and take your puppy away. The same as the people who would come and take my babies away if I didn't make the proper arrangements to have you taken care of while I'm away."

"I can watch baby Ben for you, Mommy, if you are going to watch my puppy."

"I think we will have to work something out, that is for sure. Now why don't I go run your bath so you can get ready for bed? You can try out your new lamp and read for a while after your bath, no school tomorrow. While you are having a bath, I will put the things away that we used for doing the wallpaper."

"Okay, Mommy, I will get my pj's."

"That's my girl." I kiss her on top of the head, and she gets down so I can go run her water. Once I had her in the tub, I washed her hair for her, then left her to play. She likes the water, she could swim like a fish, and we had her in swimming at a very early age. She was never afraid, so she caught on fast. Ben had put in an extra large tub just so Angel could play in it. It was a very long and wide tub, so she was happy to bathe.

Picking up the rest of the tools I had used to do Angel's room, I took them downstairs and put them back where Ben had them.

My legs were telling me they were tired from the walking today and going up and down the ladder today with the paper and now going up and down the stairs. I think I might have to get into the tub right behind

Angel. Then perhaps I will read for a while as well. All I had left to put downstairs is the ladder. Then that will be one big job completed.

I was about halfway down the stairs when the legs of the ladder hit the wall and caused the other end to swing back and got me on the back of the legs. My legs let go, and down I went. I tried grabbing for the handrail, but the ladder was in the way, and I went head over the ladder and not stopping until I hit bottom. What a racket. I woke up to Angel screaming at the top of her lungs, "Mommy, Mommy, Mommy." I could see she was in the nude and scared out of her mind.

"Angel," I manage to say. Her eyes were so large, and she wouldn't answer me.

"Angel, please! Come here to Mommy." I reached my hand out to her. She finally came and kneeled down beside me.

"Angel, I need for you to go upstairs and call 911 on the phone."

"Mommy, what is all this blood?"

"Please, Angel, get Mommy some help. Go call 911."

"I can help you, Mommy, take my hand."

"No, Angel! I knew I had startled her just the way she backed away from me. "Please! Mommy needs lots of help. You go call 911 and tell them Mommy fell down the stairs."

"Mommy, there's lots of blood."

"I know, Angel, that's why Mommy needs for you to get help. Now go tell them lots of blood." I could feel myself blacking out. Oh god, not now, I have to help Angel get help for me.

"Okay, Mommy." I saw her run up the stairs. I was slipping in and out, and I could hear she was talking to somebody. I heard her say lots of blood. Good girl was the last thing I remember thinking.

I woke up in the hospital. My mother was beside the bed, and I could tell she had been crying. I tried hard to say something, but nothing would come out, and I was out again. I felt heavy and nothing wanted to move. Then I saw Ben; he was crying also and shaking his head. "No, Kate, go back." I was so happy to see him; I was reaching for him and calling to him. He just kept shaking his head no and backing away from me. Telling me to go back.

"Where are you going, Ben? Wait for me." Shaking his head more vigorously as if he was so disgusted with me. He disappears into the mist. Why won't he wait for me? I came to again; there was another face standing over me, but I could not see clear enough to figure it out. I close my eyes again and begin to drift away.

"Kate, can you hear me? It's Dr. Adams. Come on, Kate, open your eyes and talk to me." I wanted to. I tried to, but they just wouldn't open up. I also wanted to go find Ben, and I could feel myself slipping away. The voices of whoever was calling me were drifting farther and farther away. Then everything went black.

"Will you be staying with her, Emma?"

"Yes, I'm not going anywhere."

"Please keep talking to her. That is the only way we have to bring her out of this. You can even get angry with her if need be."

"All right, I will do my best." Pulling up a chair and taking her hand, I just sat and held it and rubbed it for a long time. The tears were flowing, and there was nothing I could do about them, so I just let them come. "My sweet child, how much more are you going to be able to take? Please wake up, I need you, Angel needs you. I will be lost without my best friend. Come on, Kate, please wake up." I sang her the song "Beautiful Brown Eyes." That was her favorite song when she was little. She has the prettiest, biggest brown eyes and the longest eyelashes I think I have ever seen on anyone that wasn't fake. Angel takes after her with both.

"Wake up, my beautiful girl. Come on, Kate, you can't sleep no more. Remember, when you were in school and you hated to wake up but you had to. This is the same thing. YOU HAVE TO WAKE UP, KATE." I'm patting the back of her hand firmly that it might almost hurt. "Damn it, Kate, you have to wake up. Angel is scared to death. She needs to know her mommy is going to be fine. She is with your friend Beth right now while you get well enough that I can stay with her, but for GOD's SAKE, KATE, WAKE UP NOW." There was no movement or sound coming from her. It was like she was dead as well. This is not good, and the longer she is under, the more dangerous it can be.

The blow she took to the head was enough to do this to her, but her body is trying to heal itself. The fact that she has been in and out a few times is a good thing. Angel had told them that Kate was awake after the fall and had told her to call 911. Oh, that poor child, what she must be thinking? Seeing her mother lying there in all that blood is enough to give her nightmares for years. It was a good thing that Ben had finished that part of the basement with linoleum. It was an easy cleanup. I wanted to throw up all the time I was cleaning it. Just knowing it was my daughter's blood that had been spilled there. How do people do it when someone has been killed in their home?

The next week went by slow and no change in Kate. I almost felt like she was slowly slipping away. This would be so hard on Angel to lose her parents and her brother at such a young age.

"I think you should bring Angel in to see her."

I feel a hand upon my shoulder. Turning and looking up. "No, Alex, I don't think she should see her mother like this."

"I think it could help bring her around if she heard Angel's voice."

"Oh please, don't ask me to do that to that poor child. She has seen enough for her age already. She should be getting counseling."

"You are right to a point. But we need to use everything we can to make Kate want to fight. She could just slip totally away. Many people do that. They go into a coma and are so relaxed in it they give up on living and just slip away. Is that what you want for Kate? Or Angel?"

"No, of course not, but that child has been through hell, and now you want her in here to see her mother like this?"

"We don't have a choice, I'm sorry for that. Angel is what her mother needs. By bringing her mother around will help erase everything else."

"If that doesn't work, then you just loaded the child with another burden."

"Then we will deal with that later. We are running out of time. It is going into week 2, and it is getting more dangerous. Kate doesn't even try now like she did at first? She hasn't opened her eyes now for over a week. Has she even moved her fingers while you are sitting there holding her hand?"

"No!"

"Then why are we waiting any longer?"

Standing up, I head for the door. "Okay, okay, you win, I will go get her. You better know what you are doing, Alex. My daughter and granddaughter have been through enough in a short time. Kate still has so much to deal with when she wakes up."

"I know that only too well, and I will be here for her. God, I wish this didn't happen to Kate, but it has. Now we all have to help her to cope with it and help each other." Alex steps over closer to me and pulls me into his arms. I couldn't help but sob. He just stood there and let me cry until I could get control of myself.

"I'm sorry."

"No need to be sorry, Emma. You love your daughter, and this is a hard thing to deal with on your own. I wouldn't expect anything else from you but tears. It only shows you have a heart and care very much."

"Her and Angel are all I have, Alex. I can't bear to lose her. She is my best friend. She always has been and always will be."

"I know that, Emma. Kate feels the same way about you. She says she has felt that she has been too hard on you at times, but it was to help you get strong and to be able to be on your own. She was always worried about what would happen to you if something was to happen to her. Look at you now. You are being very strong through all this, and Kate would be so proud of you."

"I'm crumbling inside. I'm not a strong person."

"Yes, you are. You have been here the whole time with Kate and are still holding up very well. You look tired, but rest will come soon. Now please go get Angel and let's wake your daughter up so we can all get some sleep. Shall we?"

"All right, I will do this for you."

"No, you are doing it for Kate, and you and your granddaughter."

"Okay." I leave the hospital with a heavy heart. I don't want to do this to my granddaughter. Yet I don't want not to if it will help Kate. I say a small prayer to myself as I climb into my car to go and pick up Angel.

"God be with us."

I get over to Beth's, and Angel is outside playing with their little girls. One was Angel's age, and the other was one year older. They all look like they were having fun. It was snowmen season, and there were snowmen going up all over town. I had heard that the town was having a snowman contest this year, so it has everyone outside building snowmen of every size and shape and some were very colorful. I was told by the girls that they had sprinkled Kool-Aid on their snowmen for color. It looked very different. Very eye catching. The family just down from them had sprayed theirs with water, and now they look like ice sculptures.

"You girls have done a very good job on your snowmen."

"This is a family of snowmen, Grandma. Here is the mommy, daddy, little girl, and their baby."

"I see that, Angel, and they look great. I bet it was fun?"

"Yes, Grandma, it was. I wish Mommy would come home and play with me in the snow."

"I wish she could too, Angel."

"Grandma, when can I go see Mommy. It has been a long time, and I really miss her."

"Actually, that is why I'm here, Angel. I have come to take you to see Mommy." "You have, Grandma?"

"Yes, sweetheart, we have to let Beth know you are coming with me for a while." Beth came out of the door at that time. "How's Kate today?" "No change?"

"Sorry to hear that."

"I'm taking Angel up to see her."

"You are?"

"Dr. Adams thinks it is what Kate needs. I'm not happy about it. I can only hope he knows what he is doing."

"That makes two of us. Does Angel know everything?"

"I will try to explain everything on the way over."

"Good luck with that, and please tell Kate we love and miss her."

"Thank you, I will. Come, Angel, let's go now so you can get back here to play some more while the sun is shining."

"That's okay, Grandma, I don't mind not playing if I can see Mommy. It has been a long time. I have lots to tell here."

"That is really good, Angel, 'cause that is what your mommy needs. She needs her little girl to talk her ear off, okay?"

"Why would I talk Mommy's ear off, Grandma? Won't that hurt her?" I could tell by the look on her face she had never heard that expression before.

"No, honey, Grandma didn't mean it that way. I just mean you have to talk lots and lots to Mommy." We climb into the car, and Angel was quiet at first. She frowns and says, "Why, Grandma, do I have to talk so much?"

"Angel, your mommy is in a deep sleep. This sleep is keeping her from us. It is what is stopping her from coming home, and we have to wake her up. Dr. Adams says she has slept long enough. So he told me to bring you so you could help us wake her up. Would you like to help us, Angel?"

"Oh yes, Grandma, I will. I want Mommy to come home. I want to go to our house, Grandma. I like playing with the girls, but I want to go home with Mommy and you, Grandma. Please, Grandma!"

TWENTY

"All right, but first, we have to wake Mommy up."

Angel never said another word all the way to the hospital. I myself was scared for this little girl who has already seen so much, and she now has to face another of the unknown for her.

How will all this affect her mind in the years to come? Will she be strong and be able to put all that has happened into perspective, or will she be one that will lose control of her life because of all the scaring and end up having to lie on someone's sofa for 150,000 bucks an hour? Maybe keeping her away isn't the answer but having her face things that are happening head-on and deal with it. Talk a lot about it so she gets comfortable and understands that life is not a bed of roses and not all fun and games, which I'm sure Angel has already come to realize more than most children her age.

I want Kate to wake up and heal, and Lord knows, I don't want to do it at Angel's expense. What if Alex is right and Angel will be the only one Kate will respond to? Kate tried at first, but there hasn't been any sign of trying for way too long now.

"All right, Angel, hold Grandma's hand, and I will take you up to see Mommy." She takes my hand, but there is no sign that she is excited about being here. Is she scared, or is it because the last time she was here was to see Ben? Angel doesn't look around; she is just looking at the floor and following my lead. I try to hold her hand tight so she feels my love, yet not so tight or I hurt her small hand.

"Grandma."

I squat to look into those sad, beautiful brown eyes. It was like looking at Kate when she was little and she had lost her puppy.

"What is it, Angel?"

"Is Mommy going to be okay?"

"I sure pray to God she will be."

"Then I will be okay too."

I take her in my embrace and tell her, "Angel, please remember that no matter what happens, Grandma is here for you. I love you, child, more than life itself."

"Mommy loves me as big as the sky, Grandma." To her, that was ten times better than the love I could give to her.

"Oh, darling, I know she does, and that is why we have to wake Mommy up."

"All right, Grandma, I will try my best."

"I know you will, Angel. I know." I hold her that little bit longer, and I think it was more for me than her. I know it was.

"Grandma, does Mommy look okay?"

"Yes, honey, Mommy looks just fine. Except she is sleeping."

She nods her head, and we get out of the elevator. Kate's room was the second door down on the right, which I think was easier on Angel than having to walk a long hallway.

I open the door, and Angel is standing off to the side. Trying to see Kate before she enters the room.

"It's all right, sweetheart, come on in." I stick out my hand for her to take. Angel hesitates for a couple of seconds, then takes my hand and comes in behind me. She was pushed right into my side, and that was fine. I could tell now she was scared.

"Angel, it is okay, come around up front so you can talk to Mommy."

"Grandma, she looks dead like Daddy."

"No! No! Sweetheart, she isn't, you come and hold Mommy's hand. Mommy is just sleeping."

She came a little closer and was never moving her eyes off Kate's face. I take her hand and put it into Kate's. I close Kate's hand around Angel's. Angel's eyes then dart to me.

"Her hand is warm, Grandma."

"Yes, Angel, it is."

"Daddy's hand was so cold."

"That is because Daddy had passed away, honey, but Mommy is just in a very deep sleep, and we have to wake her."

"Mommy said Daddy was sleeping too."

"He is, Angel, but in a different way. His heart isn't beating. You put your hand on Mommy's heart, and you will feel it still beating."

I take her hand and place it over Kate's chest. She looks up with a smile and says, "You're right, Grandma, I can feel it."

"Of course you can." I give her a side hug. "Now we have to wake her up."

Angel starts to look Kate over, and she gets a big frown on her face.

"What is it, Angel?"

"Why is Mommy's tummy not big anymore? Where is baby Ben?"

OH GOD! No one has told this child about Kate losing the baby.

"Grandma, where is Ben?" She let's go of Kate's hand like it had burned her. I try to pull her into my arms, and she pushes herself away and starts screaming.

"Where is baby Ben, Grandma?" She is backing farther away from me.

"Please, Angel. Grandma is so sorry. No one has told you about baby Ben. When Mommy fell, that hurt baby Ben real bad, and he is now in heaven with Daddy." I have never seen such a look on a little child's face that was of so much pain.

"No, NO," she screamed. As she ran out the door. I run after calling her, "Angel, please come back and talk with Grandma." There was no stopping her; she was running so fast and into everything and knocking things over, and she just continued to scream "no, no." Nurses were watching, and people were looking out of their doors, but no one knew what to do. Christ, I didn't know what to do. The best was to try to follow her. I was pretty sure she was headed to the car. I round the last corner she took to the stairs, and Alex was running toward me.

"Emma, what is going on?" he asked as he grabs me by the arm. I broke down and was sobbing, trying to explain, but nothing was sounding like it should.

"Please calm down and tell me what this is all about."

"That poor child didn't know that Kate lost the baby, and she is hysterical over it. I have to go after her."

"Emma, you go back to Kate. I will go find Angel. The two of you are too upset to talk about anything right now. I will try to explain the best I can."

"I can't believe I was so stupid and forgot to tell her about the baby. How could I be so insensitive?"

"It's understandable, we have all been concentrating on Kate." You haven't left Kate's side, so you haven't really had the time to tell her anything." Alex leaves to find Angel, and I go back to Kate's room. I find Kate tossing her head from side to side and she has a frown across her face like she could be in pain and struggling to say something. Rushing over to her and taking her hand. "Kate, what is it? Kate, it's Mom. Please talk to me." She just keeps tossing her head, and a very firm frown is on her face.

"Kate, are you in pain?" She sort of growls out a "NO!"

"What is it, Kate? Open your eyes and tell me. Come on, Kate, open your eyes. Damn it, Kate, do as I tell you just once." I sit down on the chair with Kate's hand in mine, and I break down.

"OH, LORD, I can't take much more of this please! I need your help. My daughter needs your help. My granddaughter needs your help. I have not asked you much over the years as I know you are busy. There are people worse off than we are, I know that. I'm running out of steam, and I don't think I can do this on my own any longer." Putting my face down into the side of the bed, I let it all go, and I weep like I haven't wept since my husband passed away.

The soothing hand rubbing on the back of my head was comforting, but that doesn't wake Kate up nor does it help me with Angel. I found it only made me sob all the harder. I knew I should get a hold of myself because this wasn't going to help Kate either. Except it felt like I didn't have control of my body and it was just having a real meltdown. How can one person sob so hard and long?

"Mom?"

I held my breath. Did I hear right? Was that Kate calling me, or was it my mind playing tricks on me?

"Mom, are you okay?"

I jerked my head up, and it was Kate's hand that was on the back of my head. Kate was looking at me with a worried look on her face.

"Oh, sweetheart, yes, I'm okay, yes, yes, oh, baby, I'm fine" I start to kiss her all over her face, and my tears are flowing silently now, but they are still flowing.

"Mom, you are going to drown me."

"Thank God."

"No. Mom, you really are going to drown me."

"I'm sorry, but I'm so happy you are awake, Kate. It has been a long time."

"How long, Mom?" she whispers.

"Kate, it has been two weeks. Two very long weeks."

"Mom, where is Angel?"

I thought I could hear Angel crying.

"Mom, where is she?" Kate's voice is so weak she is hard to hear.

"She is here. She is with Dr. Adams."

"Is Angel okay, Mom?"

"When she sees you, she will be just fine, honey."

"I could hear her crying, Mom. Why was she crying?"

At that moment, Kate put her hand up on her tummy. She starts to shake her head no and closes her eyes.

"Kate, please! Stay looking at me. Please, Kate, talk to me."

Her tears were flowing silently now, and she was rubbing her tummy. I try to take her into my arms and soothe her, but she would not respond to me.

"Kate, I'm sorry you lost the baby. I know you and Angel wanted baby Ben more than life itself. But, Kate, once again you have a little girl who needs her mommy. She doesn't want me or her friends, Kate. She wants her mommy. She needs her mommy."

"What did they do with baby Ben, Mom?"

"Not now, Kate?"

"Yes, now, Mom, I want to know. What happened to baby Ben."

"I had him cremated for you, Kate. You know they can't hold a body too long, and Dr. Adams didn't know how long it was going to take for you to come around. I knew you would want to bury him with Ben once you were well. I sure hope I made the right choice for you?"

"You did, Mom, thank you. Would you please get Angel?" My daughter sounds dead inside. Her voice is not the voice of my Kate.

"Yes, I will." Standing up off the bed and turning around just in time for the door to open and Dr. Adams comes in. The pleasant surprise that was on his face as he came in to the side of Kate's bed.

"Well, well, looks like our sleeping beauty finally decided to wake up." He takes Kate's hand and feels for her pulse. Pulls out his penlight and looks into her eyes and gets her to follow the end of his light with her eyes.

"Are you up to something to drink and eat?"

"My baby."

"I'm so sorry, Kate, there was nothing I could do. You had already miscarried him by the time the paramedics got to you. You were hemorrhaging badly, and we tried the D & C. It did not help, and I had to do a hysterectomy. You lost a lot of blood, Kate. We gave you a transfusion, Kate, but you have to help yourself get built back up now. You have to eat. You are going to be very weak, and I will keep you in here until I am happy with how you are gaining your strength back. You will be fine."

"A hysterectomy?"

"Yes, Kate, I had no choice, or you wouldn't be here now."

"You should have let me die." She turns her face away from them and stares at the wall. Dr. Adams straightens up his shoulders and, with a pissed-off attitude, ties into Kate, "Don't talk such foolish, Kate. Angel needs you. She misses her mommy and is already in such a state seeing how she also has lost so many that mean just as much to her as they did to you. Now I'm sorry for all that has happened to you. You had better learn to live with this and be here for your daughter. Who by the way is sitting with the nurses waiting to see her mommy. This little girl has seen her share of pain and losses for her age and has been through hell and back. I know you have to. As a parent, you have to be there for this little girl who is so strong. She is worried about her Mommy Kate. Now do I go and get her, or do we just let her think that her mommy doesn't *love* her? What is going to be, Kate?"

Kate wouldn't answer; she just lay there looking at the wall. Dr. Adams turns to leave, and Kate knew in her heart that Angel needed her as much as she needed Angel. The pain is so great.

"Bring her in." Dr. Adams just kept walking, and I was right on his heels. When I knew the door was shut, I gave him a blast.

"Just what the hell do you think you are doing? You want Kate to give up and go back into the coma? Why would you talk to her like that?"

"She wants to see Angel now, doesn't she? Sometimes you have to practice what is called tough love, Emma, and you are going to find out you are going to have to do the same thing as I am. There is nothing more wrong with Kate other than she is weak from the loss of so much blood. Mentally she is also weak but not to the point that we can't snap her out of this. Emma, she is going to mourn the loss of her child, and rightfully so. Kate also has another child who needs her mother. Not her grandmother or friends or her doctor. Her mother, and the more we stress that to her, the better it will be. For her and Angel and you. We can sit by and watch her feel sorry for herself. That is not doing her any good. She has to learn to live again, Emma, the same as you had to when your husband died."

"This is just so much for her in such a short time."

"You're right, it is. If we let her sit idle, she will be months or even years getting back on track. Maybe even end up being committed, is that what you want for her and Angel?"

"No, of course not."

"Then work with me here. Let's go get Angel and take her in to see your daughter."

"All right."

He tucks his arm in mine, and we set off to get Angel. We find her in the nurses' lounge, and they had made her a cup of hot chocolate, and it looked like she had been spoiled by the goodies that were all lying on the table in front of her. I went over to sit beside her, and she moved away. That rips my heart.

Alex was over talking to the nurses, and I knew they were discussing Angel.

"Mommy is awake now, Angel. Are you ready to go see her?"

She just shakes her head no.

I raised an eyebrow and say, "You're not going to see Mommy? Why not? She wants to see you."

She sits with her head hung down.

"Angel, Mommy really misses you, don't you miss Mommy?"

"Yes."

"Then let's go see her." I reach out my hand to her, and she doesn't move, so I put my hand down.

"Mommy won't talk to me now."

"Yes, she will, sweetheart. Mommy is waiting for you."

"No, she won't, it will be just like when Daddy died."

"Oh, honey, it won't be, Mommy is okay."

She jumps up off the sofa and turns on me with such vengeance. "No, she's not! Grandma. Mommy is not okay, and she won't talk to me." She turns around and goes over to Dr. Adams.

"Dr. Adams, will you take me to my friends' house now please."

He squats down so he can talk to her eye to eye. "For sure you don't want to talk to Mommy?"

She shakes her head no. Dr. Adams looks over at me. I could feel the tear slide down my cheek.

"Okay, but I have something to do first. Would you please wait with your grandmother until I come back?"

TWENTY-ONE

"Okay." Angel comes back over and sits on the sofa beside me. This time she is closer, but I don't make a move to hug her or anything. She is angry with me for something right now, and I will just have to wait to see what happens. Dr. Adams left and had been gone for a while, then the nurse got a call and she left. The silence in the room was so unnerving. I felt like I could jump out of my skin at any given time.

Angel sat there looking at the floor, and she could have cared less that I was in the room.

"Angel, are you going to tell Grandma why you are angry with me?"

She is thinking about it. I knew it was just a matter of time. "Grandma, why didn't you tell me that baby Ben died like Daddy. You said Mommy was okay that she was just sleeping. Grandma, you lied to me."

"I guess in a way I did lie to you. Grandma didn't mean to lie. I was so worried about Mommy, and I wanted so bad for her to wake up I forgot that you weren't told that baby Ben had died. I'm sorry for that. It must have been very sad for you to find out that your baby brother has gone to heaven to be with Daddy."

"Uh-huh."

"I'm so sorry, Angel, Grandma's brain just is so tired."

"It is, Grandma?"

"Yes, honey, it is. Now that Mommy is awake, Grandma is going to go and get a good night sleep."

She now snuggles up to me. "Grandma, can I sleep with you?"

"I think you could. Should we ask Mommy if that would be okay?"

"Mommy won't care."

The door to the lounge opened up, and a wheelchair was pushed in. Alex had brought Kate to Angel, seeing how Angel wasn't going to see Kate. Kate wasn't strong yet, but Alex was determined to get these two together again. Angel could not see the door, so it was going to be interesting to see how she reacted to this.

"What won't I care about, Angel?"

Angel sat up straight and just stared straight ahead. It was like she thought she had heard a ghost.

"Angel," Kate calls to her as Alex brings Kate around the side of the sofa. Angel's eyes get huge, and she is looking like she has seen a ghost. Kate was very pale, and she is thin. With losing the baby and the extra weight since. So to Angel, she could very easily be seeing a ghost.

"Mommy?"

"Hi, honey." Kate reaches out to take her hand. "Come here, give Mommy a big hug, would you?"

Angel never moved.

"Mommy really needs one of your bear hugs, Angel."

Angel gets up and moves very slowly toward Kate. No one knows what she was expecting. Perhaps one day we will find out, but for now, we can just speculate that she wasn't sure whether that was her mommy or not. Angel finally gives in and hands her hand over to Kate. Pulling her in tight to her body, she takes a deep breath, and the smell of Angel's hair makes her moan.

"Oh, baby, Mommy misses you. I love you as big as the sky."

"You do, Mommy?" Angel asks as if she wasn't sure of her own existence anymore.

"Of course, sweetheart."

"When you coming home, Mommy?"

"As soon as I can, Angel, as soon as I can."

Alex gets down on one knee and takes Angel and sits her on the other.

"Your mommy has to stay with us just a little longer so we know she will be strong enough to walk and take care of you. Mommy has to eat lots now so she can get stronger again."

"I can make Mommy chicken noodle soup."

"You can?"

"Yes, Daddy showed me how when Mommy was sick with baby Ben." Her voice wavered, and she dropped her eyes to the floor.

"That is good to know, Angel, 'cause when I let her out of here, she will need someone to take care of her. I'm trusting that I can count on you to help me make Mommy better. Can I?"

"Oh yes, I will take good care of Mommy."

"Good, now that we have that solved, should we take Mommy back to her room so she can eat and rest?"

"Okay, can I push Mommy?"

"You sure can, Angel, don't you worry about anyone. They can move out of your way."

"Okay." She giggles. What a lovely sound. We all go back to Kate's room, and the nurse helps her into bed. Alex takes her blood pressure and checks her pulse and her eyes one more time.

"Looks like my patient here will be just needing to eat good, and she should be good to go soon. Now I will leave you all alone. I have sick patients waiting for me." He leaves, and I follow him out of the room.

"Alex, thank you so much."

"You're welcome, Emma."

"I'm sorry I questioned you about your work."

"No need to be sorry, Emma, you were just concerned about the ones you love." Giving me a hug and then moving on to another one sick at hand. I had to be grateful that my daughter has him for her doctor.

Going back inside, I find Angel up on the side of the bed lying with Kate. Kate was stroking her hair, and I could see that Angel had been crying. I guessed they must have been talking about the baby.

"Angel, I think it is time that we go and let Mommy rest. We will come back first thing in the morning."

"Mommy, can I sleep with Grandma tonight at our house?"

"If Grandma wants you to, that is fine with me."

"Let's get going then, Grandma is very tired too." Kissing Kate good night was not coming easy. I was afraid she might not wake up again.

"Thank you, Mom. I love you."

"I love you too, my sweet child, and I will see you in the morning?" I raise my eyebrows to her, and she knew what I meant.

"Yes, Mom, I will see you in the morning." As we were leaving, Angel sort of hung back. She was hesitant to leave her mother now that they were talking.

"It's okay, Angel, Mommy will be okay, and we are coming back right after breakfast."

"We should have breakfast with Mommy."

"Then we will have to see what we can do about that. Let's go home have our baths and snuggle by the fire with a hot chocolate. In the morning we will see where we can get breakfast and bring it up and eat with Mommy."

"Okay, Grandma. Mommy, we will be back for breakfast, okay?"

"Okay," Kate calls out to her. Now that she was alone, she would grieve for her son that she has lost. One day you are awaiting the arrival of a new baby; then the next, it has been taken from you in a blink of an eye. There will be no little Benjamin Parker, like his daddy. He has gone before us to be with the good Lord. "I hope, Ben, that our son is with you safe and happy. You have no idea what this has done to Angel and myself. We were hoping that Benjamin Jr. was going to keep you alive and with us for many years to come. Just maybe that is why the good Lord has taken him from me. It's not that I was trying to replace you with your son, but just to keep your face visible so we wouldn't forget what you look like. A picture is all we will have to cherish. We will hold it dear to us. It would have been great to have a small warm body that looked like his daddy to hold. Oh, Ben, why?" I can't stop the sobbing, and it was coming from way down inside, and I had to let it go.

Knowing that there will never be another baby is the emptiest feeling a person could have. You feel like you are hollowed out inside. Is this how pumpkins feel? To know that Angel will always be the only child I will ever have makes her truly my *angel* sent to us from God. I hope she knows how special she is and always will be.

Still sobbing when Dr. Adams came to do his evening rounds. I must have used up two boxes of tissue paper, and my throat and stomach hurt as the sobbing was so hard and heavy.

"Kate, I can't give you anything to ease this, you know that."

Chocking back a sob, I was finally able to answer, "I have to face this sooner or later, and drugs won't make it go away. Why is this happening to me? What more can he take from me? Angel?"

"No, Kate, I don't think that will happen. This was just another horrible accident."

"I thought that when I didn't miscarry after being so sick like Angel that this baby was going to be strong and healthy."

"Kate, your baby was strong and healthy. You took an awful bad fall, and no one's pregnancy would have withstood it."

"Why didn't I just leave that damn ladder where it was for the night?"

"Kate, it could have happened at anytime. People fall all the time. I'm sorry about all this, and I do know how hard it is on you. I truly believe that you and Angel will be all right. You two are survivors if I have ever seen one. You now have to look ahead as hard as that may seem to you right now. You have to think about Angel. That little girl has been through a lot for someone her age. I think you should think about taking a holiday. You and Angel going somewhere that you have never been. I don't mean to a place where you and Ben have been with or without Angel. Start a new life, Kate, with you and Angel, maybe even with Emma."

"With Mom?"

"Yes, Kate, do you know how special you and Angel are to that lady? She never left your side. She would die if anything happened to you or Angel. The three of you should do some traveling and get reconnected."

"Mom likes to be on her own."

"We all like our space, Kate."

"We always would invite her, but she would always say she was busy. When she comes around, she never stays too long, a couple days at the most, and she would have to leave."

"Kate, that was when you and Ben were a family. She didn't want to intrude or be the third wheel as they call it. Now that it is just you and Angel, you should include her. I think you all need time to heal and, like I said, get reconnected. It will do you all the world of good. Emma and Angel are very close. I can tell the way they are with each other."

"Yea, Mom thinks of Angel as her china doll. She has from the time Angel was born. There has been a special bond between the two of them. I hope it will always be like that."

"What about you, Kate?"

"About me, what?"

"What kind of bond do you have with your mother?"

"What kind of bond?"

"Yes, Kate, are you and your mom like Emma and Angel?"

"I really don't know. It has been a long time since we really did anything together. I guess I've always just thought of Mom as Mom. I respect her a lot. I love my mom."

"So it wouldn't hurt for you to get to know more about your mom and maybe find out what she would like to do or where she would like to go. It's not too late to build a special bond between the two of you. You might already have it. You just have to figure it out."

"I have never thought about it. I never thought Mom as being lonely. She is always busy. Mom has never been one to sit around. She always felt like it was a waste of time."

"She stays busy 'cause she is lonely. Bet she is busy right up until she falls into bed."

"Yea, she does. I remember that when I was at home still."

"Take her traveling, Kate, show her how much you love her."

"Thank you, Dr. Adams, for the talk. I think I will."

"Please promise you will do more than just think about it. It will do you good as well. I say take six months and just travel."

"Six months?"

"Is there a reason why you can't?"

"School and the house and Mom's friends"

"So far I haven't heard anything but excuses. School you can take with you. What a better learning experience for Angel to see some of this great world we live in."

"Great world?" I say that with a grain of salt.

"Yes! Kate, the world is a beautiful place, and you have to show Angel that there is greatness out there. It may not wipe out all the sadness she has seen, but it will show her that there is good after bad. It will give her more of an opportunity to see things differently than just staying in that house where she has had nothing but sorrow."

"That house has been all we have known."

"That is true, and now it is time to spread your wings. You know Ben would say, 'Do it, Kate.' What do you have to lose? I'm going to go now. Hope you are feeling better. I will check with you in the morning. Please try to get some sleep. I will send you something to help you sleep if you would like?"

"No, thank you. I will be fine."

"All right then, good night."

"Thank you and good night." I lay there for most of the night thinking about what I should do. How would I ask my mom if she would like to just give up everything and travel with Angel and me? Dr. Adams is right. Ben left me well provided for, and the mortgage was paid off the week following his death. I could arrange for direct payment for the utility bills.

Angel would learn a lot about the world. But where to go? What part of the world would we want to go see first? Where would Angel want to go? Where would Mom want to go? Where would I want to go? I always said I would like to see Australia. Now wouldn't that be something? Yea!

I doze off for a while, but there were so many questions going around in my head.

The night was long. I had asked for Ben to guide me in my answers; nothing was coming to mind, so I took it that this was something he was wanting me to do on my own. He no longer was going to be making decisions with me. It was time I learned how to stand on my own two feet.

The chatter coming down the hall was very familiar. Angel was alive and well, and everyone was knowing it.

"Good morning, Mommy, Grandma and I brought you breakfast from Mac's. It is still hot. Just like you like it, Mommy."

"Then how can I say no. Come up on the bed, and we will eat."

"I might spill your coffee?"

"No, just put it right here on the table."

"Good morning, Mom."

"Good morning, Kate. Did you sleep well?"

"Yes, I did."

"You don't look like it. I want to say you look like hell, but that won't get you up and about."

Kate chuckles. "Leave it to you, Mom, to say it as it is."

"I'm sorry?"

"Don't be, that is what makes you special, and that is why I love you as I do." Leaning over and kissing Kate on the top of her head. "Thank you, Kate, now let's eat our breakfast before it all gets any colder. Come on, Angel, Grandma will help you get up here beside Mommy."

"I'm hungry, Mommy."

"Me too, what did you bring me?"

"An egg muffin and a coffee."

"Just what I needed, thank you so much."

"This is a whole lot better tasting than hospital food, right?"

"Yea, Mom, it is. But not as healthy."

"Who says?" They laugh and get right down to eating.

TWENTY-TWO

"Mom, there is something I want to ask you."

"What is it, Kate? You all right?"

"Oh yea, Mom, I will be fine." I reach over and take Angel's hand. "We will be just fine, won't we, Angel?"

"Yep, Mommy, we will."

"That's my little trooper. In fact, this question that Mommy has for Grandma is also for you, Angel?"

"It is?"

"So what is it, Kate?"

"Mom, if you were to travel, where would you like to go?"

"To travel?"

"Yes, Mom, to travel."

"Well, I don't know, Kate."

"Come on, Mom, there must be someplace where you would like to go more than another."

"I have always thought I would like to see a real kangaroo." Now this has Kate laughing. It was such a great sound to hear my daughter laughing so soon after all she has been through.

"What is so funny, Kate?"

"'Cause that is what I would like to do as well."

"Me too, I want to see a real kangaroo. Can we, Mommy? Can we?"

"I think the three of us should do some traveling and go see those kangaroos."

"Are you serious, Kate?"

"I sure am, Mom. Unless you are tied up with something else?" I saw tears form in her eyes.

"There is nothing that could stop me from going with you and Angel. If you are really serious, Kate."

"Me too, Mommy. I'm serious." I couldn't help but pull Angel in for a hug.

"I couldn't be more serious, Mom. As soon as Dr. Adams tells me I can go home, we are taking a holiday. The three of us."

"I think that will be great. For how long?"

"Six months, maybe a year."

"What about Angel's schooling? Your house?"

"I can get some schoolwork Mom to take along. But wouldn't this be a schooling all in itself?"

"It sure will, what will the school say?"

"I don't care, we are going for as long as we want. What do you say, Angel?"

"Yippee, yippee, we are going to the kangaroos."

"See, Mom, you don't have to worry."

"All right then, I will arrange to close my apartment up."

"Good, now we all agree we are going to see the kangaroos, RIGHT?"

"YES!" they cried together.

"Mommy, can Grandma take me to the park when you have a nap?"

"That is totally up to Grandma."

"I would love to go to the park with you, Angel. The walk will do us good. The sun is shining today, and Mommy is doing great. It is a great day all around."

"I'm happy that we are all going to go on a holiday together. Mom, we haven't done anything together for an awfully long time, and it is due."

Bending over and taking her in my arms for a long overdue hug. "I love you, Kate, more than you will ever know. You are my world. You and Angel." I just hugged her as close as I could.

"I'm sorry, Mom, for not being there for you all this time."

"No need to be sorry, you had your life and I had mine, what there is of it? Now we need each other again, and we have to be lucky that we have this option. We can't look back. We must look ahead and move on. As painful as it will be at sometimes, it is what we all have to do, to survive. I'm here for you and Angel anytime you need me. Just call."

"I know, Mom, and I can't wait for us to take this trip."

"Me either, dear. Now maybe you should rest. I will take Angel to the park for an hour or so. We will be back."

I wanted to say I trust you will wake up, but I will just keep that fear to myself.

"Maybe now I will sleep knowing that I have made some decisions. The excitement of our plans will be all that would keep me awake now."

"All right, see you in a bit." Kissing her on the check and turning to get Angel's hand, I see her watching Kate closely.

"Are you ready, Angel? Give Mommy a kiss, then we can go and let Mommy sleep."

Angel goes over and gets up on the side of the bed so she can kiss Kate and hug her. "Mommy, you will wake up again, won't you?"

"Oh yes, sweetheart, I sure will. Mommy's head is healed from that bang now. You go with Grandma and have a good time. I will see you when you come back. Remember always, Angel, Mommy loves you as big as the sky."

"I love you that big too, Mommy."

Off they went to the park. Angel was happy, and she skipped and sang her little songs all the way to the park. It didn't take her long to find friends to play with. It looked like she knew them from school and they were just talking up a storm. I had overheard Angel telling them about Kate losing the baby and how we were all going to go see the kangaroos.

I sat on a bench and pulled out my pocketbook that I had in my pocket. I like to keep one in my pocket when going to the hospital. You never know when the person you are going to go see is sleeping or not. It does help kill time. Angel was busy with her friends, and there was no reason why I couldn't read for a while. It would give Angel the time she needed to be a carefree little girl. It would do her wonders.

I must have read for about half an hour, and I would glance up to see what Angel might be doing. The girls didn't stray too far away from where they first met. They ended up over on another bench and sitting there talking like us older women would do. I'm sure the girls had many questions for Angel. They would want to know how Kate lost the baby and when she would be home and when Angel would be leaving on her trip.

I could tell by the look on their faces that they were having a very serious conversation. Angel seemed to be handling it all in stride.

I saw this tall gentleman approaching the girls, so I watched, and they all answered his question and didn't seem to mind that he was there. He was talking to Angel, then next I saw him come around the bench and kneeling down in front of Angel and was giving Angel a hug. The hug lasted a little longer than I thought it should, so I get up and I walk over to where the girls are.

"Angel, are you okay?"

The gentleman looks up at me with a look of concern on his face. Standing up and sticking his hand out to me, he says, "I'm very sorry to hear about Kate. Is there anything I can do for her?"

"I don't think so. She has Angel and me looking out for her. Thank you for asking just the same, Mr.—"

"Sanders. Jake Sanders, madam."

"I'm Kate's mother, Emma."

"I thought so your daughter looks very much like you. She is a very pretty lady as well."

"Thank you, she is."

"This is just a horrible thing to happen. I know her and Angel were looking forward to having this baby."

"Yes, we all were. Now we will move on, and unfortunately for Kate, she will never be able to have any more children."

"Oh, that is too bad. Is she okay with that?"

"She really doesn't have a choice. It was her life that was on the line. She may have times it will bother her, but she just has to remember how lucky she is to have Angel."

"I understand. Can she have company?"

"She sure can anytime of the day. She didn't sleep well last night, so we came to the park to give her some rest time."

"Kate isn't sleeping well?"

"Kate just had a lot on her mind last night, and now that she has some answers, I think she will settle down and sleep well."

"That is a good thing then. I will go up after supper and see her. What is her room number?"

"I think she would love the company. She is in room 210. I won't be taking Angel back after supper. I would like for her to start getting a good night sleep on regular basis."

"It sounds like all of you need to catch up on your sleep."

"We are faring pretty good considering."

"Please if you ever need any help, call me. Here is my card."

"Oh, thank you, Mr. Sanders."

"Please call me Jake and promise you will call. I can help Kate do things around the yard."

"I will be sure to let her know, and I will be sure to call if I see she could use a hand with something I can't help with. Kate is pretty independent. It is really hard to get her to ask for help."

"I gather that when I met her. She is a very proud woman."

"She is that all right, and I'm proud of her. She has handled a lot over this last year."

"She is lucky to have her mother."

"I hope she feels like that."

"Grandma, are we going now?"

"Yes, Angel, we are going now. We will go see Mommy like we promised her, then we will go home and relax."

"That sounds like a very good idea, Grandma."

"I think your grandma is a very smart woman."

"Yes, she is." Angel takes my hand and looks at Jake as if Jake wasn't telling her anything she didn't already know.

"Now, Angel, you mind your manners. We will be seeing you around then, Jake, and thank you again for your offer to help. I'm sure Kate will enjoy your company." Angel and I headed back to the hospital. We didn't stay long. The nurse was wanting to take Kate for a short walk just to see if she had the strength to be able to take a shower on her own. So they walked us out, and we waved good-bye through the big window and watched as the nurse turned her around and was headed back to her room.

"Mommy keeps that up, and she should be coming home soon."

"I can't wait, Grandma."

"Me either, sweetheart."

"I'm glad you will be staying with us now, Grandma."

"Oh, now I don't think that I will be doing that, Angel."

"Why not, Grandma? Mommy gets lonely when I'm at school."

"Maybe she does. Mommy is going to have to figure that out on her own. Now get into the car." Staying with Kate and Angel never crossed my mind. I always thought of Kate as one of the most independent persons I know. I just could not see us living under the same roof for a long period of time. That comes from being so much alike.

"I think we will have an early night, Angel, then you and I will go over to my apartment and check on things."

"Okay, Grandma. Can I still sleep with you?"

"You really want to? Don't you miss your bed?"

"I miss you more, Grandma." I reach over and take her hand and give it a squeeze.

"I miss you too, sweetheart."

"If you lived with us, Grandma, then you wouldn't miss me so much."

"You are right about that."

"Please, Grandma."

"We will see how we all settle down when we come back from our holidays. Then maybe, just maybe, Mommy and I will talk about it."

"I can't wait to go see the kangaroos, Grandma."

"Me either, I can't believe that after all these years, I'm going to do what I always have wanted to do."

"How come you didn't go with Grandpa?"

"Grandpa was busy working, and it was something we would likely be doing now if he were still with us. Grandpa always wanted to go to Australia. So I guess I better see enough for both of us."

"Maybe Grandpa already seen it."

"How do you figure that, Angel?"

"You told me long time ago that Grandpa was an angel now."

"Yes, he sure is."

"Well, he has wings, Grandma, and he could fly there."

"You are absolutely right. Bet he has already seen Australia."

"You still coming with us, right, Grandma?"

"Oh yes, Angel, I wouldn't miss this for the world. To take a trip like this with you and Mommy is a dream come true. We must take lots of pictures so when you get old like Grandma, you will always be able to remember what we did together. You will be able to show your friends when we get back."

"Grandma, will you help me with scrapping them?" Chuckling at how she sees scrapbooking.

"I sure will, I love to scrapbook, Angel."

"Will you show me how to do more of it, Grandma?"

"You bet, and I have bought more tools, so it is more fun now than it was back when you were three."

"That's cool, Grandma, thank you."

"So we better make sure we get a large stack of pictures."

"Mommy always takes lots of picture. Everywhere we go."

"I know she does, and that is a very good way to be. Now you'll always have pictures of you and your mom and dad."

"Knock, knock," Jake says as he pushes the door to Kate's room open. She had just finished having a snack and was looking out the window. Evening was falling, and it always looks colder in the winter evenings. The people walking by were pulling the coat collars up and trying to tuck their faces in out of the wind. That too always feels colder at night.

"Hi, Jake, come on in. How are you?"

Going over and taking Kate's hand, he couldn't help but think how fragile she felt and looked. Yet she had a very bright smile today.

TWENTY-THREE

"I'm great, Kate, the question is, how are you? I'm so sorry to hear what happened. I know how much you and Angel wanted the baby."

"Thank you, Jake. I'm fine, it will take some time to get over."

"Yes, it will, and I hope it won't be too hard on you?"

"It would have been worse to carry him full-term then lose him or even after he was with us for a while. I know in my heart he is with Ben and so he is okay. I think of it as though the good Lord has made it so we aren't to be lonely. I have Angel and Ben has Ben Jr."

"You had him named?"

"Oh yes."

"Are you having a service for Ben Jr.?"

"When I get out, we are just going to lay him to rest with Ben. It won't be really a service, just Mom and Angel, Dr. Adams, and myself."

"Would you be offended if I were to be there?"

"Jake, you want to be there?"

"Yea, Kate, I would like to be there for you and Angel. Maybe even for Emma."

"You met my mother?"

"Yes, I did. She is a very lovely woman. I see where you get it from."

I know I was blushing. I tried to pass it off as just general chitchat. Jake had an easy way about him that I felt pulled to. It was like when Ben would be playing with Angel and she would run and climb on my lap to be safe. I got that feeling from Jake that he was a safe place to be.

"They never told me they saw you."

"Guess they had other things on their minds today. Angel was busy with all her friends at the park, and Emma was reading. Yet she never let

Angel out of her sight for a minute. I never did know how my mother would do that as well?"

"Do what, Jake?"

"She would be reading, yet she knew what we were up to and would always call us on things we weren't to be doing. When I'm reading, I need peace and quiet, no distractions."

"That's me too, I read when Angel has gone to bed. I also don't like distractions. I lose sight of the story if I don't have just reading time. I see people reading on their lunch break or their fifteen-minute coffee break. That is not for me. I like to get right into the story. I want to be able to enjoy it."

"Well then, sounds like we have something in common."

Laughing at Jake's comment. "It sounds like it."

Getting up and going over to the bed, Jake takes me by the arm and helps me. I was grateful as I don't feel all that strong.

"Not so steady on your feet yet, Kate?"

"No, Dr. Adams says it's from losing so much blood. It will take some time. I did have a blood transfusion but only half of what I needed. It was to help my body do what it is to do."

"Is it working?"

"Yes, they check my blood twice a day, and they say it is coming up. It is just a very slow process."

"Not to mention scary."

"You have that right. Poor Angel will have nightmares for a very long time." "Why?"

"When I fell, she was the only one with me, and I have no idea how long it was before we got help. I knew she was already seeing a lot of blood because she had told me before I blacked out. Dr. Adams said I had already lost the baby by the time the paramedics got there. I have no idea what all she saw. Maybe she will talk to me about it when we go on our holiday."

"Oh! You're going away, are you?"

"Yes, Mom, Angel, and I are going to go to Australia."

"When?"

"As soon as the doctor tells me I can."

"How long you going for?"

"Don't know for sure, six months maybe."

"Six months!"

"Well, none of us have a reason to rush back, so we will make it a very special trip. We hope to see and learn a lot. It will be Angel's education after all."

"I guess Angel won't be in school."

"I'm going to get some math to take along. The rest will be based on what we see and do."

"That is great, sounds like fun. I'm jealous. That is one place I have always wanted to go as well."

"Hey, me too, so if I'm going, so can you."

"What about your house?"

"I will see to getting someone to keep an eye on things."

"If you don't mind, I could do that for you, Kate?"

"No, Jake, you don't have to do that. I'm sure I can get a teenage boy who needs pocket money to deal with my house."

Picking up my hand and smiling like a nervous teen himself. "I will make you a deal, Kate. If you promise to send me a postcard from all the places you visit, I would gladly watch out over your house free of charge."

"I can send you postcards even if you don't watch my house."

"You would?"

"Sure, even if it was just to rub your nose on it."

"Oh, so now I see how you play. Dirty!"

"Yep, that's me, a dirty player, so you better be careful." We were still laughing when Dr. Adams came in.

"Now I haven't heard this young lady laugh like that for a very long time. It warms my heart to hear it. Your friend here should have come out of hiding a while ago."

"Dr. Adams, this is Jake Sanders." Up until now, we forgot that he was holding my hand, and I think we both blushed when he let go to shake Dr. Adams's hand.

"I don't believe I have seen you before."

"I haven't lived here long, and I don't go to doctors very often. Last time I was twelve with my appendix."

"That is a long time between visits all right."

"Guess it is, but I like to leave room for the real sick. So short of breaking something, I don't bother you fine folks."

"I wish everybody felt that way. It would cut down on our health care bills. Plus not to mention all the waiting time."

"So, Kate, how are you feeling?"

"Besides feeling guilty for being here, great I guess."

"Now, Kate, you know we weren't talking about you. You had a very serious fall and almost lost your life over it. You need to be here."

"Kate, you didn't say it was that serious. I knew you lost the baby. But sounds like there was a lot more to it than that."

"Oh yes, Kate was in a coma, and she hemorrhaged badly. We almost lost her." "Oh, Kate!" He picked up my hand again and held it so gently.

I saw the sad look that came into Jake's eyes. It almost brought tears to mine. What a softhearted man he is. I wonder why he isn't married. Or maybe he is. I never asked him.

"She is on the road to recovery now, and by the sound of her laugh, she has come a long way in a couple days. Keep this up, and you will be going home sooner than we thought."

"You don't want to rush her to go home. Kate won't rest there."

"I see you know Kate well."

"No, not yet, but I hope to get to know her, well."

"Kate, did you think about what we talked about?"

"Yes, Dr. Adams, I sure did. I also talked to Mom and Angel."

"I'm glad you're talking about everything now, Kate."

"We are leaving as soon as you say I can."

"You are leaving?" Dr. Adams has the biggest frown.

"Yes! We are all going to Australia."

"You're kidding?"

"No! I'm not, as soon as you let me go and say it is safe, we are out of here."

"Well! I will be damn, Kate Parker does listen. I'm glad to hear it. You are also going?" he asked Jake.

"No, the three ladies are going on their own. I, sir, will be taking care of Kate's house while they are away."

"Sounds like you have everything under control and plans are all made. I will get out of your way, and you two have a good evening. Kate, it won't be long, and you will be on that big silver bird and getting the holiday you so deserve. I want postcards from wherever you are. Got it?"

"You too?"

"What does that mean? You too."

"Jake wants me to send him postcards of all the places we go."

"Good, so while you're writing out one, you can do two. I will talk to you tomorrow." He slipped out as fast as he came in.

"Nice, Doctor."

"He has helped us a lot, and he really cares about his patients."

"I can see that. If I ever need a doctor, hope I can get him."

"He has almost been like a father to me. He is there always anytime day or night. He gave us his home number the first day we brought Angel to him. We never have used it, but the fact that I have it makes things not seem so bad. 'Cause I wouldn't call him over silly things, and so when we do need him, well here I am." I spread my arms out across the bed.

"I hope you won't be needing him for a very long time after you are out of here, Kate."

"That makes two of us." I was kicking around the idea of asking about a wife.

"Since my wife died, I haven't had to spend much time in a hospital."

"I'm sorry to hear that, Jake."

"It's been ten years now, so I'm fine with it. Oh, I have missed her, and it was very rough at first. It took about five years before I went out anywhere except to work."

"I have been out and about with Angel. She has kept me alive."

"We never got a chance to have children. Grace was diagnosed shortly after we were married, so she fought for a long time. We never thought about having a child. The doctors told us right from the beginning not to have children. That it would have shortened her life a lot sooner. We just enjoyed us for what time we had."

"I'm so sorry, Jake. That must have been hard on you to watch her like that."

"It almost killed me as well."

"Then I'm lucky that Ben was taken so fast. It was a shock, but I never had to watch him suffer. That too would have killed me."

"It is very hard to see someone you love in so much pain and you can't do a damn thing for them. I now have my dogs, and they are good company, for the most part. I'm finding that I miss having human conversations more now than I used to."

"I love talking to you, Jake, so when we get back, you sure are welcome to stop by anytime for a visit. I can even make coffee."

"Now that sounds great to me. You know I should come over before you leave so you can show me what is normal at your place, so I will be able to tell if someone has been around while I was away."

"Good idea, I never thought of that."

"By any chance, do you have any pets to take care of?"

"No, we don't. Not yet anyways."

"Are you thinking about letting Angel have a puppy?"

"I think it is something I should really consider. I think she should have some kind of playmate. Seeing how the two-legged ones are out of the question. I best think about the four-legged ones. It will be something at the top of my list when we get back, that is for sure."

"I think you would make Angel very happy if you got her a puppy."

I know it won't be just any puppy. It will have to be like that little one she saw at the park."

"Those are easy to come by. They seem to pop out at my place on a regular basis. Do you prefer male or female."

"I myself females. Angel will want the black and white just like she saw."

"There are always a couple black and white in the litter, so she should be safe." "We will check to see what you have happening over there when we get back." "Sounds like a plan to me, Kate. I think I should go now so you can get some sleep."

"Jake, would you take me for a walk to the doors and back first."

"If you think you can do it, I sure wouldn't mind."

"I have to work at this so I can get out of here."

"I think you have to make sure you are strong enough, Kate. Don't rush yourself. You will just set yourself back. Now take my arm and hold on, and we will go for a stroll up and down the hall."

Doing as Jake had said, I take a hold of his arm, and he puts his hand on top and tucks my arm close into his side. We walked slowly and chatting about nothing really and yet a lot. It was nice walking with someone like this again. I hadn't realized how tall Jake really was, or I just didn't remember when I met him at the park. I could get a kink in my neck if I were to look up at him for any length of time. I found myself wondering what kind of dancer he might be. I bet he could twirl a girl around the dance floor with such ease you would feel like you were floating. Now that is something else I haven't done for a long time. Ben and I used to dance at home. We never like to get a babysitter, so we would move furniture and put on our own tunes. Dance till we couldn't dance any longer. It was great.

"I hear those wheels turning, Kate. What are you thinking so hard about?"

I stopped abruptly and turned to face him.

"Do you like to dance, Jake?"

TWENTY-FOUR

"Dance?"

"Yes, dance."

"Well, let's see." He takes me in his arms and hums a tune while we dance down the hall of the hospital. I was right. He was so graceful that anyone could follow him. I did exactly that. He turned me around, and we headed back to my room dancing all the way. Stopping, he bows and says, "So what do you think?" The staff all start to clap. I felt my face turn red.

"I think you are a mighty fine dancer, Sir Jake."

"I think the same of you, Madam Kate. When you get back, we will have to go dancing."

"Sounds like when we get back, we could be terribly busy."

"Yes, it is starting to sound that way. Do you mind?"

"No, I don't, it will be good to be back busy. We may be tired from the trip, but it will all be for a good cause."

"Now let me help you back into bed."

"All right, thank you."

Tucking me in and kissing me on the cheek, he says, "Good night, Kate, sweet dreams."

"Good night, Jake, and I hope you sleep well too."

"I think it will be the best sleep I have had for a long time. Thank you for the dance, Kate."

"You're welcome and thank you too."

After he left, I couldn't help but lie here and think about what we just did. It was so out of the normal for me. It felt good to do something that you just don't do. We didn't harm anyone or cause any undue stress to either of us, so it was great. In fact, it was so sweet of him I think I would like to get to know him better. With that thought in mind, I know I fell asleep with the biggest grin on my face.

The next week went by so quickly. I ate well; my blood came up to normal. Every day Jake came up and would walk me up and down the hall so my legs would build up strength. They no longer felt like they were made of rubber.

The nurses asked if we were going to dance one more time for them the day I was going home. My mother's mouth fell open, and she said, "What are they talking about, Kate?"

"Here, Emma, if you don't mind you take Kate's bag, and we will show you."

"Oh, all right."

"Jake, no."

"Kate, yes." He takes me into his arms and says, "You ready, my dear?"

Away we go. This time the tune he hums has a little more get-up-and-go. I found myself thinking our dance ended too quickly. The nurses were clapping and cheering us on. We had them on ignore.

"Where did you learn to hum like that?"

"I used to play drums in a band. That is how I met Grace."

"You hum very nicely, I must say."

"Thank you. I have to say though I would love to dance with you to something other than me humming."

"I rather enjoyed our dance, thank you."

"Oh, me too, I just want to really dance with you, Kate. I haven't wanted to dance for an awfully long time, but it feels right to want to dance with you." He leans down and places a light kiss on my lips.

"Now when did you two have time to learn how to dance like that?"

"I've been here teaching her."

"I'm impressed."

"Now, Mom."

"Well, I am, I haven't seen you dance for a long time, Kate. I haven't seen you look so happy for a long time. I'm glad Jake is teaching you how to enjoy life again. Thank you, Jake."

"You're welcome. Now can we take her home and get her settled before Angel gets home? Angel will be surprised to see you at home today after school instead of in here."

"It will be great to be home again."

"I bet it will."

"I have some things I have to do, Kate. Is it okay if I'm not there right away?"

"Oh sure, Mom. I will be fine until you get home."

"I can always stay with Kate, Emma, until you get there."

"I will be just fine. I won't need a babysitter." That cuts through me like a knife. Realizing that it was true, I won't ever need a babysitter again. Jake saw the pain go across my face with those words spoken.

"I know myself I will be in need of a coffee. How about you, Kate?"

"Yes, I will." I knew I didn't sound as convincing as I had hoped I would. I climbed into Jake's truck and waited for him and Mom to finish whatever it was they were talking about.

Jake got in, and we drove quietly to my place. On the way there, I felt this heavy feeling come over me. It almost made it hard to breathe. The ray of sunshine that I was feeling has left, and the gloom has taken over. Surely it can't be all over the fact that I wouldn't ever need a babysitter. I thought I came to terms with that in the hospital?

"You're awfully quiet, Kate. Are you all right?"

"Yea, I think so."

"So why so glum all of a sudden?"

"I really don't know." Was Ben trying to send me a message? Is there something I need to know? Maybe about Jake. I turned and was watching him. When he turned and looked at me.

"Did I do something wrong, Kate?"

"No, of course you haven't."

"You can talk to me, I'm a very good listener."

"I haven't known you long, Jake, but I do feel as though I could talk to you. That isn't the problem."

"Try me and let's see what it is that is bothering you."

"I don't know, I got this real heavy feeling in my chest. I thought I was happy about going home. I am happy about going home. This might sound dumb to you. I almost feel like Ben is trying to send me a message and I'm not reading it properly. I don't know what else it could be.

"Is he upset because of you? Is he finding this unsettling to him? So he is making me uncomfortable? I wouldn't think that Ben wouldn't want me having a friend to talk to. Him and I, we talked all the time. He knows how important it is to me to be able to communicate with people. I really enjoy your company, and I'm not doing anything disrespectful. I promised myself that I wouldn't think about dating another man for at least a year after he died."

"That is respectful, Kate. I don't have a problem waiting."

"What are you waiting for?"

"To date you."

"To date me?" I chuckled.

"Yes, Kate, I'm going to take you dancing, so I would consider that a date. Wouldn't you?"

"Don't friends hang out and do those kind of things too?"

"I guess some do, I never really thought about it until now."

"I really like you, Jake, as a friend. I feel I could use a good friend after all of this, and you seem to fit the description, sorry."

"Don't be, I'm honored. I would love to be your friend, Kate. I also have needed one. I think what it is for me is that you don't know anyone that I know. So we don't have anyone pushing us for more than what we want. I'm very comfortable talking to you. You don't give me all that sad, pity stuff. I had, had all I could take. I know they're my friends, and they think they're doing me a favor by setting me up with their friends and all. It wasn't what I was wanting. I needed time to be alone. To think about what I wanted to do now that Grace is gone. I was feeling like I was been pushed and pulled in every direction. That was one of the reasons I decided to move. I knew no one here, and it has been great. I haven't been lonely until about a month ago, and I think I finally was able to let go of Grace, and now I can move on. Moving help me to let go. I'm in a totally new place. It has nothing for memories for me, so I can start new. I'm looking forward to it."

"That is great for you, Jake. I never let my friends do anything stupid 'cause I was the stupid one. I refuse to have anything to do with any of them. I felt like the third wheel, so I just stayed away. I'm hoping our holiday will help me start new. I don't know when I will be able to move on from Ben. To be able to love someone else like I love him. I just don't know. What about Angel? I have to be careful about who I bring into our lives. I just can't go off half-cocked and not think about Angel and what my decisions will do to her. She is very vulnerable right now, and anything could happen to destroy her. Trusting could come too easy for her, or she could be totally hard to deal with. Either way it is going to be up to me to make all the right choices. I may never have another man in my life the same way Ben was. I have to be able to trust a stranger with my daughter. I have heard of so many horror story about stepfathers it just makes me cringe to think about anything like that happening to Angel."

"What I've seen of Angel and I've watched how she behaves around people when she is out among strangers, I don't think you will have to worry. I also think she would tell you if something wasn't right. It is something you could talk to her more about and make her more aware now that it is just you and her."

"You're very right, I better do that. Thank you, see, that is why I need a friend to help point some of these things out."

"I'm sure your mother will be doing the same."

"You're probably right about that. Not too much gets by Mom." Pulling up into our driveway gave me a very sinking feeling instead of a good one.

"What is it, Kate?"

"Nothing, Jake, I'm fine."

"Okay, I will bring your bag in."

"Thank you." Getting out of Jake's truck seem like it was a very hard thing to do.

My legs just did not want to move yet. I was fine at the hospital. I saw Jake watching me, and I didn't know what to do.

"Here, Kate, let me help you. The truck is a long way off the ground for you."

I know he said that for my benefit, not to cause any more stress.

"I'm sorry, Jake, I don't know why my feet and legs feel like rubber."

"Maybe the way you were sitting. Let me help you inside before Angel gets here. She may knock you down with glee, so you should be sitting when she comes home."

"You're right, she will be hyper, that is for sure."

We open the door, and there it was. The picture all came flying back at me as I was falling down the stairs. I was chocking back a moan.

Jake pulls me into him tighter. "I'm sorry, Kate, you have to do this. I don't think there is an easier way except face on."

"I know. I didn't think it would be like this after all this time. I can't help knowing my son died right there." I point to the bottom of my stairs.

"That is where you fell, Kate?"

"Yes." I turned my face into his chest and weep silently.

"I knew you had fallen, but no one said where. I took it that you had fallen off the ladder. Come now let me help you up the stairs then. You don't have to see this right now."

All I could do was nod. We got up into the kitchen, and Jake sat me at the first kitchen chair we came to.

My house was dead silent. The radio I always had playing was off, and it was so eerie in here I just had to ask, "Jake, would you please turn on my radio? It is above the stove."

"I sure will, Kate. You want the news?"

"No, I want noise."

"Oh, all right."

We sat and listen to the radio for a bit. Then Jake got brave enough to ask, "Kate, when is the baby's service?"

"Tomorrow at ten thirty."

"You don't mind me being there, do you?"

"No, I don't mind, Jake, but you really have done enough. You don't have to be there too."

"That is what friends do, Kate."

"It's not really a service. I just want to lay Benjamin with his daddy. It is something that has to be done now that I'm out. Mom had him cremated, so I could deal with it when I was ready, and I don't see any reason to drag it on. Nothing is going to bring him back. I just want for Angel and I to be able to move on. I want to plan a trip with her and Mom without any more tears. Do you understand, Jake?"

"Yes, Kate, more than you know."

"I'm so sorry, of course you do." Reaching out to take his hand. "I didn't mean it like that."

"I know you didn't, Kate, and I'm fine, and I want to see you and Angel fine as well. Believe me when I say you will be. Time heals all things. It just takes longer for some versus others."

"You're right, I know, our holiday will surely help with that."

"I envy you. I wish I were going too."

"Hi, Mommy, hi, Mommy."

"Hello there, sweetheart, and how was your day at school?"

"It was fun, Mommy. My friends all want to come see the kangaroos with us."

"They do? Well, you tell them the best we can do is take pictures to show when you get back."

"We have to take lots, Mommy, 'cause they will want one."

"We can do that, Angel, and Mommy is going to buy a movie camera so we can watch it with Jake when we get back. How does that sound?"

She giggles and says, "We will be in the movie, Mommy?"

"Yes, you will, and it will be so neat 'cause you will have it forever."

"You want to watch our movie, Jake, when we get back?"

"I would love to, Angel."

TWENTY-FIVE

"Jake, why don't you come too?"

"Thank you for asking, Angel. I'm going to take care of your house and yard so you and Mommy and Grandma can go and have a great holiday without having to worry about anything."

"That's very nice of you, Jake. Why would you do that?" She has a frown and has her head cocked to the side as if she was in total disbelief.

"That is what friends do for each other."

"They do?"

"Yes, Angel, they do."

"Mommy, when Jenny went on a holiday, we didn't do that for them?"

"That is because they were only gone two weeks. We don't know how long we are going to go for."

"Okay. Grandma bought pizza for supper, Mommy, she says we have to fatten you up."

"She did?"

"Yup. Jake, you going to have pizza with us?"

"Thank you for asking, Angel. But I have to go now. I just wanted to stay with your mommy until you got home to take over."

"Oh, Jake, you're sure welcome to stay."

"Thank you, Kate, but I really have to go. Another time we will have to do this." "You sure?"

He stands up to leave. "Yes, I'm sure." Jake hugs me and says, "I'm not far away, call whenever, please take care."

"Bye, Jake. Thank you for all your help."

"You're welcome, Emma, hope you make this lady here listen to you."

"Oh, no worries about that. Mom carries a big stick."

"Okay then, I feel good about leaving now." We all laugh about it as Jake leaves.

Over our pizza and tea, Mom and I discuss what we are doing about Benjamin tomorrow morning. We were not dragging it out. We do need to put a closure to this so we can all move on. Dr. Adams was going to be there to say a few words of farewell. Short and sweet.

Angel never said a word; she just sat and listened. Taking everything in. The evening went well, and we turned in early so we could face the next day with all the energy we needed.

At ten thirty, we were at Ben's grave site, and there had been a perfect little rectangular hole made on top of him. Dr. Adams stood holding this perfect redwood caskets with brass handles. Mom had made the right choice. Off to my left, I saw Jake coming up to stand beside me. It was a relief to know I would have someone other than my mom and daughter to lean on, knowing that they were feeling the pain as much as I was. We stood holding each other as our silent tears fell like rain. While Dr. Adams said our farewells.

"Oh, God in heaven, we ask you to please see that little Ben is united with his father and that they walk hand in hand in eternal happiness. Although we never got to know him, we all loved him just the same, so the pain he leaves behind is felt by many. So we ask you again to please take care of them both until the rest of their family are able to join them. In Christ name, we pray. Amen."

We all laid our flowers on top, and I turn and hug Dr. Adams. I held on to him a little longer than normal, saying to him, "Thank you for being my father, my doctor, and my friend."

"You're welcome anytime, Kate." He hugs Angel and Mom and shakes Jake's hand, patting him on the back.

"Thank you for being here for them, son. I must go now." Then he was gone. Feeling hollow and empty inside and numb to the outside world. Taking one last look at what should have been, and then we all turn around and leave the cemetery. Jake asked if we would like to go for an early lunch he was buying. So we went to the all-breakfast dinner. I wasn't wanting more than toast and a coffee. I noticed that no one else really ate anything big either.

"I must say you sure look good in a suite, Jake."

"Thank you. I think you look great all the time."

"Thank you, Jake."

"Mommy, what are we going to do now? Do I go to school after lunch?"

"Do you want to go to school? You sure don't have to."

"I think so,"

She says as she hangs her head, "God, my daughter was down."

"I think I will go see about getting our plane tickets and see how soon we can fly off to Australia."

"Really, Mommy? Can I come too?" Right on this is what my daughter needs most of all.

"You sure can, that way you can help me pick out the best deal." Now she sits up and gets to eating her lunch. Jake looked at me and I at him. He raises an eyebrow and smiles.

"I think you might have hit the nail on the head."

"For all of us."

"Yes, Kate, I think Jake is right."

"Me too, I'm sad today, but I want to make things better for all of us, Mom, so I think the sooner we do this, the better."

"I believe you are right, Kate."

"Are you coming with Angel and I to see what trip we want to take?"

"Yᴇs, I am."

"Sorry, we are leaving you behind, Jake."

"No need to be sorry, I will be here when you get back. You girls go and have a fantastic time. Just don't forget where you live. Otherwise, I have to go shopping for new friends again, I would hate that." We all break down with laughter. Finishing up, Jake left to go home, and Mom and Angel and I went over to the Fly Anywhere Office to see what we could get as a suitable holiday package for three. With no time limit, after all, who had to rush?

After one hour, we had found the perfect package, and we could fly out Friday evening. This was super. It was giving us enough time to get done what we had to and arrange everything with Jake. We won't have time to think about changing our minds. Not that any of us had thoughts of doing that. The shorter the wait the better. I was now pumped to go. I hadn't been this excited about anything for a long time. I think it has been well overdue. Angel too, this was going to be a great experience for her as well as for Mom. I don't think my mom has been on to many planes or has gone too far from me. She never talks about before I was born, so I can't rightfully say. I think she would have said something if she had gone to any interesting places.

Yes, this is just what the good doctor had ordered.

Jake came over that evening to see how we made out. While he was there, he checked over our yard so he would know what was normal and what wouldn't be.

"I think this should be a fairly easy job. Hope the pay is good?"

"What kind of pay might that be?"

"Maybe supper cooked by Kate Parker."

"I think that could be arranged when we get back."

"You mean I have to starve until then?"

"Oh no, just keep doing whatever it has been that you been doing. You don't look worse for wear."

Everyone laughs, and Angel jumps in to save Jake. "Would you like me to make you a bowl of chicken soup?"

"Well, that would be nice, Angel, but I'm just teasing your mommy."

"Okay, I'm going to watch TV in my room now, Mommy."

"All right, did you pick out the special clothes you want to take with us already?" "I can do that now."

"Oh, you are multitasking."

"Yep, just like you do, Mommy."

"Hope you get better at it, then I am starting so young?"

"Me too." Way she goes.

"She has come around quite nicely since this morning."

"Yes, Jake, she has. She was so excited at the travel agency that she was almost too much. The women working there were great with her. They answered all her questions and showed her all kinds of pictures. She was so happy."

"Good, that is what you both need. To be happy again."

"I'm sorry we just met and now we are leaving."

"Don't be sorry, Kate, everything happens for a reason."

"I have told her that all her life."

"Mom!"

"Well, I have."

"Sometimes we don't see the reason for many years to come, but we do in the end."

"It doesn't make sense to me, Jake, but like you say, maybe I will get some answers later."

"Everything has a way of working out. One day something will happen, and you say so that is why. Right now nothing makes sense, and your full of 'oh, God, why me.' This feeling you will carry around with you for a very long time. I know right know you're not thanking him for anything. Right now you don't even pray at night when you go to bed. You are mad as hell at him, and you don't think you will ever forgive him. You will, and you will say to him once again, 'Thank you, Lord.'"

"Right now I don't even want to talk to him. He has taken everything from me that I love."

"You are wrong, Kate. He has left you Angel. You and Angel have unfinished business, and until it is done, you will always be together. I believe that we are all put here to serve a purpose, be it big or small. We are not the ones to choose our fate. We all live on borrowed time. From beginning to end, so live each day to the fullest because you will never know when it is you he is calling."

"How did you get to be so wise, Jake? I always feel so much better after we have talked.

"I too have had losses in my life and big ups and downs. But look at me, I'm still as strong now as I ever was, and I'm happy again and living like I want to. Me and my dogs. Which speaking of them, I best get going, they will need outside time before bed."

Getting up and going to the door with Jake was easy. He made everything seem easy.

"Thank you, Jake, for your time and for keeping an eye on our home while we are away." Going into his arms felt so natural.

"Have a safe trip and really try to enjoy it, Kate. This time you are taking to be with Angel and Emma. Make the best of it and one you will talk about and remember for years to come."

"I will, Jake, thank you." Hugging him a little extra longer and not feeling ashamed of doing so.

"Remember to drop me a postcard now and again. You have my business card. It also has my e-mail address. So don't be a stranger while you are away. I know you are going away to forget, but I hope I'm not on that list yet! I hope I'm on the start over fresh list."

"I promise I won't forget to keep in touch."

He bends down and kisses me ever so lightly on the lips. Almost so lightly that it made me wonder if it was something I had wished for Jake to do.

"I will miss you. Good night and good-bye."

"Good night, Jake, and good-bye." Closing the door and leaning up against it, I stood wondering. Should I have asked him to take us to the airport?

Would Ben approve of Jake as a friend. Has Ben guided Jake to find and watch over Angel and myself? Why would we meet him now, at a time when we could use some strong support if Ben didn't guide him to us?

Could it be just a coincidence? Mom had left as well to go home and do the rest of her packing. When she was done, we were on the phone for hours.

"You know, Mom, you should have just thrown your bags in the car and came back. We could have all left from here."

"I guess so. I know I won't be able to sleep. Flying makes me very apprehensive." "That makes two of us. Good thing we will have Angel to keep our minds occupied."

"Is she sleeping already?"

"Has been for hours. Just you and me losing sleep over taking a holiday." We laugh and talk for another hour.

"I think I will try to sleep now, Kate, you should too."

"You're right, I will. Good night, Mom."

"Good night, Kate."

I tossed and turned. Keep looking at the clock and time seems to be dragging. I close my eyes, but they just pop right back open, and here I lay staring at the ceiling. I wish I had laundry to do or something. I have read that after fifteen minutes, if you haven't fallen asleep, you should get up and find something to do. Now it has been two hours, and I don't feel any sleeper now, then when I came to bed. I think I will do that. Climbing out of bed and going out to the kitchen thinking I'll make myself a hot chocolate. I was just filling up the kettle when my doorbell rang. I dropped my kettle and made a mess. Standing there looking at the door and not knowing whether I should open it this time of night. The last time I had a caller this late. Ben had been killed.

"Kate, you there? Honey, it's Mom."

"Mom! I raced to the door and pull it open harder than I had to."

"Kate, what's wrong, are you all right? You look like you have seen a ghost?" "What are you doing here at this time? You scared the hell out of me?"

"Couldn't sleep no how so thought about what you said, so here I am. Whatever you have in the kettle, is there enough for two?"

"Of course, Mom. I'm sorry, come in out of the cold."

"One thing about Australia right now, it is summertime there."

"That's right, I can't wait."

"Me either, I will take summer over this cold any day."

"What about Angel, Mom?"

"What about her, Kate?"

"Christmas, we will be missing Christmas, won't we?"

"Oh, I don't know."

"If it is summer there, doesn't that make it July or something like that, or are they that many months behind, or is it ahead? Oh god, I don't know."

"Maybe we can ask someone on the plane?"

"We are going to have to. With so much going on, I totally forgot." "Understandable. We will find out and go from there."

"Guess we will have to." Drinking our hot chocolate and waiting for the time to go by so we could wake up Angel and go to the airport. We have to be there one hour before our flight time just to be checked on board. Since the 9/11, they say it takes a long time to get through. I haven't been anywhere since that happened, so I don't know what we are in for. Guess it doesn't matter so long as we know we are going to be flying safe.

Getting Angel up at five thirty and getting toast and juice was as easy as making pie. She was up and so full of energy, and Mom and I were looking forward to the sleep on the plane. We had like a sixteen-hour nonstop flight. This scares the hell out of me. I'm thinking of taking some gravel; that way, it will make me sleep. I don't want to miss too much of the excitement with Angel, so I will play it by ear and see how things go. Maybe Mom and I will sleep in shifts; that way, Angel will have one of us to share things with about the trip. It won't be much for her to share if she has to say. Yea, Mom and Grandma slept all the time.

The lineup at the airport wasn't too excessively long, but it was still timeconsuming. Once we were all checked out, they told us we could go to the small cafe on the corner. There we would hear our flight being announced for boarding. The airport had all kinds of shops in it. It was almost like going to a mall. Going to the cafe, we were so busy chatting and the excitement that was in the *air*. We did not see Jake coming up beside us. He reaches out and grabs my arm, saying, "Good morning, Kate."

"Hey, Jake, didn't know you were coming to the airport?"

"I didn't know either, but I had a restless night and thought, hell, why not come see you three ladies off."

"You coming too, Jake?"

Squatting down and looking Angel right in the eyes. "You don't know how bad I wish I were coming with you. I will miss you while you are gone."

"I will miss you too, Jake." She falls into his arms and hugs him so tight. It wasn't a quick hug. She was very sincere about what she had told him. "Will you come and have a hot chocolate with us, Jake?"

"If Mommy and Grandma don't mind. I would love to."

"Can he, Mommy? Can he?"

"Grandma and I would love to have hot chocolate with Jake and you." We walk to the cafe and all sit down together as though we have done this many times. People passing by would have taken us as a family. It was a good feeling to feel like that again. It wasn't something that wouldn't be happening anytime soon or maybe never. Angel is my first priority. I have to make sure she is safe and happy. Happy is not quite the word I would use to describe her right know. Maybe overzealous and hyper would be better words to describe her at this moment. I kept asking her to keep it down, and Jake just kept encouraging her. They were laughing back and forth; it was good for Angel. It was probably good for Jake too if we knew the truth. I found myself wishing he was coming along. Angel seems like she has really taken a liking to him. I guess it was safe to say we all have.

TWENTY-SIX

Our flight was being called, so Jake walked us back to the loading exit, and we all hugged and said our good-byes, and we were off. He had said he would watch out the big windows until he saw our plane lift off before he would leave the terminal. We were well on our way; the seats we had didn't make it, so we could even see the windows, never mind Jake. I felt sad at this moment because I knew Jake was sad and was going to be lonely while we were gone. It seemed like it was a punishment of some kind for Jake. He is so happy to meet new friends, then we up and leave. This could not be helped; it was something we had too do. Once again Mom would say, "Just remember, Kate, everything happens for a reason." I don't think Jake would want to hear that right now.

Angel was in such awe that she was on such a huge plane. She didn't know what she wanted to do first. Once we were up in the air, she could get out and walk around. We had learned from the flight attendant that Christmas was celebrated there the same time as we do. Christmas is celebrated on December 25 all around the world. We were going to get to celebrate it in a whole new way than we were used to.

I managed to sleep for a while, and then Mom slept. We done this a couple of times each and never once did Angel settle down enough to have a nap. She was wearing us out along with everyone else on the plane. When she sat to watch the movie of Tarzan, I had hoped she would fall asleep. Nope, not on your life. Then they played a movie on different places in Australia, and that wound her up like a seven-day clock. The people on the plane were very good about her. She wasn't doing any harm, but she wasn't missing anything either. The older people got a real kick out of her, and of course, she was getting spoiled by all of them. I would hear them say,

"Come here, Grandma has this and Grandpa has that." Angel just took it all in and went from grandmas to grandpas and seemed to make them all happy. Ben would say, "That's our little trooper."

Our time was going by fast, and whenever I could, I would send Jake a postcard. I did if we were staying in a place for more than a week. I would always let him know where we would be going to next. Tried to share our holiday with him. I had doubles of our pictures printed, and I would send him off a pile to look at. I'm sure the one of Angel in the kangaroo pouch has to be our best one yet.

In his notes back to us, he sounded very pleased to get them and was anxious for more to come. His little notes went from saying, "Dear, ladies, and signing, your friend, Jake" to "Dear, Kate, I'm missing you always, Jake." In the end they were coming back as "My darling Kate, missing you, love, Jake." As his notes got a little more personal, I quit reading them to Mom and Angel. I would just tell them, "Jake says hi, and he misses us."

"Tell him we miss him too," they would say. So I guess I would have to say that our courtship started while I was in Australia. By mail we were dating, sort of. I could tell Jake was very delighted to hear back from me in such a manner. His letters spoke loud and clear. This was making it harder to be away, and even Angel was wanting to go home. We did make it to six months. I guess after seeing all, we had seen there was nothing left to do but go home and share it with your friends.

"Mom, what are you wanting to do?"

"Kate, this has all been very nice. I have really enjoyed being here with you and Angel, and I hope I never forget the fun we have had together. I have to say, though, I wouldn't mind going home. Spring will be coming shortly at home, and I do like to do my flowerpots."

"I know you do, Mom, and I like to do my yard work. It has been super to be in warm weather for so many months. It has been a great break away from the usual. Even with the days we had rain, it has still been great. I don't think Angel even missed the snow. Maybe at Christmas time, after that, it all seemed to be normal for her."

"That is one thing about a child, they adapt fast."

"They do, Mom, and it is a good thing. So we go home then?"

"I'm ready to go home, Kate."

"Home it is then. Tomorrow we will book our flight."

"I think I will turn in and get a good sleep. Good night, Kate." She comes over and kisses my cheek.

"Are you okay, Mom?"

"Yes, I'm just tired."

"You look tired, Mom. This has been too much for you."

"I'm fine, and I enjoyed our holiday more than I can tell you. I love you too, dear."

"Good night, Mom, and I love you too."

I sat up a little longer. I decided I would reread the letter I had received from Jake. Jake's handwriting alone would make any woman want to read his letters. He had to have had the nicest handwriting I have ever seen. I was almost embarrassed to write him back. I always made sure to print it whenever I sent him anything. He had such a romantic touch to his writing I would just sit and smile at it and I could almost vision him sitting and writing this. I have read on how you can tell a lot about a person just by their handwriting. Wish I knew what Jake was saying. Maybe in my heart I already do.

My darling Kate,

I can't tell you how much I miss you in such a small space. I dream of the day that you will be back here beside me. I never thought that my heart would be able to feel love again. I thought that after I lost Grace that it was all over for me. I always thought she was the one true love that everyone talks about. Now I think she was just a stepping stone for me in waiting for you. Please don't get me wrong because I loved Grace with all my heart and I know a part of me died that day with her. The part of my heart that she left behind now beats because of you. I know, Kate, that this is so soon after meeting you, but I guess this is one of the times that it was love at first glance. I hope you believe in this as much as I do. I hope that I haven't misread you and scared you off. That is the one thing I don't want to do. You have to be the three most extraordinary women I have ever met.

Not ever having children of my own makes me know how lonely life is without them since I have met Angel. She is just that, an angel without wings. She makes a person smile and feel good even if you don't want to. That she gets from her mother. Kate, you make me feel alive again, and you make me want to do things like I haven't wanted to do in a very long time. I have been lost without you. They say absence makes the heart grow fonder, and I do know now what that means.

We dance so well together as if we were made for each other. I want to dance through the rest of my life with you and Angel at my side. My darling Kate, I pray that you will give us some thought as well as a chance to be more than just friends. I know life throws unexpected things in front of us, and we are left to determine which way we want to go and what we want to do with it. I think this is one of those times. I would like to see it through. I await patiently for your arrival. Loving you more with each passing day!

JAKE

I must have read his letter ten times, if not twenty. I am feeling a lot like he does. My heart also has felt something, and it too beats better when Jake is around. I know we dance well together. I felt the pull then, and it wasn't uncomfortable. It was a soothing feeling and one that I know I could get to love. It is almost like getting a second kick at life.

Because I felt the same as Jake. Ben was it. He always had been right from the beginning. We were happy, and we thought we were the one true love that was meant for us. I never ever thought of a day without him in my life. We complemented each other; we didn't drag each other down. As a couple we looked great together, and we worked well together. We were always told what a beautiful couple we were. When we danced, it was like we fit like a glove together. Now that part of me is gone; it died that day with Ben.

Could I have that with Jake? Would we complement each other and be a goodlooking couple, or would we look like the odd couple? What about Angel? How would she really feel if Jake were to be a bigger part in our lives? Angel, hell, what about my mother? Would she take to Jake? She and Ben were very close and always had been. I don't recall them ever having any kind of disagreement. He knew Mom was strict, and he respected her for that. Others just thought of Mom as being old-fashioned; Ben did not. He knew she had morals and was setting high standards for me and expected him to abide by them. Ben had no problems doing so. He felt that was what made us who we were, and has made me who I am today. There are stepping stones to take in life, and you do it by respecting yourself and everyone else. I can only hope that I do as great a job with my daughter as my mother has done with me. I want her to always be able to walk with her head held high and be proud of who she is and how she got there.

TWENTY-SEVEN

We were up and at the airport earlier than we had to be. I took this to mean that we were all anxious to get home. Our flight home seemed like it was taking longer than when we left. Sitting back, I realized that the flight itself wasn't even bothering me. I was thinking about Jake and wished I had told him when we were leaving. Perhaps he would have met us at the airport. Angel sat looking out at the clouds. The sky was a beautiful bright blue, and the clouds looked like cotton candy. It was like we could just reach out and take a handful. I was thinking, if this is heaven, then it will be great to be here.

"Mommy."

"Yes, Angel."

"Is where Daddy and baby Ben are? Is this heaven, Mommy? It sure is beautiful." "I think so, Angel, or part of it, and you are so right. It is so gorgeous up here." "I can't wait to come see Daddy and baby Ben. I wonder where they are?" "Oh, Angel, heaven is such a huge place. I wouldn't know where to start looking." "Me either, Mommy." She sat with her face right in the window, and I knew she was looking very hard for some sign of Ben. Angel said nothing the rest of the trip home. I was thinking. I hope this is as close to heaven she will get for many many years to come. Angel fell asleep, and I woke her up so she could buckle up for landing.

"Angel, it is time to put on your seat belt. We are home now."

"We are, Mommy?" she says in a sleepy voice. The time difference is going to kill us for a couple of days. We were getting our bags, and I could tell Mom was having a hard time with hers.

"Mom, are you all right?"

"I'm just tired, dear, nothing that a good night's sleep in my own bed won't fix." "Did you not sleep well last night?"

"No, I sure did not. Think I was just excited about coming home. Now I will just go home tonight and drop dead."

"Yea, we will also be having an early night as well."

"Mommy are we going to eat at the small cafe before we go home?"

"Oh, I don't know? Mom, what do you think we should do?"

"We do have to eat, so we could do it here, and then we don't have to stop anywhere else on the way home."

"Okay, let's eat here."

Angel had gotten some of her life back, and Mom and I were watching a little boy trying to get his mommy's attention. When Angel let out a yell "JAKE" and took off on the run, he was running as fast as she was, and he scooped her up, and they twilled around and around. He was laughing and hugging her, and she was hugging him back so hard I thought she would surly choke him. Mom and I just looked at each other.

"Did you tell him we were coming home tonight?"

"No, Mom, I did not. " Looks like Angel is happy he is here.

"You think?" Emma had the feeling she knew how Jake knew they would be here, and she must remember to thank him the next time she saw him.

"Hi, Jake."

"Hi, Emma, how was your flight?"

"Long, and I'm glad to be home."

"How about you, Kate?"

"Long, and I'm also glad to be home. How are you, Jake?"

"Great now, and I'm glad that you are all home safe and sound." We all laugh.

"I missed you, Jake,"Angel says as she squeezes his neck and kisses him on the cheek.

"Oh, Angel, and I have missed you and your mommy very much." He pulls me into his side and kisses the top of my head.

"We are going for something to eat. Would you like to join us?"

"Would I? You bet." We all seem to get our second wind. Jake just had that way with him, especially with Angel. I'm sure she talked nonstop for the first twenty minutes. I thought poor Jake. Yet he seem to be taking it all in, and I could see him glancing at me from time to time with the biggest grin.

Mom was quiet. It didn't bother her too much. I knew she was tired, so we just let Angel get it all out. We did get to say a few words occasionally. Most of the time, we just laughed at her. Like when she was trying to tell Jake about being in the pouch of the kangaroo.

"When I was in the mommy kangaroo's,tummy I could feel her heart beeping."

"You mean beating, and you were in her pouch, not her tummy. Now you should eat and let Jake eat too. We have to get Grandma home, she is very tired."

"How were you able to get, Angel, in a pouch of a kangaroo?"

"It was a very huge kangaroo, and I was scared of it. But it was one that had been bottle-raised and was the family pet. Their children rode in the pouch when they were all very young. I felt Angel was too big. I let her be in it only long enough to be in the picture. The pouch looks like very heavy leather, but I wasn't taking any chances. They are an amazing animal all right."

"That is my favorite picture of you, Angel, and I had it made really big and have it hanging on my wall for all my friends to see."

"You do, Jake?"

"You bet I do."

"We should get going so we can all get to bed early."

"Can I ride with Jake, Mommy?"

"I don't—"

Jake cuts me off with a "I don't see why not. I'm going your way, and I would like the company. Just one thing, I have to stop for puppy food." Jake thought this would really get Angel's attention, but she didn't catch on.

Kate did. "You had?"

Jake put his finger up to his lips to quiet Kate. He was going to surprise Angel tomorrow.

"All right, Angel, you be a good girl. Mommy and Grandma will see you two at the house." We part,ways and I watch them walk away. Jake has her by the hand, and he was laughing at whatever she was telling him.

"It looks like we will be getting a puppy after all."

"I think it will be good for Angel to have a puppy, Kate. I know you didn't want to have to worry about an animal. All children should have a pet of some kind. It gives them a true friend, and it teaches them responsibilities."

"You're right, Mom, I will see what Jake has for puppies. Angel already put in her order for a black-and-white female. I think these are earlier than Jake had planned for." I look over at Mom, and she has her head back and her eyes are closed.

"Boy, you are tired, hey, Mom?"

"Yea, I am, nothing that a good night sleep in my own bed won't fix. Guess I'm too old to go chasing halfway around the world."

"Come now, you're only sixty-one. That isn't old."

"Maybe not to you, but to me I am old."

"I'm sorry, Mom, I shouldn't have kept you away so long."

"Don't be sorry. I enjoyed myself with you and Angel, and this is something we will remember for the rest of our lives. All those pictures I hope Angel will share with her family someday. You should scrapbook them with her, Kate. You always do a great job and make them so interesting to look at."

"I will. I want Angel to scrapbook with me. I think she is old enough to learn and to put her own stories with the pictures."

"She catches on quick, and it will help her to relive her holiday."

"Me too, it will be fun. You going to join us? We will do it after supper. I will set up the spare bedroom. That way we don't have to put everything away each time. I hate doing that. This way we can just carry on the next day. We'll have fun, Mom."

She didn't answer, so I look over at her and see that she was sleeping. I reached over and took her hand in mine.

"We played you out big-time, Mom." It didn't take long, and we were pulling into my driveway. She was all embarrassed that she had fallen asleep.

"It's okay, Mom, you told me you were tired. Guess you really meant it. I will make us a good cup of coffee. That is one thing in Australia they don't have."

"If you don't mind, Kate, I just want to go home?"

"Are you sure, Mom?"

"Yes, I am, Kate."

"I will put your bags in the backseat for you then. Oh, it's nice to see the green grass peeking though. I was afraid we were going to come home to a big pile of snow yet."

"No, spring should be well on its way."

"I would say it is here."

"We will have to work in our yards soon."

"We have a couple of weeks yet to wait on that. We have to recuperate from our holiday. Guess we came home to rest up."

"I know I sure have too. Like I said one good night sleep in my own bed will be all I need, Kate. I will see you tomorrow."

"Yea, Mom, come over whenever you get up, okay?"

"I will, might not be until noon."

"That's okay, I hope Angel will sleep in that long too. Love you, Mom, drive safe." I hug and kiss her good-bye.

"I will, dear, good night."

I watched her drive away, then went in to make a pot of coffee. I'm sure Jake will have a cup with me when he and Angel get back. I was thinking they must have a lot of dog food to buy. Then I heard Jake's truck, and I could still hear Angel chatting and laughing. My god did that child not give Jake a break? Poor Jake, bet he won't offer to take her along next time. I turn to see them coming through the door, and Jake has Angel up on his shoulders.

"You better duck, Angel, or it could hurt," Jake says to her.

"Jake she is too big to be doing that with. You are going to hurt yourself." "I hope I can carry more than Angel, or I'm not much of a man."

"Yes, you are, Jake. You are a big man."

"Thank you, Angel." He slips her around and down on to the floor like there was nothing to it, or her. Ben had started having trouble doing that with Angel because she had gotten so big. Now that I look at Jake, I realize just how much bigger he is than Ben was. I had always thought Ben was a big man. Guess he was average 'cause he would look small standing beside Jake. Jake is not a heavy man by any means, but he is put together very well.

"All right there, miss, I want you to unpack your dirty clothes for me, thank you."

"Aww, do I have to do that now, Mommy?"

"Please I want to start some laundry tonight."

"Okay, Mommy. Thanks for the ride, Jake." She blows him a kiss, and off she goes.

"Well, now I think you have won her over. You even get a kiss blown your way."

"Yea, I did, but I would rather have this one." He cups his hands alongside of my face and comes down to kiss me. My head is spinning, and I want to pull away. But my body just leans into him, and I drink in the kiss he is giving me. When he finally comes up for air, all I could say was "wow."

"Wow is right. I would say I'm sorry for doing that, Kate, but I'm not."

"Me either."

"You're not?"

"No, Jake, I'm not. I have missed you too. Now let's get our coffee, and we will go in and sit by the fire and catch up. Good thing it is gas, all I have to do is flip the switch and we will have heat."

"That sounds good, but I don't think we need that for heat."

"Maybe not, but that is what we will have to settle on for now."

"Oh, really?"

"Yep, and after I pour our coffee, I will go see what Angel is up to. She is being so quiet."

"Here then, let me get our coffee."

"Thank you, I will be right back." I find Angel sound asleep on top of her blankets, cuddling her teddy bear that we had left behind, and she had missed him something awful. I just covered her up and kissed her on the forehead. "Guess tomorrow will be another day, sweetheart." I pick up her dirty laundry that she had piled by the door. I closed the door a little to keep most of the light out. The dark bothered her since Ben's death.

"Angel, okay?"

"Yes, Angel is sound asleep, guess she was as tired as Grandma."

"Maybe I should leave, Kate. You are probably as tired as they are."

"I'm tired, Jake, but I really want to visit with you. I have missed you."

"Okay, Kate, I would love to stay and visit with you as well. I also have missed you." We go in and sit by the fire. Jake sat in the big chair. I sat on the sofa. We sit and look at each other as though we were now lost for words.

"You should have seen Angel in Australia. She was like a child in a candy shop. She didn't know where she wanted to go first. Every day was like Christmas to her."

"How was your Christmas for you?"

"For me, it is like Christmas hasn't come. Who has Christmas without snow?"

"We will have to make up for it this coming Christmas. I want Angel to show me how to make snow angels with two sets of wings."

"She told you that?"

"Yes, she did, why?"

"I'm telling you, they don't look like two sets of wings by the time she is done." "Now who says they don't? How many angels have you seen?"

"Good point. The ones in the pictures are always beautiful."

"Of course they are, and so will Angels double-winged ones be."

"She will be happy to know you like her angels. Once Christmas was over, the rest of our holiday was great. I could tell Mom was getting tired. So it was no surprise to me when she said she wanted to come home. When I asked Angel, she also wanted to come home. None of us wanted to wait another day. Guess the saying. There is no place like home is so true."

"I haven't travelled a lot, Kate, but I would have to agree. It is a great feeling to walk back into your home after being away for any length of time."

"Yes and no."

"I can understand how you must feel right now, Kate. It won't feel this way all the time, Kate. You can't say coming home has never felt great."

"You're right, Jake, our home was a happy home at one time. That seems like such a long time ago. Nothing good has happened for so long that I hate to come home. I feel like there is a weight that settles on my shoulders as soon as I come through that door."

"Kate, have you thought about moving?"

"Yes. for a bit. But this is Angel's home. It is all she has ever known to be home." "Angel is very young, and she can make memories and become attached to another home. If you feel like this. How do you think Angel feels? She has also had her share of sadness in this home. You don't think that every time she goes by the room that was to be the baby's room that she doesn't think of the terrible day. Or every time she goes by the stairs where you fell and all the nightmares it brought to her isn't weighing on her shoulders? Remember how you felt when I brought you home and you had to face the stairs?"

"Oh, Jake! I didn't think of that. You're right, I will talk to Angel about moving. It will be the best for the two of us.

TWENTY-EIGHT

We sat and talked for hours, and we got to know more about each other. I was able to tell Jake more about Angel's childhood and about the relationship that her and Ben had.

"I don't think bringing another man into my life is going to be that easy. On him or Angel."

"So me asking you to consider us as more than friends is out of the question? Is that what you are telling me, Kate?"

"I don't know, Jake. I see how she reacts when you're around, and I think sometimes it would be okay. Then I wonder what it would be like if you were around always. She is okay for short term. Maybe she would feel threatened if you were around on a steadier basis."

"You telling me that you have considered us more than just friends?" He gets up and comes over and sits on the sofa with me.

"I do feel the pull too, Jake. I just don't want it to be on a rebound thing. Relationships like that don't work for long periods of time. I do have to consider Angel in all the choices I make now. 'Cause it isn't just me."

"Of course you do, to a point, Kate. You also deserve to be happy, and you are too young to be left on your own. When there is a willing loving man that wants to share his life with you. Angel is going to grow up and move out on her own, and where does that leave you? If you pass it by now?"

"You're right, Jake, but Angel is still going to be my responsibility for a few years yet. I would hope."

"So why can't she be our responsibility? You don't have to do this on your own."

"Jake, you don't know what you are asking?"

"Yes, Kate, I do. I love you, and I'm asking you to be my wife."

"WHAT?"

"I would like you and Angel to marry me, Kate. I have never been a father to my own or a stepchild. All I can promise you is that I would try to do the best I can in making a great husband and father. The husband part I think I have down pat. The father part will take some training, but I do think I could do it without a lot of trouble or mishaps. There maybe times you would have to guide me and maybe even pick me up when I stumble."

With that said, Kate takes his face in her hands and says, "Yes, Jake."

"Yes, Jake, what?"

"Yes, I will marry you. Angel and I will marry you."

"What? Are you sure, Kate?"

"Oh, I'm sure." Kissing him to seal the deal. When I backed away, he had this stunned look on his face.

"Jake, are you OKAY?"

"AWW YEA."

"You sure? 'Cause you don't look okay?"

"I can't believe that you just said yes."

"Have you never been told that you shouldn't ask the question if you didn't want to hear the real answer."

"I wanted to hear that answer, but guess I was more prepared to hear a 'sorry, I can't.' Not a yes."

"SO?"

"So what?"

"JAKE!"

"OH, Kate, you have made me so happy. I want to jump and shout, but I would wake Angel up so how about this." He kisses me until we are out of breath.

"WOW!"

"I think we've been there already, Kate." We break out with laughter.

"There is one other thing, Kate?"

"What is that, Jake?"

"I would love to be able to ask Angel myself."

"Oh, I don't know, Jake, if that is a good idea. This might be too confusing for her to understand."

"Well, if we see that it is, then you will have to help me. I think it would be best if I ask her, then she won't think I'm trying to take you away from her because I will be showing her that I want her too."

"Jake, I love you, I didn't think I would ever say this to anyone but Ben. I could not see myself ever loving another man. You have made me feel alive again and, yes, loved. I think you are the kindest man I have met in a very long time. You are my kind of man. I know we haven't known each other for very long, but you make me feel like I have known you for years. I feel deep in my heart that you will make a great replacement father for Angel. But because I feel this way doesn't mean Angel will, and we have to be prepared for that. It could hurt, Jake."

"I'm a grown man. I'm sure I can take whatever Angel throws my way. I don't want to replace her father. I just want to help see her grow up. If I get lucky and reap the same pleasures as Ben would have, then I will take that as a gift he has given to me. Everything in life has risk, and I'm more than willing to take them with you and Angel.

"Kate, you have no idea how long I have fought this feeling because I thought that Grace was the only one for me to love and I had promised myself that I would never betray her. When we married, it was forever. I didn't believe in anything, but from the time we met, my heart has been like a volcano waiting to blow. This might sound silly to you. I went and talked to Grace and asked her to please send me a sign if I were doing something wrong. There has been nothing but good feeling for me, so I know she is okay with this. I'm totally okay with this. I don't want to pass up my second chance at happiness. I so want to share it with you and Angel."

"Jake, you make it sound so simple."

"I don't mean to. This has to be easier than combining two families."

"Guess so, hey. Not too many of them work out."

"So it is a good thing there is just Angel."

"Maybe it will work out for us."

"I'm going to give it my best shot."

"Me too. I want to also promise you something else, Jake."

"What is that, Kate?"

"I won't ever compare you to Ben or criticize how you do something 'cause it wasn't how he would have done it."

"Thank you, Kate. I will make you the same promise. I know everyone is different. That is what makes the world go round."

"I think we are off to a good start."

"I believe you could be right. So when could we get married?"

"Oh, I don't know? You want it to be soon?" Jake gets down and kneels at my feet.

"Kate, I have waited a long time to find love again, so if you say I have to wait longer to show you just how much I love you, then I guess I will just be like my puppies and lay at your feet and beg."

"Now that is cute."

He pulls me down on to the floor, and we lay next to the fire. Talking about plans of our future. "You were going to sell your house, Kate, are you still?"

"Yes, I will talk to Angel about it tomorrow. After all, we won't be needing two houses."

"I will also sell mine."

"Why, you just bought it not that long ago?"

"It was good for the dogs and me but not to have a family in. We will all go shopping and find one that will suit us all. Maybe we should find one with a suite so your mom could be closer and we could watch out for her." Sitting straight up like a bullet and cupping my mouth. "What is it, Kate?"

"Mom, Jake, I never thought about Mom."

"What is wrong with your mom?"

"Nothing is wrong with her, but what about us getting married? What will Mom think? Better yet what will Mom say?"

"Why don't we ask her tomorrow? After all, it is a little late now. Even with the streetlight shining in like this, I know it's not morning yet." He pulls me back into his arms and kisses the hell out of me.

"You know I could do this to you forever?"

"I think Angel would complain."

"Oh yea, you're probably right as always. So tell me when we all get moved in together, does Angel still get to pick her puppy?"

"Good question? That will make for three dogs. That is a lot for one house."

"Then we must find a very big house with a very huge yard. I think Angel should still get her pick of a puppy, or she could see that as something

I have taken away from her right off the get-go. Could be trouble number one, if not number two."

"Jake, she will have to learn that it won't always be her way. That is life."

"I know, but could we start a little slower on that part of it."

"Oh, I can see how this is going to be, Mr. Pushover."

"No, I don't want to be a pushover, but let's not have an upset to get us off on the wrong foot."

"I will tell you what. Let's see how all this is going to plan out. Us getting married and moving. If we can find a place that will be suitable for three dogs, then we can rethink three dogs."

"When you say three dogs like that, you make it sound like a lot of dogs."

"Jake, it is a lot of dogs for one family."

"They're small dogs, Kate."

"Dogs are dogs, big or small."

"You've noticed that too."

"Jake, I'm serious."

"I know you are and you're right. We will play this one day today."

"Thank you." We laid there and must have fallen asleep because Angel was shaking me and saying, "Mommy, Mommy, why you on the floor?"

"What?" I raised my head and look around. Jake wasn't anywhere to be seen.

"Mommy, why are you sleeping on the floor?"

"Aww, I was just laying by the fire and guess I fell asleep." Throwing the cover off me that Jake must have put on me and getting up to go to the washroom. I felt like a kid that just got caught with her pants down.

"I will be right back out, Angel."

"Okay, Mommy." She looks at me like she really didn't believe me, and I know that made me blush. Good thing Angel was too young to understand what blushing was all about. It is not a good thing to lie to your children, and it is really hard when it feels like they know you are lying to them. I wonder if this is how they feel when they get caught with their hands in the cookie jar. I must remember to thank Jake for leaving me in such an awkward position. I must also remember to thank him for the pillow and throw. Making coffee and not wanting to look Angel in the eye was starting to get to me. I wanted so much to tell her about Jake and me getting married. I wanted to share this exciting news with my best friend, my daughter. I know she is only seven, but she is my best friend.

"Mommy, why are you being so quiet? Are you sick, Mommy?" I could hear the fear in her voice, and that tore at my heart.

"Oh no, Angel, I'm not sick, sweetheart. Mommy just has many things going on in her head, and I have to talk to you about them."

"Like what?"

"Well, I was thinking that we should sell this house."

"You were? Why, Mommy?"

"You know, Angel, I know it has been the only home you have known and it might be hard for you to move and start over. The thing is, sweetheart, this house makes Mommy sad now. Daddy isn't here anymore, and now we can't use the baby room. I think we should sell it to someone who could use it. You and I worked too hard in that room to waste it. Maybe there is a baby boy out there that really needs a room. We could find a new place and make a whole new life for us, and we could just start all fresh. Do you think you would like to do that, start fresh? We could leave all the sadness behind. We could get to be very happy again like we used to be. What do you say, Angel? Please tell me how you feel about this."

She sat drinking her milk and looking at me but through me. I hate when she does this, but I know she is in deep thought when she does. "Mommy."

"Yes, Angel."

"Will Grandma still find us and come see us?"

"Of course she will. Maybe we can find a big place, and Grandma could come live with us."

"That would be cool, Mom."

"You would like that, Angel?"

"Oh yes, Mommy, then Grandma wouldn't be so sad."

"You think Grandma is sad?"

"Uh-huh. How about Jake, Mommy, will he still come visit?"

The doorbell starts ringing, and Angel jumps down to go answer it.

"Hɪ, Jᴀᴋᴇ." She runs and makes a jump for him, and he was lucky enough to catch her.

"Hi, Angel. You know you are almost too big to be doing this I might drop you one time." Giving her a big hug.

"No, you won't, Jake." She snuggles into his neck.

"Does Mommy have coffee made?"

"Yes, I do. Come on in, and I will get you a cup."

"Jake, will you still come see us when we sell the house?"

"Aww yes, you bet." He looks over at Kate and was surprised to hear that they were already talking about such serious things so early. So this opened the door he was needing.

"You know what, Angel, I have something to ask you and your mommy, so can we all sit down and have our coffee and talk?"

"Okay." Angel gets very quiet, and Kate looks at Jake with a "what are you doing" look.

"Come, Kate, and sit with us." He reaches out and takes Kate by the hand and pulls her over to the chair beside him and Angel. He could tell Kate was reluctant to do this, and now he was wondering if she hadn't changed her mind. It had only been three hours since he covered her up and left, not wanting Angel to find him on the floor with Kate. There was a time for everything, and now was not the time.

TWENTY-NINE

Kate slid in on the chair but looked like she was ready to take off in flight at any time.

"Kate, are you all right?"

"I already asked Mommy that."

"You did? Why is something wrong, Kate?"

"No, nothing wrong, Jake. We can talk later, you go ahead, I'm fine."

He looks at her and raises his eyebrow in wonder. "Well, Angel, I was wondering if you and your mommy." He reaches out and takes Kate by the hand. "If you would marry me?"

"What does that mean?"

"Have you not been to any weddings?"

"Yes."

"You have?"

"Yup, we have, right, Mommy?"

"Yes, we have, Angel."

"Those ladies look like princess in their white dresses."

"They sure do. Would you like to be a princess someday, Angel?"

"Oh yes, when I big like Mommy, I will be a princess. My dress will be big and shiny."

"When you are a princess like that. That means you are getting married."

"Oh."

"I want you and Mommy to be my princesses."

"You do, Jake?"

"Yes, Angel, more than you will understand. You have grown into my heart, and I want to spend every day with you and Mommy."

"You can come and visit all the time, Jake. Can't he, Mommy?"

"Yes, he can, Angel."

"See, Jake, it is okay."

"Thank you both for that, but that isn't what I want to do?"

"It isn't?"

"No, Angel. I want to be in the house with you every night and every day. I want to sleep in the same bed as Mommy and help Mommy look after you and help Mommy with cutting the grass and doing what needs to be done around the house. I want to be able to take you to school and take you shopping and buy you pretty things and spoil you like crazy."

"You do, Jake? Why?"

"Because, Angel, I now love you and your mommy very much and I want to help make you happy."

"Do you love me as big as the sky?"

Jake looks over at me, and I nod. "Yes, I sure do and maybe even bigger."

"Oh, that's lots."

"Angel, you and Mommy make me happy, and I want to be with you always. Not just for a coffee, but always."

"But Mommy and me, we going to sell the house."

"That's okay, we can go looking and find a new one that we can all live in. It will be fun to go house shopping."

"Grandma too."

"I sure hope so, we have to ask her."

"Jake, do I still get a puppy?"

"Yes, Angel, you still get a puppy."

"Okay, Jake, I will marry you." She hugs him hard and then looks up at him and asks, "Do I have to wear a white shiny dress?"

"I'm afraid so, Angel, otherwise, I can't marry you."

"OH, YIPPEE, Mommy, we getting married."

"So it seems, Angel, are you happy?"

"Oh yes, Mommy, I am."

"All right then, I guess I should make some breakfast. Jake, you having breakfast with us?

"Yes, Mommy, we married him." This brought out the laughter in all of us.

"I will have breakfast with you two beautiful ladies only if you promise me something. Well, two things." Kate and Angel look at each, then back at me. "I mean it, I need two promises."

"Do we give Jake his promises, Angel?"

"But what is it? Maybe I won't like it?"

"You're right, Angel, maybe we won't like it, so we should ask him what they are before we say yes. So, Jake, what is it you want us to promise you?"

"Number one, I want for you two to promise to always be this happy. Second, this is a big one and is probably very hard for you two to do, but I hope you will try."

"What is it, Jake?"

"Well, now, Angel, I want you to promise that you will come house shopping with me after we eat?"

"Can we, Mommy? Can we? Please, Mommy, I promise to be happy."

"Jake, are you sure you want to do this already?"

"I haven't been more sure of anything in a very long time, Kate. But marrying you and buying a new house is where I want to be."

"Me too, Jake."

He scoops Angel up and twirls her around as she snuggles deep down into his neck. I know she has missed Ben horribly, and I hope she continues to build a tighter relationship with Jake.

"Of course you too, Angel. Now let's eat so we can go shopping." Our breakfast went by fast. I think we were all too excited to get going that no one wanted to eat more than it took to make our tummies feel okay for the moment.

"Is Grandma coming with us, Mommy?"

"I don't know. Grandma hasn't even called. I will call her before we leave and see what she is up to. She might be too tired yet to chase around looking at houses. Maybe if we find one we really like, then we can take her to see it."

"Remember, Kate, we should look for one that Emma can have her own living space but still be with us." I go over and wrap my arms around Jake's waist.

"How were we so lucky to find you?"

"That goes both ways, Kate, thank you." He kisses the top of my head.

"While you two are getting dressed, I will give Mom a call."

"Okay with us."

"Yep, okay with us, Mommy." Angel takes Jake's hand, and they head for the door. Mom answers on the third ring.

"Hi, Mom."

"Good morning, Kate."

"You just getting up, Mom?"

"Yea, still feel a little washed out. How about you and Angel?"

"We are great, Mom. What are you doing today? Did you want to come hang out with us?"

"No, darling, thank you for asking. I have some things to do today. Perhaps I will catch up to you later."

"Mom, are you all right?"

"Yes, Kate, I'm fine. I just have some things I have to do. If it doesn't take long, I will pop over when I'm done."

"All right, Mom, we will talk to you then."

"Kate, is there something you want to tell me?"

"Not right now, but when I see you, we will talk."

"All right, dear, I love you."

"I love you too, Mom." Running out the door to catch up with Jake and Angel. They were already in the truck and acting like this was something we do all the time. It felt so good to be a family again. I know some women don't need a man to complete their lives, but I'm not one of them. I do like all the comfort they bring me, and the company that we share is like no other.

"Was your mom going to meet us somewhere?"

"No, she has things she wants to do. She said if she is done early, she may come see us then."

"Did you tell her the good news?"

"No, I don't want to do that over the phone."

"Oh, so that is how it is."

"Yep."

"Hi, does Dr. Adams have time to see me today?"

"Yes, Emma, he does. If you will just take a seat, he should be just a few minutes."

"Thank you." Sitting in this waiting room wasn't where I wanted to be. But the time has come to make some changes, and I know Dr. Adams will be the one to help.

"Hello, Emma, and how are you?" He comes over and takes me by the arm to help me up, and I moan a little.

"I'm sorry, I didn't mean to hurt you."

"I'm fine."

"Come on in, and we will talk."

I found the walk to his office to be a bit unnerving. The last time we did this was shortly before Kate, Angel, and I left for our holiday. I had my checkup then.

"Now, Emma, tell me how are you feeling?"

"I have been getting very tired."

"Has this been going on a long time?"

"Just the last couple weeks of our holidays."

"Is that why you came home?"

"No, it was Kate's idea. She was ready to come home, and I wasn't arguing with her. I can't tell you how glad I was when she mention she was ready to come home."

"Emma, have you talked to Kate about any of this?"

"No, and I'm not going to."

"I really think you should. Kate has the right to know."

"I have the right to tell who I want to, and I don't want her to know anything, yet."

"Okay, I will give you a checkup and do your blood test."

"I want you to come back and see me at the end of the week, and we can talk more once I have all your results back."

"Okay, I will rebook."

"When do you plan on telling Kate?"

"Not sure yet, I'm going over to see them later, if I can stay awake."

"Good, tell her I said hi and I would like to see her and Angel."

"Don't you dare tell her anything."

"As much as I would want to, I can't and you know that. She will be furious with me when she finds out and she knows I didn't tell her."

"It won't be the first time for Kate to be mad, and it sure the hell won't be the last."

"You're right on both accounts, still doesn't make it right."

"It is what I want that matters."

"You are right again. Don't you want your daughter at your side?"

"No, not like this."

"This is when you will be needing her the most."

"Maybe."

"Did you make those other arrangements for me that we talked about before I left?"

"Yes, I did. Jackie said anytime you need her, she is there."

"That's good 'cause I think I will be going to see her very soon."

"You do?"

"Yes, I do. They say if you are tuned into your body, you will know a lot more than your doctor will."

"I believe that as well, Emma. You are the only one who can tell me how you feel."

"I feel like hell."

"You look tired, but you still look good, Emma."

"Thank you for that. If I had more time, I would give you a run for your money." "That would have been great, Emma. I'm sorry we missed our chance."

"Me too, Alex."

"Remember to come see me on Friday. In the morning should be good."

"Thank you, I will."

He pulls me into his arms and hugs me for a very special moment. I have not been hugged this way by a man since my husband passed away. There had been a few lookers, but no one made my heart race or even made my skin tingle to the touch, so I never persuade them. So I had a lot of friends, and they are all very good friends. The suppers and the dances were always enjoyable. None of them pushed for more than I was willing to give, and we were always comfortable with each other. I guess over the years, I had gotten used to my space, and I didn't want to share it with anyone else. I loved my husband deeply although he was not the love of my life. I had walked away from that many years ago. But he did give me a good life, and I in return gave him respect and love. I hurt for a long time after he passed away. We had become very good friends as well as husband and wife. At first, I couldn't see anyone else in his bed with me. Then I guess it just got easier for me to be alone, and I didn't miss not sharing my bed with anyone. I suppose the odd romp in the hay would have been nice if that was all I wanted. I was never a one-night-stand kind of woman, and not finding anyone that I wanted under my roof on a steady basis made it easy to be alone. Not having a small child at home was one of the reasons

I never needed a man. Kate was with Ben, and they had Angel. I found I was happy to be alone. I always knew I could go visit when I was lonely. My time was my time, and I enjoyed every minute of it. I always stayed busy from morning till bedtime. I did a lot of volunteer work. It took me a while to get into it, but once I did, I found there were more people out there that needed me; if the truth be told, I did need them as well. Or at least that's how I felt, and it brought me great pleasure to be able to make them happy with whatever little thing I could do for them. These people had all become my family; some I got so attached to that it hurt just as much when they passed away. But dying is a way of life, and we all have to come to terms with it sooner or later. Most of us wish for it to be later.

I had my special times with Kate and Angel, and I will always have that to remember. I hope that they will hold on to those memories as well. Memories are made for a reason, be it good or bad. Most of the time, it will be our good memories that see us through the bad times. Some memories you can almost bring back to life. Those are the ones that you relive over and over. Special occasions are meant for building memories.

THIRTY

As we approached the driveway that had huge overhanging evergreens that were shaped to grow together at the top, which made it look like you were driving through a covered bridge. It took my breath away.

"Kate, Angel, this is it."

"Oh, Jake, the grounds are beautifully kept, and this driveway is just so pictureperfect."

"That is why it is perfect for us. We can get married here and start our new life as one."

"Oh, Jake, I don't know. This will be more money than I can afford."

"Please, Mommy, I like it."

"Me too, Angel, but it will take more money than we would ever have. Selling my house and yours won't buy this place."

"Now look, Kate, we will have three dogs we are going to have to have a big yard."

"Jake, get real. This is more than a big yard. This is someone's mansion."

"Let's go look at it before we really decide one way or another."

"Everyone's yards here are so well kept it makes me feel like I live in the slums of town."

"Maybe they all pay for the same groundskeeper."

"Must be, we couldn't afford it, and so our yard would become a laughing stock of the neighborhood."

"Well, thank you for the vote of confidence."

"I'm sorry, Jake, but really."

"Yea really." We pull up and just sit there and look around. There were people moving around off at a distance.

"Is there someone going to meet us to show us around."

"Oh yea, that won't be a problem. Come, we can get an early start. That way we won't feel pressured into buying."

"All right, Jake, but I know I can't afford this place."

"Kate, you won't be alone anymore."

"Well, unless you were born with a silver spoon in your mouth that you haven't shared with me, then I know it is out of reach. Also not realistic."

"Don't spoil the fun, let's go look around." We climb out of the truck, and Angel takes off on the run.

"Angel, come back here."

"No, Kate, let her go. She looks so happy just to be able to run."

"Maybe so, but it isn't our place to let her do that."

"How else will we know if it is what we want if we don't try things out?"

"Jake."

"I'm serious, Kate."

"Me too." Angel look like she was a mile away and still running, then she disappeared around a corner.

"Jake, I don't like not being able to see her all the time."

"Relax, Kate, she is fine. We will catch up to her soon." We kept walking, and I was up the speed of my pace to be able to catch up to Angel. Coming around a corner, there were people out back around a pen, and Angel was in there like a dirty shirt.

"What in the world?"

"Let's go see." Walking over to take a look at whatever it was that was so amusing it had Angel's full attention. This man turns around and spots Jake and right away comes to shake his hand. "Mr. Sanders, I'm so glad you came today. Look what we have gotten." He turns around and points to the pen. There lies a beautiful black pony. It was trying so hard to get up.

"Looks like it just arrived?"

"Yes, sir, it did, we got to watch this one being born."

"Well, you're lucky than Pete 'cause that doesn't happen very often."

"No, sir, it doesn't."

"Mommy, look at the baby horse."

"Yes, Angel, I can see, it is beautiful." Looking at Jake and trying to pay attention to what Angel was talking about. Jake knew these people. These people knew Jake.

"It sure is, Mommy, can I have one?"

"They get really big, Angel."

"I know, Mommy, but they have to or you can't ride them."

"You want to learn to ride a horse?"

"Oh yes, Mommy, please. Jake, please can I have a pony too?"

"I don't see why not, but your mother and I will have to talk about it first. Right, Kate? Kate, you okay?"

"Yea, Jake, I'm fine. I also think there is more we have to talk about." Kate gets very quiet. She listens to all these people talk to Jake like they know him very well and for a long time. The one man had snow white hair and could hardly walk, but he had spirit.

"Are you going up to the house, Mr. Sanders?"

"Yes, we are. I want to show Kate and Angel."

"Is Ms. Kate the new lady of the house, Mr. Sanders?"

Lady of the house? What the hell is she talking about?

"We will see, Lizzy."

"Yes, sir, Mr. Sanders." It was like she knew she had just stepped over a line and knew enough to back off. My head was in a daze, and it was like I was having a beautiful dream. I looked at Angel, and she didn't seem to be too concerned about anything. She was having a blast.

"Kate, are you ready to check out the house?"

"Come, Mommy, I want to see the castle."

"Castle, yea sure, let's do that."

"Kate, you okay?" Jake asked again with a frown.

"I think so." As we walk up to the castle, as Angel calls it, I pinched my arm just to make sure I was a wake. Angel skipped and jumped and danced all the way. Getting to the front door, we saw it had the biggest lion heads on each side with a nameplate above that read, "WELCOME TO THE SANDERS ESTATES."

"Wow, Mommy."

"Wow is right, Angel."

"Jake, do your folks live here?"

"No, Kate, not anymore." He pushes open the door that looks like it was going to be a three-man job, but Jake made it look so easy, as if Angel could do it on her own.

"What do you mean? Not anymore?"

"My folks have both passed away, Kate."

"So this is WOW." Kate enters the house, and she could not say anything but "wow!" Whatever room she entered or whatever she saw. She and Angel had the same answer, "wow!"

"You two ladies don't know any other word than *wow*?"

"Jake, I have to sit down."

"Okay, Kate, we will go into the sitting room. Lizzy will bring us some iced tea." "Are you kidding me? Lizzy will bring us iced tea?"

"Yes, she will, Kate, in about five minutes." Putting my hand out to catch myself if I were to fall instead of sitting. The blood is now pounding in my ears. Angel is sitting there with her big brown eyes taking this all in. This room was almost bigger than my entire house. He calls it the sitting room. Angel was right, it was a castle; all they were missing are the knights in shining armor.

"Kate, are you okay?"

"No, Jake, I'm not, and I hope you can explain because I feel like I have just walked into a new century. I'm not comfortable, and I want to know if I'm in a dream?"

"I'm sorry you're not comfortable, and no, you're not in a dream."

"Then please explain all this." Kate waves her hands around the room. Just then as on cue, Lizzy comes in with the tray of iced tea and snacks.

"Here you go, Mr. Sanders. I thought maybe the little miss would like cookies with her juice."

"Thank you, Lizzy, that was being very thoughtful." Lizzy hands us our iced tea and gives Angel her cookies.

"Thank you," Angel said in barely a whisper.

"Will there be anything else, sir?"

"Not at this moment. We would like to be left alone now please."

"Yes, sir, I will see that you are not disturbed."

"Thank you, Lizzy."

"You are most welcome, sir, miss." And she bows to me and leaves the room. I have never been bowed to in my life. Or made to feel like I was a person of some high mucky muck.

"I'm sorry, Kate, I can tell you are not happy at all."

"Happy has got nothing to do with it. I'm lost for words, Jake, plain and simple."

"I wanted to give you and Angel a surprise, that's all."

"Surprise, Jake? This isn't a surprise. This is like being taken through a time warp. Does this really belong to you?"

"Yes, Kate, it does. I'm sorry, we can leave if you wish we don't ever have to come back. That would be fine with me. I don't come very often anymore. I thought it would be a great place to finish raising Angel. That's all."

"That's all? Jake, look around, we have never been close to a place like this, never mind live in one."

"I'm sorry, Kate. Like I said, we can leave if you would like."

"What I would like is for you to explain this. I thought all you had was that small house that you are living in. Who are you really, Jake?"

"I'm nobody special. My grandparents owned this place, and they turned it over to my dad who turned it over to me. It is really simple, Kate."

"There is nothing simple about this, Jake. It would be a lot of work, which I couldn't keep up with and you either."

"That is why there are other people here. It is their jobs to do it all."

"All the time, Jake?"

"Yes, Kate, all the time. They are like us, and their family just keeps replacing themselves as they get older. Their grandfather that you saw out there today is 102 years old. He came with this place."

"I don't know if I could live where you and." I didn't know how to finish this, so I just shut up and looked down at my feet.

"Oh my god, Angel, we still have our shoes on."

"I'm sorry, Mommy."

"Don't fret it. You're okay. I took you by surprise, so we will let it go this time."

"The answer to your question, Kate, is *no*. Grace and I never lived here. She died before my parents, and I never wanted to live here alone. It needs children and dogs to go along with the horses. We agreed that to have three dogs, we needed a big place."

"Yes, we did. Isn't this a little bit of an overkill?"

"Maybe. But it should be enjoyed by my children, Kate."

"There's just Angel and that all there will be. It's too big for one child."

"Angel will have lots of friends. She could make this place hum with laughter. Please, Kate, I want to give you and Angel the place you deserve. This is so you and her."

"We can't afford a place like this, Jake. The expense alone is more than what I will ever have."

"Kate, this place is paid for and has been since my grandfather had it, and there is enough money put aside to take care of this place and all the workers for Angel's lifetime and then some. My grandfather was a very smart businessman, and he took care of everything. We just have to enjoy."

"I would feel like I was living off of you. Ben left me well provided for but not for this."

"You can use your money for things you and Angel will want. Let me put a roof over your head. It is here and it is calling for Angel, we might as well use it. This place needs some young blood and laughter in it. It will be Angel's in the end and her and her children will have a beautiful home always. Would that not make you feel good knowing that when you're gone, your daughter and grandchildren have been provided for?"

"You would leave this to Angel?"

"Oh yes, Kate, I will. One thing it will be set up, so no matter what man is in her life, they can't take it from her nor will he be able to get money on it. It will always be clear of all banks, and she will always have a home as well her children and theirs."

"Jake, that is too much."

"No, Kate. Angel is my daughter now, and she deserves whatever I can give her. It will be rightfully hers."

"Jake, that is so sweet of you to say, but you better think about this. This isn't something to take lightly."

"I know that more than anyone, Kate. If I don't have someone to hand it down to, it will go to the workers. It didn't take much thinking about, Kate. I love you and Angel more than I thought I would ever be able to love again. So this place becomes yours and hers. If I should die, it will be yours whether you want it to be or not. So please take what I'm offering you as my wedding gift to you and Angel. I would sooner see it belong to people I truly love than the workers. Don't get me wrong, I'm very fond of all of them and they will always have a place to live so long as this place stands. Which short of an earthquake there shouldn't be a problem?" He takes my hand and says to me, "Kate, with all my heart and soul, I want to put you into this home and make you the happiest woman on earth. You deserve some happiness in your life for once."

Tears are rolling down my cheeks, and I didn't want that to happen. "Jake, just marrying you will make me very happy. I know Angel will be happy too. Right, Angel?" We look over to where Angel was sitting, or should I say where she had been sitting.

"OH MY GOD, WHERE DID ANGEL GO?" Jumping up to run out to find her. Jake grabbed my hand and held me back.

"She is just fine, Kate. We will go to her in just a minute, but first tell me we have a deal and you will take the wedding gift I'm offering to you and Angel. Please, Kate, make me the happiest man on earth."

"Jake, I don't want you to be sorry for this later."

"That will never happen, Kate. We have been brought together for a reason."

"Mom tells me that all the time that things happen for a reason even if we can't see it at the time. It will show sooner or later, and that's when we say so this is why."

"Yes, Kate, this is why. I lost Grace, and you lost Ben, so this could become us. I feel so good about it all, and I know Grace is settled with it. I want to put her to rest now and have a new life—one that is full of love and happiness, not just memories. My memories will always stay within my heart, and I promise you from this day forward there is no more Grace to be mentioned. It is you and only you. Angel too of course, so what do you say, Kate?" The tears are flowing so hard you would have thought I hurt myself. Jake takes me in his arms where I feel so safe and loved how could I say anything but "YES, JAKE, we will accept your gift and your love. We have been so blessed in meeting you. There is one more thing I have to do."

"What is that, Kate?"

Looking up to the heavens, I say, "Thank you, Ben, now rest in peace."

Jake pulls me closer and kisses me ever so gently. "Now let's go find Angel and then let's go find Emma. Do you think this is big enough for Emma to live with us?"

"Oh, Jake, Mom will be so excited. She also deserves something great in her life."

"She has you and Angel. Yes, this too." We go and find Angel back out at the pony. Jake knew she would be there.

On our way home, we told her about the big house and that we would be living there and that we were getting married on the lawn. The driveway was going to be like the isle of the church. Once decorated, it would be even more beautiful than it already is.

"Mommy, do all princess live in castles like we will."

"Yes, honey, they do."

"Mommy, I love the castle."

"I'm glad, Angel, and we hope you will be very happy there?"

"That grandpa, he says I can have my own pony."

Jake and I look at each other.

"He did?"

"Yes, he said all princesses have ponies."

"Well then, princess, it looks like you will be getting a pony to go with your puppy. You are going to be very busy, little girl, taking care of these animals."

"Jake, could I have a black one like that baby one? He is almost blue, that grandpa said."

"He is that all right. If you had one, what would you call it?"

"Beauty, just like the book."

"Okay, he is yours."

"Jake!"

"What? He is mine to give to whoever I want."

"Oh, thank you, Jake. I have to tell Grandma so she can come see him 'cause he is beautiful."

Jake and I break down with laughter. Angel talked nonstop, and it seemed that. That grandpa as she calls him had told her a lot about horses. I got an education on them, and Jake agreed with the things she was told, so I knew my daughter, our daughter, was in good hands when it came to that grandpa. It was nice to know Angel would have someone to call Grandpa again. All children need to have grandparents in their lives it makes them richer at heart.

THIRTY-ONE

When we got home, there was a note on the table from Mom. She said she would drop by a little bit later, had other things to do.

We sat around the table and making arrangements for our upcoming wedding. Angel was so excited she was just bouncing off the walls.

"Mommy, did you see the princess bed in the castle?"

"I sure did, and I think it is too big for you?"

"I'm growing, Mommy."

"That you are, Angel."

"What will I do with my bed?"

"I think we will take it to the giveaway shop. That way another little girl can have a nice bed."

"My canopy bed is like a little princess bed, right?"

"It sure is, but now you are going to be a big girl. We can put you into a big bed."

"Okay, Mommy. My toys too?"

"Don't you want to take your toys?"

"I will have a puppy and a pony. I won't need toys anymore, Mommy."

"What about on rainy days and you have a friend stay over, what will you do if you don't take your toys?"

"Hummm. Guess I better take them then."

"I think so."

Jake sat and listened, not saying too much, but you could tell by the look in his eyes his admiration for Angel. I have heard where another man has a hard time taking on another man's child, but I don't think that is going to be a problem here. If anything I will have to watch and make sure Jake doesn't go overboard in his giving to Angel.

Oh god, what am I talking about? Look what he has already given to us without a blink of an eye and no second thoughts. Angel will always look at it as her castle.

This week went by fast, and we still hadn't seen Mom. We were taking her out on the weekend even though she knew nothing of our pending wedding or our move. I just told her I had something I wanted to share with her whenever she had time.

"Go right on in, Dr. Adams is waiting for you."

"Thank you." Sitting down and thinking, "God, hope this won't take long." When Alex came in, taking my hand in his and saying, "Hi, Emma, how have you been?"

"Hi, Alex, same old thing. Tired all the time."

"I'm very sorry, Emma, but things have gotten a lot worse since you went on the trip with Kate. I know you said you didn't want any kind of treatments. But really it would have slowed it down."

"I saw my mother go through this with treatments, and it was horrible. She wasn't my mother in the end, and she was so sick the whole time. I'm not sick, I'm tired. I will not do that to Kate."

"I know, Emma, so now we deal with it your way."

"That's right, it is going to be my way. I just want you to tell me what I'm to be expecting to deal with as time goes on."

"Ovarian cancer is not as nice one to get. None of them are. Ovarian is usually caught too late when a woman is as healthy as you were and had no need for a doctor. By the time signs start to show, you're hooped. I'm sorry for that."

"Thank you, not your fault. Now tell me what I'm to look forward to."

"You are going to get a whole lot sicker, Emma. It has spread through all your organs, and you don't have much time. So whatever you have to get in order, I suggest you do it this coming week."

"I have everything taken care of."

"Does that mean Kate too?"

"I'm not telling Kate."

"Emma, PLEASE!"

"No, end of story."

"What will happen in the end to Kate when she finds out?"

"Nothing will happen. She will accept it and move on. She has been down this road so many times already that she will know how to handle this. I will leave her a letter, it will explain it all. She will understand in time."

"You know this is against all my good thinking."

"It's my thinking you have to worry about. Now I want to have everything settle so I can go to see Jackie end of next month."

"By the end of the month, you will be in really bad shape, Emma. Kate will know you are a very sick woman by then."

"Okay then, I will be gone in two weeks max, how will I be then?"

"You will probably be very weak and not keeping anything down. This last half of stage 4 goes very fast."

"All right, so you are telling me that I don't really have any good time left."

"I'm so sorry, Emma."

"Thank you for being honest, and I will let you get back to more patients that you can help." Getting up to leave and the floor wanted to come up and hit me in the face. Which it would have done if Alex hadn't caught me. He just stood there and held me for whatever time I needed. I hadn't really cried about this. I guess I was hoping today he would tell me it all magically disappeared or there had been a mistake made in my test results. It didn't happen that way, so the tears came, and there was no controlling them. I tried to apologize for crying, and Alex just said, "Let it go, Emma, it's okay to cry. I'm here with you now, and I will be till the end."

"You will?"

"Of course. I owe Jackie a visit, and this way I can be with you too. She is a hell of a nurse, but she is not your doctor."

"She will be okay with this? Why does she do this?"

"'Cause she is a super person, and as a sister, I couldn't have asked for better. She has done this for me for a few of my patients who didn't have family to be there with them."

"Jackie is a very good sister, Alex."

"Yes, so I can be with you as much as possible and not get in her way."

"Good thing all your family was in medicine?"

"Just us left. Dad was a doctor, and Mom just took very good care of us."

"That would have been nice."

"It has been. So you do whatever you need to do. Then I will take you down to see Jackie."

"You will, Alex?"

"Yes, if you're not letting Kate be with you through this, then I'm going to be there whether you like it or not. You are not going through this alone. Do you understand?"

"Thank you, Alex." Hanging on to him like he was my lifeline. Hell, he was my lifeline, has been for some time now.

"I will call you later to chat."

"All right, thank you. I'm going over to Kate's now."

"Please, Emma."

"No."

"Okay, okay. We will chat later for sure." He kisses me on the cheek.

"I don't think doctors are supposed to do that."

"I'm also your friend."

"Thank you for being here with me."

"You don't have to thank me. Now are you steady enough on your feet to make it out to your car, or would you like me to walk you out."

"Thank you, I will walk myself. We don't need people talking."

"Don't worry about other people, Emma, worry about yourself."

"It's too late to worry about me, Alex."

She leaves him standing there thinking, *God, I wished things could have been different for her. I wouldn't have mind having her for my wife. Didn't think I would ever think that after being taken to the cleaners with the first wife. Why did it take so long for us to find each other again? I don't think Emma is anything like that. If things went sour, she would have just left, like she did before and the same as she is now. Not wanting to cause anyone any pain or put anyone through the hell she will be going through. She is one fantastic woman and what a waste to be taken so young.*

Emma gets out to her car and doesn't remember if anyone said hi or if she had even seen anyone on her way out. Getting in behind the wheel hit her again, and she just let it come.

"Dear God, please give me the strength that I will need to get through this. I don't want Kate to be able to tell anything is wrong. Today will be my last visit with my daughter and granddaughter. So please help make it a good one. You are calling me home, so please grant me this." Pulling out of the parking lot, she then heard horns blowing and she saw people shaking their hands at her. "Yea, well, let's see how well you will do when your number is up, asshole." Pulling off to the side of the road to have a talk with myself before going any farther. "Now, Emma, get a hold of yourself, it's no one's fault. You have to pay attention to your driving, or you could kill someone else." Getting out the wipes and wiping down her face and taking some slow deep breath to calm herself down before heading over to Kate's. Thinking, *God, I don't know if I can do this?* Emma drives on over to Kate's and sat outside for a moment to gather her thoughts. What was she going to tell them about not being around? Knowing that she will be able to keep in touch with her cell phone. Thank God for texting, Kate won't be able to tell by my voice that I'm sick.

Getting up to the door, she could hear all kinds of chatter and laughter. Yes! This is what I want to remember, Not Kate and Angel crying over me. But laughter. She could also heard Jake and knew he was a lot of why there was laughter in this house. He made Kate and Angel happy; just maybe they will work something out between them down the road. She rang the doorbell, and Angel was the first to get to it. She had been warned about saying anything. Kate and Jake want to talk to her about it first.

"Hi, Grandma, come in. Jake is having supper with us."

"Hi, sweetheart, I can hear that."

"Do you want some, Grandma?"

"No, thank you, dear, I just had a snack downtown."

"Hi, Mom." Kate comes over and hugs me. Then she stands there looking at me. I wasn't sure what I should say or what she thought she saw. So I waited her out.

"Have you caught up on your sleep, Mom?"

"Yes, I think so, but by the end of the day, I'm ready for bed."

"Well, you have always kept yourself busy right up until you fall into bed."

"I'll have you know I fall into the bathtub first."

"Come sit down, I will get you some tea."

"That would be great, Kate, thank you."

"Hi, Emma, and how are you?"

"Hi, Jake, I'm great, thank you for asking."

"You getting over the holiday?"

"Yes, I am. It's taking me longer than Kate and Angel. Guess age has something to do with it."

Kate brings the tea around and setting it down, then she goes and stands by Jake and has her arm around his shoulder. Smiling like she was the cat that had just swallowed the bird.

"Okay, Kate, you want to tell me what you are smiling like that for."

"Jake and I have something to tell you."

"Me too, me too."

"Wait your turn, Angel, please."

"All right, I'm listening, Kate."

"Were getting married. Now before you say anything, we want you to know we have thought it over well. Right, Jake?"

"Yes, we have, Kate."

"Yes, we have," Angel pipes up and puts in her two cents.

"Well, this is a welcome surprise. When and where?"

"We are getting married out at Shady Lanes Estates. The date we are not quite sure of a 100 percent yet."

"Who do you know out there? Those are big places, Kate, and to rent one would cost you a fortune."

"We have our own, and we thought we would get married there to start our new life together."

"You bought one of those huge places? How?"

"Not really. Jake owns one of them."

"What? Those belong to very rich people, Kate."

"Yes, Mom, I know. We will be moving there this week."

"Jake!"

"Yes, madam?"

"Would you please explain what my daughter is talking about."

"It's simple. I own the one that belongs to Sanders."

"The Sanders estate is you? Just wait till I sit down." Mom slides in on the other chair beside Angel and is looking like she is in a dream of sorts. So I go around and put my hand on her shoulder.

"Mom, are you all right?"

"I can't believe this. My daughter and granddaughter are going to be living with the rich."

"You better believe, Emma. I want Kate and Angel to get what they deserve out of life, and I want to give it to them. I want them to be happy again."

"I thought you had a house just down there somewhere." She waves her hand over her head in the direction of Jake's house.

"I do. I bought that small house for just me. I didn't want to live in the mansion by myself. It needs a family and pets."

"Well, I'll be damn. My little Kate is going to be living in a mansion."

"Me too, Grandma."

"Yes, of course you too, Angel." She wraps her arm around Angel and pulls her into her side.

"Grandma, it is a castle."

"It sure looks like one from the road. I'm very happy for you all, if this is what you all want."

Yea, we do, and we would like you to live with us too. There is plenty of room, Mom."

"Please, Grandma, please."

"That is very kind of you, but at this moment, I can't."

"Why not, Mom, you have nothing to hold you to the apartment."

"No, I don't, but I will be leaving in a week's time or so."

"Oh, where are you going? We just got back."

"I'm going out to the coast to take care of a friend who is sick. She called to see if I would mind."

"For how long, Mom?"

"As long as she needs me to."

"You will come back for our wedding, won't you, Mom?"

"She is pretty bad off, Kate, and I may not be able to get away."

"But, Mom! I can't get married if you're not here with us."

"Now, dear, of course you can. Something like this comes along only once in a lifetime, and you and Jake deserve each other. Remember, I have always told you things happen for a reason."

"No, Mom, I won't get married without you at my side."

"Mommy, we won't be princesses?"

"Yes, you will," Jake cuts in.

"Kate, we will be married this coming weekend. That way Emma will be here, and everyone will be happy."

"We can't do it on that short of a notice?"

"Yes, we can, I have more help than I know what to do with, so this week they will earn their keep."

"You sure, Jake?"

"Very sure, now everyone, relax and enjoy your tea. Later I will make calls, and tomorrow you girls go shopping for your dresses, and we will be just fine."

"Okay, Jake, I have to go see Dr. Adams tomorrow."

Emma turns white and holds her breath while waiting for Kate to continue. "Why is that, Kate, something wrong?" Emma holds on to the side of the table so tight her knuckles are white.

"No, I want him to give me away. After all, he has been the closer person as far as being a father to me. I would like to ask him, so he can make time for it."

"That is a very good idea."

Kate notices Emma and can see something is not sitting right with her. "What is it, Mom, you don't look well?"

"Nothing, honey, this is a lot to take in. First, our holiday and now this. It has all been like living a dream."

I go around and wrap my arms around her and say, "I know it has, Mom, and it feels so good. I'm glad you came on the holiday even if we wore you out a little bit. It is one Angel and I will always remember."

"Me too, sweetheart. Thank you for asking me to go with you. Now what can I do for the wedding?"

"Nothing, Mom, except get lots of rest so you can enjoy it with us before you leave to go take care of your friend. She hasn't any family that can do this for her?"

"No, she is from the old country, so not too many of her family made it over. She is the last one left here."

"Oh, that is too bad."

"Yes, it is. But I shouldn't be too long."

"Remember, your place is with us then, and if you want, we can move your stuff while you're away."

"I will think about that and let you know. You have many things to deal with right now. You don't need mine to worry about."

"Yea, but these are all good things, Mom, for a change."

"I know, sweetheart, so enjoy it."

"We will, Mommy." I kiss her and hug her close. She feels thin.

"Is it my imagination, Mom, or have you lost weight?"

"No, dear, I think at this age, they call it muscle mass or some silly thing. I still weigh the same. I had my checkup and all is fine."

"Good, I'm glad to hear that. We don't need any more hospitals for years to come."

"You are so right, my dear. Now I think I will go and please call and let me know what I can do."

"We will, Mom." Kate kisses me good night, and I couldn't help but hug her a little longer than usual.

"I'm going to get Angel ready for bed."

"I will walk your mom out, Kate."

"Thank you, Jake." Jake takes me right to my car, and I hug him and thank him.

"Thank you, Jake, for taking care of my little girls. I'm so glad that you have found each other. I really think you are what they needed in their lives. I know this is soon, but I can see the love in your eyes for those two, and their love for you. I wish you all the best."

"Emma, I know you aren't telling Kate everything. I saw all these signs with my wife."

"Just leave it alone, Jake, please."

"You know where to find us when you're ready."

"Yes, I do, good night."

"Good night, Emma."

THIRTY-TWO

J ake was on the phone when I came out from putting Angel to bed. "The workers at the house will have the yard all done up. I will go out tomorrow and let them know what we expect them to do."

"Expect them to do, Jake. I don't even know what we might want to do yet. This takes some planning. It doesn't happen overnight."

"We have to have it ready for Saturday."

"Saturday? Jake, what is the rush?"

"Your mother is going away to help someone who is very ill, and she could get called away sooner. I would like her to be with you when we get married. I know it would mean a lot to you. I don't want to have to wait until she comes back before we can get married."

"I won't get married unless my mom is there."

"I know that, so we get it done this Saturday."

"Do you think we can, Jake?"

"Yes, Kate, we can, I have lots of help available, so let's decide tonight on what you want for flowers and whatever else so I can let the staff know tomorrow."

We sat up most of the night, and Jake drew the layout of the yard, so I knew what I had to work with. We didn't go big and splashy. It was going to be elegant and small. After all, we both had the large wedding once, and there was no need for it again.

I took Angel shopping the next day, and we got the dresses. Hers was a white sparkly full-skirted princess dress. It had so much netting under it that it stood up on its own. Angel loved it, along with her sparkly shoes. For myself, I got an off-white evening gown with a hat. They both had sequins on them, but not too much that I couldn't just wear it to a simple dance.

Angel thought I should get one like hers. I told her not at my age. Princess gowns were for young girls, and she was happy with that. She twirled around and around in the store I thought she would make herself sick.

Going to the flower shop to see what they had for flowers so that Jake's yard men could get them arranged. These were the only two things besides getting our hair done that I had to do. Jake had the rest under control.

This week went by mighty fast, and I had texted back and forth with Mom and kept her in the loop. It was a good thing for texting; you could still carry on with whatever you were doing yet have a conversation with someone at the same time. She had her own hair appointment so wouldn't be coming with Angel and me.

Jake and I had listed our homes, and I had three lookers already, and the second one looked like a buyer for our house. It was a young couple waiting for their son to be born, so of course, they loved the baby's room. Their baby was due in four weeks. We would have to move fast if they wanted the house. With the wedding and all, we were going to be very busy. For as busy as we were, it didn't seem to bother me. I took each day as it came, and we did what had to be done that day, and that's all there was to it. Jake was a very organized man, and I think that was the biggest help of all. Jake wasn't worried about selling his small house. He said he would rent it out if nothing else came of it. Myself, I didn't want that headache.

Moving was going to be simple because we didn't have to take anything but our clothes and just things we really wanted. What wasn't staying with the house was going to the secondhand store. We were starting over totally fresh. There wasn't going to be any Ben or any Grace among us. Other than Angel and Jake looked at her as another me, not Ben. Although he didn't have a problem with it. After all, she was Ben's daughter, and now he would have the great pleasure of raising her and loving her as his own. He planned on doing the best he could for Angel. He wanted to give her the moon if possible. This was going to be all so new to us and hard to get used to. Jake would make a decision and go with it, no questions asked and no second-guessing. Where I was always thinking and rethinking. It used to drive Ben crazy, and my mother. My mother used to be like Jake and always knows what she wants and goes for it. She never second-guesses herself. Mom always told me it was a waste of time, and your first instinct is always the best. She always told me that when doing exams at school.

Go with your first choice. If you change it, it will be wrong. It took me a few times to trust what she was saying. I finally learned in school to do as Mom said, but in my life, I haven't been so good at it. Perhaps Jake will teach me how to stick to it.

Our plans fell into place just like they were supposed to, and I believe it was all because Jake was like Mom. He made a decision and stuck to it.

Our big day came, and the yard and all the trimming looked fantastic. The huge trees that grew over the red brick road going up and turning into a huge circle in front of the mansion looked like they were a covered bridge done up with lights and the biggest white bows I have ever seen. These bows also had lights through them.

We had decided to get married in the evening. It wouldn't be so hot; everyone would enjoy being outside. The hundreds of mini lights everywhere made it look like something out of a fairy-tale story. After all, wasn't this a fairy-tale wedding? As Dr. Adams walked me through the trees, I couldn't help but think I had somehow become Cinderella. Angel was skipping along in front of us and tossing out red rosebuds. Jake said red was the sign of love and he would like the path to his heart done up in red rosebuds. How could I argue with that?

"Kate, are you going to be okay living in a dead woman's house?" This took me by surprise, and I stumbled and he caught me. My eyes must have been as big as saucers.

"Well, are you?"

"She never lived here."

"Really?"

"Yes, she died before Jake's parents. He never wanted to live here alone."

"Then I won't say anymore on that subject."

"Thank you." Everything went as planned, and Mom was there, and she seemed so happy for us. Yet she seemed so sad.

"Ladies and gentlemen, Kate and Jake wrote this, and so we will share it with you. It is totally not your usual wedding vows but will do.

"Today we stand at a milestone in our lives. Behind us are all the struggles and challenges that we both have conquered along our way. Before us lies a new beginning filled with thrilling possibilities. Today we both have chosen the path in which we both want to take, so we will go for it and are hoping for your blessing. Starting over is the bravest kind of beginning there is, and we have learnt that it is never too late to start over. With this said, I now pronounce them man and wife. Everyone, please help me welcome them to a new beginning as Mr. and Mrs. Jake Sanders. Jake, you may kiss your bride."

Everyone starting clapping their hands and shouting and whistling. I knew I went red in the face, and don't ask me why. We mingled with the crowd, and everyone was having a good time. We had parted ways for a while, and I had talked with my mom and later saw Jake talking to her, and then he took her into his embrace as though in comfort. I had thought about going over to see what it was all about, but I knew Jake would tell me later. Angel was having the time of her life, and her eyes would dance with excitement every time someone called her a princess. Before I knew it, Jake was back at my side, and I decided to mention that I was concerned about Mom.

"Jake, my mom looks sad."

"She is, sweetheart, she is worried about her friend. There is nothing we can do about it. Please will you just relax and enjoy our wedding?" Jake knew he had to get Kate off the subject.

"You're right, I'm sorry."

We went on with the crowd, and then Mom came to say good-bye. "Jake, Kate, I must bid farewell. This old body is telling me it is time to turn in." She takes me in her arms and holds me like she used to when I was sick. It always gave me comfort knowing my mom was there. I think that no matter how old you get, a mother's hug is something no one can replace, not even a husband. A mother's hug is always full of unconditional love. It makes you feel safe, secure, and like you can take on the world.

"I love you, Kate, more than life. You must know that and always remember whatever I have done, I've done it from that love."

"I know, Mom, and I love you the same. You have been my life, my rock for so long, I would be lost without you. I'm so glad we were able to get married today so you could be here with us. It wouldn't have meant the same to me without you."

"You and Angel have been my world, and now I must share you with Jake, and I don't have a problem with that. He is now going to be your rock, and when you need to, you lean on him all the way. "I will, Mom."

"Kate, promise me."

"I will, Mom, I know Jake is a very good man, and Angel and I are very lucky to have met him."

"Yes, you are. I'm glad that I will be able to rest easy, knowing he is taking very good care of my girls."

"We look forward to you living with us, Mom. Angel will be in seventh heaven having her grandma living in her castle with her."

"We will see how things go, Kate." With that said, she turns to Jake and hugs him as she does to me.

"Thank you, Jake, for coming into my girls' lives and loving them as you do. I feel relieved that Kate and Angel will be taken very good care of. I never dreamt in a hundred years that my girls would be living in such a grand home and with such a grand lifestyle."

Just then Angel came running up to her grandmother. "Grandma, Grandma, are you sleeping in our castle tonight with us?"

Getting down so she could talk to Angel eye to eye. This was something Mom always does even when I was a child. She said people didn't seem so scary to children if you got down to their eye level. "I'm sorry, sweetheart, not tonight, Grandma has to go and finish packing."

"Where are you going, Grandma? Is Mommy and me coming with you?"

"No, you're not. I'm going to go take care of a friend that is sick. You have your new life to start here with Jake and Mommy. Please remember, Grandma loves you as big as the sky."

Angel had joined in. She always knew what was coming. "I love you too, Grandma, and I hope your friend gets better soon so you can come home to our castle."

"Me too, Angel, me too." She hugs Angel, and I could see a tear just hanging on as she got back up and bid us farewell and left. I saw Dr. Adams come and meet her part way and walked her to her car. It was nice to see him hugging her. I wish those two would get together.

"Mommy, I'm going to go play again."

"Okay, you be careful and be a good girl."

"I will, Mommy." And away she went.

"My mom is so damn sad, Jake. I'm worried about her."

"I know you are, sweetheart, but this is something she wants to do. We had best get back to our guest."

"You're right as always."

We went and mingled some more, and it wasn't long before our guest had all left and we were in tucking Angel into her big bed. She gave us some attitude as she didn't want to take off her princess dress. We had to promise that she could wear it again tomorrow. After she settled down, it was like five minutes and she was out.

"Now, Mrs. Sanders, should we turn in to our room?"

"Oh, that sounds good to me, Mr. Sanders."

He took me down the hall to what was to be our bedroom, and when he opened the door, I could only stand and stare.

"Well, what are we waiting for?" He scoops me up and carries me in over the threshold. Setting me back down ever so gently.

"Jake, this is bigger than my whole house was. Not to mention beautiful."

"Thank you, and it is all yours, my dear."

"It's ours."

"Yes, it's ours."

"The bathroom is over there, the shower is on this side."

I go to have a bath, and everything was laid out. My, what a beautiful room. I got so caught up in looking at the room I almost forgot Jake would be waiting for me. How does one get used to all this? I had to pinch myself to see if I were dreaming. This is so overwhelming. Oh, Angel and I could get so spoiled. I'm glad Jake got to know us while living in that little house. He knows we love him for who he is, not for what he has.

Looking up to the heavens, I just had to say, "Thank you, Ben, I'm sure it was you who brought us together and what a wonderful person you sent. We will try to make you proud. I will always love you, Ben, good night." I had placed my hand over my heart and held it there for a few just to be sure Ben knew he was still part of me. My bath was sweet and too short as I knew Jake would be coming soon to find me. Guess that wouldn't be so bad; the tub was plenty, big enough for two. Hell it looked like it would hold four. Going out, I could hear very soft music playing, and I found Jake pouring us some champagne.

"Here you go, love."

"Thank you, Jake."

"A toast to Mr. and Mrs. Sanders." We raise our glasses and drink.

"Now please may I have a dance with my wife. I have waited a long time for this dance."

"Yes, you may. I would love to have a dance with my husband."

We danced and danced and went on to having the most marvelous wedding night anyone could have imagined.

After we had been living there for a couple of weeks, I had come downstairs to hear Angel and Jake deep into a conversation. They would always make breakfast Saturday, and for some reason, it seemed like it was taking them forever today, so I decided to check them out.

"Jake, now that you married us, can I call you Daddy." Then she hangs her head. "Sorry."

"Don't be sorry, Angel. You already have a daddy."

"I want a real daddy, one that will come to school on Dad and Daughter Day. My dead daddy can't do that."

"So what do you do on those days, Angel?"

"I sit out and watch everyone else."

The tears are sliding down my cheeks as I watch Jake go around the table and take Angel in his arms.

"Oh, baby, we will have to talk to Mommy about this. I don't have a problem being your daddy, but Mommy might."

Wiping my face, I was going to try to slip in like I hadn't heard anything.

"Mommy might what?"

Both Angel and Jake were surprised and didn't know what to say. Jake puts Angel back on the chair and comes around and wraps his arms around me, kissing me so lightly.

"Good morning, Kate."

"Come now what might Mommy do or not do?"

"Go ahead, Angel, tell Mommy what you just told me."

She hangs her head, and I wanted so badly to take her in my arms and tell her everything was okay. I wanted her to be sure this is really what she wanted. So I go over and kneel down in front of her. Taking her face in my hands and bringing her eyes to meet mine.

"Angel, tell Mommy what is making you so sad?"

"I want Jake to be my daddy. I want to call him Daddy. I want him to come to my school and be my daddy." Now she is sobbing. Taking her into my arms. I could almost feel my mother and Ben with me.

"You have a daddy, Angel."

"No Mommy, my daddy is dead. He can't come to my school no more, and the kids laugh at me because I don't have a daddy."

I almost chocked on those words. I never knew the kids were saying anything. Angel never said a word.

"Oh, sweetheart, why didn't you tell me."

"Tell you what, Mommy, you already know I don't have a daddy anymore. I want Jake to be my daddy, please, Mommy."

I look over at Jake, and he is crying about as hard as Angel. God, what do I do?

"OKAY, OKAY, you want Jake to be your daddy?"

"Yes."

I look over at Jake and say, "Do you want to be Angel's daddy?"

"Yes, I do, Kate."

"Are you two sure of this?"

"YES," they both yelled at me at the same time.

"Okay, no need for yelling. It is settled, Jake, you are now Angel's daddy."

"Kate, are you sure?"

"Yes, Jake, I'm sure."

"Mommy, for real? Jake can be my daddy?"

"YES," I yelled back at the two of them.

"Okay, okay, you don't have to yell at us, Kate. We get it. Thank you." And he kisses me and reaches over and takes Angel into his arms and twirls her around and says to her, "Now will my daughter show me how to make pancakes?"

"YES, DADDY, I WILL. I LOVE YOU, DADDY." She squeezes his neck until he was play chocking.

I wouldn't have been able to live with myself if I had refused Angel this one request. I was pretty sure Ben would be okay with it when he saw how devastated his little trooper had been over this.

THIRTY-THREE

We had gone ahead and had Angel's name changed to be Angel Parker-Sanders. This was a very special day for Angel as it made her feel like she belonged and was whole again. There would be no more father-daughter days missed.

We kept in touch with Mom on a daily basis, and she was getting good at texting and fast. She had one of the old phones where you had to punch the same number three times to get the letter you wanted, and I couldn't believe how fast she had gotten.

She said her friend was failing fast and was glad to be there with her. We told her we planned a trip out her way soon.

We ran into Dr. Adams now and again, and it always seemed as though he was headed out of town each time we saw him. He said he was going to see a friend. I had wondered if he had taken up with a lady out of town and didn't want any of us to know. Yet I'm sure he wouldn't move away. He has people he has taken care of for years, and I don't think he would ever let anyone down.

I had thought many times it would have been nice for him and my mother to get together. But he was her doctor, so it stayed that way.

Running into him today was somewhat different than the other times. He did look tired, and he seemed to be in a real hurry today, and if I hadn't felt like I was prying into his private life, I would have asked what the hurry was all about and maybe even teased him about having a heavy date waiting for him who obviously was wearing him out. We had our quick chitchat and the usual "how was everyone?" and he was gone. Even when he was talking with me, he seemed like he was already gone. He is a dedicated man; I have to give him that. I hope to talk to him longer next time.

"Alex."

"I'm here, Emma."

"I want you to know how happy I am that you arranged for Kate and I to have that time together. I hope that those memories will get her and Angel through the hard days that are ahead of them."

"That daughter and granddaughter of yours, they are very resilient people, Emma.

You have to be proud of them."

"Oh, I'm proud of them, Alex, and I'm so happy that Kate and Jake found each other. I totally believe in things happening for a reason."

"I believe in that too, Emma. As hard as it is for me sometimes to see the reasons."

"I know, Alex."

"Like now, why you? You should still have an easy thirty something years, and he's taking you so soon. We never got our chance."

"Oh, Alex, you're so sweet, but we did have our chance." She puts his hand up to her frail lips and lightly kisses it.

Emma sits most of the time in the two-seated love seat recliner; she felt it was easier for her to breathe. Her breaths are shallow and short. Alex knows the signs, and he knows Emma doesn't have much time. He knew she was fighting it, and that was the reason she wouldn't sleep in the bed. As if sitting up was prolonging her life. How he wished that was true. Jackie and Alex had her apartment all set up for taking care of the dying. The government helped them out with a lot as it was all for people who didn't have families to take care of them or for the ones who, like Emma, chose to die alone. This was the first time Alex spent most of his time there. Usually, he turns the patient over to Jackie and stops in once in a while to check more on her than the patient. He had taken a leave of absence until Emma's ordeal was over.

"My darling," he says to her as he pulls her close to him because he is sharing the love seat with her.

"I'm asking you one more time. Can I call Kate for you? She would be here in a few hours."

Even though he knew she didn't really have that much time. Shaking her head back and forth and whispering, "Alex, you promised me you would see this through with me."

"And I am, Emma, I just want you to be sure that is all. I don't want for you to have any regrets."

"There's no regrets, Alex. Just stay here with me and hum those beautiful songs you know."

"All right, Emma, I can do that." Alex hums all the old favorite tunes that he and Emma knew. The ones that they danced to whenever they had the chance to go out. They never went out in their hometown. Neither one wanted to be the talk of the town or someone's breakfast conversation, so they always went out of town. Their friendship had seen them through many things, and they were both annoyed at the fact that they have been cheated out of their time. They both knew that was what Kate had wished for and always had planned on them being together. Thinking they had lots of time yet. Guess this is when the saying "You snooze you lose" comes into play.

Neither one regrets the time they had as they enjoyed themselves totally. They were both happy about their arrangement at the time. They also knew they had done a very good job of keeping their secret between them and them alone.

Alex knew he was going to be very lonely, and it was going to be hard for him. He loved Emma more than he loved anyone in his life, and he knows when she goes, she will be taking his heart with her. He also knows how hard it will be every time he sees Kate. Kate and Emma look so much alike; he knows when he looks at Kate, he will be seeing Emma. He always felt that when he saw Kate, he was seeing Emma in her younger days. They were both strong, beautiful women.

Alex knew he would have to keep himself together so he wouldn't betray Emma's trust in him or their secret. He also knew he had other people counting on him, so curling up and dying with Emma wasn't going to be an option.

Where he was going to pull his strength from, he had no idea. Alex also knew it wasn't going to be a pretty picture when Kate finds out he knew Emma was dying and didn't say anything to her. Although she knows that a doctor can't rightfully say anything about any patients without costing him his job.

He pulls Emma in even closer if that was possible, and he falls asleep with her in his arms. Dreaming of the last time they went dancing and smiling to himself at the memory of Emma. Oh, she is such a smooth dancer and such a joy to have in his arms. So carefree and easygoing. She knew there was time to worry, and she knew there was time to relax.

He learned that when Kate was in the coma, just how strong-minded Emma could be. He was also concerned about her health at that time. He knew she wasn't getting the rest she needed, and she knew it would play hard on her health and was willing to take that chance 'cause her daughter needed her at her side. It tore at his heart watching her with Kate and feeling like he couldn't do a damn thing for her. The same thing as he has been feeling these last few days.

"Alex. Alex, wake up." Jackie is shaking his shoulder.

"Alex, she is gone. Emma passed in her sleep."

"OH, my darling, NO!" Pulling Emma into him closer, he breaks down. His deep convulsing cry tore at Jackie. She had known that Alex had loved Emma for a very long time. She used to ask him all the time what was stopping him from marrying her. Alex would just say, "It's not time yet." Now it will never be time. Jackie held them both for a bit, then left Alex to be alone with Emma while she made the arrangements that she and Emma had talked about and had written down so that Kate could see that her mother's wishes had been carried through.

Emma had her angel statue where her ashes were to be put into and given to Kate. It was four and a half feet tall and beautiful. She wants Kate to keep it in her garden. Emma loved her flower beds and wishes to spend the rest of her time there among the roses. She would often say, "I will be the thorn among the roses."

Alex sat with Emma in his arms for the better part of the morning.

"Alex, we have to call now."

"I know." The tears were still falling, but his cries of despair had stopped even though Jackie knew that he would still have times when it would all come back to him and he would break down again. All she could do was let him know she was there for him and that she loved him. At this time, it didn't feel like she had much to offer that was going to take the pain away that Alex was feeling. She knew he was going to be full of regrets for not marrying Emma a long time ago. She knew that they spent all their spare time together and the time that Emma was gone to Australia with Kate and Angel almost killed him. He knew it was shortening up his time with her, but it was something that she had to do, and he loved his

Emma enough to help set it all up with Kate. Many times after they left, he had wished that Kate wouldn't have bitten on his suggestion. He had wished he hadn't been so persuasive with Kate. When Emma called him and said they were coming home early, he knew his Emma was in deep trouble. Alex was angry with himself for letting her go. He knew it would wear her down too fast. Emma had told him she did not want to sit around and wait to die, and if she had any say in it, she wasn't going to. Many times he had thought about getting on the plane and joining them. It was a tug-of- war in his mind. His love and respect for Emma and their secret won out. Jackie and Alex went ahead with the arrangements as planned and was trying to figure out just how he was going to call Kate and tell her that her mother had just passed away in her sleep when Kate didn't even know her mother was sick. He had Emma's cell phone in his hands when it went off, alerting them of an incoming message. Alex damn near threw it across the room. Jackie stooped down and picked it up, handing it back to Alex. He just sat there and looked at it.

"Go on, Alex, read it and see what Kate has to say."

So he flips it open and reads,

Hi, Mom, I know you must be busy, for I haven't heard from you in a few days. So I thought I would let you know we will be there in two days. If this is a problem, please let us know. We have finally gotten everything settled and rearranged with the two places. We got all your things moved in to the south wing so you will have lots of sunshine for your roses. Hope you will be rested when we get there so you will be able to show us some of the special sites. That is if your friend will be okay to be left alone for a while. We are hoping your friend is well enough that we can bring you home with us. This seems funny to be taking a honeymoon now, but guess we can call it whatever we want. Seeing how you were at our wedding, we feel it is only fair that we share our honeymoon with you. Angel is so excited to see you as Jake and I are. Text us when you have a chance.

Love you, Mom, see you in a couple of days.

Running his fingers through his hair and looking at Jackie and saying, "Guess I have two days to figure out how to tell Kate her mother has passed away."

"Oh, Alex, you only done what Emma wanted. Kate will be mad at you at first as I think we all would be. That will be normal. But she will finally come around. From what you tell me of this young lady, she is a very wise one, and if she is anything like Emma, then it will be fine and she will forgive you."

"Forgive me? I don't deserve for Kate to forgive me. I should never have let Emma talk me into this. How could I have let her?"

"Because number one, you loved her, and number two, she also was your patient and you were seeing her last wishes carried through."

"How is Kate ever going to trust me again? As a doctor or a friend."

"Tell me, Alex, if Emma had chosen to be in the hospital and said no to any intervention when it came to prolonging her life. What would you have done?"

"I would have carried out her wishes. I wouldn't want to see her suffer."

"So that is just what you have done. You saw her last wishes carried out."

"Oh, Jackie, you know this is different."

"To a point it is. It is a very small point, Alex."

"Her daughter has been lied to."

"No, she hasn't, Alex. Kate never asked if her mother was sick. So there was no need to tell her. In her texting, she would ask Emma how she was doing, and if she was getting any rest. She was told the truth to both these questions."

"Her daughter was cheated out of time with her mother and a chance to say goodbye. Oh god, Jackie, no matter what you say, it won't make me feel any better about this." He runs his hands through his hair and weeps. Jackie sits down beside him and pulls him into her embrace. Stroking his hair and she hugs him for as long as it took for him to get himself together. Alex finally fell asleep, so Jackie just covered him up with Emma's blanket. What else was a sister to do? They had come and got Emma, so they could cremate her and return her to Alex later tomorrow. He would have her here with us when Kate arrived.

Jackie knew this was going to be hard on Alex, and it wouldn't surprise her if he gave up his practice. She would do whatever she could and within her power to talk him out of it. After all, what else would he have now that Emma is gone. His practice had always been his life. Even when he was in medical school, he talked about the girl he met and how she was the love of his life. He loved his practice, and in the end, it came first, and he had lost her. Later he had met another and married, but she couldn't take all his time that he devoted to his practice. It was a messy divorce as she took him for everything she could. She had said he owed it to her for all the neglect that he had given her. How he made her feel like anything but a woman.

Meeting Emma did him a world of good, and he got that old spark back in his eyes, and he did more with Emma then he had done with any women. He still held his practice with pride, but he had learnt that he needed someone also that he could enjoy himself with. Perhaps the messy divorce had stopped him from marrying Emma. Jackie knew Alex, and so she also knew that the regrets that he was going to carry was going to pull him way down and could possibly kill him. She would have to pray that he won't turn to the bottle as their father had done when their mother had died. Jackie felt that perhaps she should move back with Alex so she could be there for whenever he fell apart. They were close, and she felt she must make that suggestion to Alex.

THIRTY-FOUR

Alex slept all that afternoon and woke up around 1:00 a.m. I could hear him fussing around out in the kitchen and knew I wasn't going to get any sleep now until he went back to bed, which wasn't likely to happen anytime soon. Putting on my housecoat and going out to join him, I walk over and wrap my arms around his waist. He was only six and a half feet tall, and here I am pushing five foot nothing.

"Do you feel better now that you had a little rest, Alex?"

"Not really, I still have Kate to deal with. As far as being sleepy, I'm fine."

"You have put in some long days with Emma."

"Yes, I did, and I don't regret a minute."

"I know you don't. Alex, when people love each other like you and Emma did, nothing is too hard to do for them."

"You're right, I would have given her my right arm if need be."

"I could tell."

"I only wish she would have had cancer where she could have had some kind of transplant or surgery and survived."

"That would have been nice, Alex, and I'm sorry you are hurting so much."

He takes his glass of milk and kisses me on top of my head. "Let's sit down."

"Okay, I will put on a pot of coffee first." Jackie gets busy making coffee and cutting up some banana bread. She knows Alex isn't going to eat a meal but will pick at this if it is sitting in front of him. Sometimes she has to chuckle to herself remembering that's what her mother would do in a time like this. People don't want meals but will snack. Bringing it all over to the table and looking at Alex, she sees a man that has aged considerably over the last three weeks. He has got the brightest crystal blue eyes that she had ever seen in a person. She herself got her mother's brown eyes and had always wished for their father's eyes as Alex had.

"What time is Kate going to be here?"

"She should be rolling in around five this afternoon."

"This is going to be the first time that I'm going to be lost for words. I have dealt with a lot of deaths over my years of being a doctor, and even when it came to losing Ben, I was able to help Kate through it. I don't think I will be able to give her the strength this time that she will be needing. This is one time I will have to let Kate down."

"Oh, Alex, you're not letting her down. She has a husband now to draw strength from. It shouldn't have to be you. You have to also mourn Emma, and this is natural, you know that."

"I have been Kate's shoulder since her and Emma moved to town."

"Yes, you have and a very good friend you have been to them."

"A good friend would not be in this mess right now. Kate should have been at her mother's side. Oh, Jackie, what have I done?"

"Alex, she may be mad at you for a short time, but she will soon realize how much you loved her mother and you done what anyone in your shoes would have done."

"Mad, Jackie! Good God, Kate is going to be devastated to say the least, and I helped create it. If she never talks to me again, I won't blame her. Even though I know I deserve it. It will tear what is left of my heart out. She has been the closest person to being a daughter that I have ever had, and Angel has been like my granddaughter. Never in a million years did I ever think I would be the cause of such pain to the two people I love the most in this world. Excluding you, my dear sister."

"Alex, please don't do this to yourself. You're not being fair. You done everything that Emma wanted, and you had to go by the book on some of it, seeing how she was not just your lover, she was also your patient. No one is going to be able to hold you accountable for your actions. Please, Alex, you are going to have to forgive yourself for this. Knowing you loved Emma like you did and that she had trusted you to see her wishes through, should be all Kate is worried about."

Alex sits there and just shakes his head. He knows deep down inside he has done the right thing but is torn between the love he has for both Emma and her daughter and granddaughter.

Loving Emma was an easy thing to do, so doing what she asked of him came easy at first. As Emma got sicker and her time was running short, he had often kicked himself for agreeing to go along with Emma's plan. He knew she was doing it to save Kate and Angel from all the pain of watching her mother and Angel's grandmother pass away. But what about the shock this is going to bring to them. Just out of the blue, they are going to be told, "Sorry, your mother and your grandmother is dead." Where is the justice in that? Kate sure the hell won't see it that way. The ringing of the doorbell brings Alex back to reality.

"Alex, can you get the door? I'm in the bathroom."

"Got it, Jackie." Stumbling to the door and pulling it open, he saw Kate and Angel standing there.

"Surprise!" came from her mouth, but she was obviously the one who was more surprised.

"Dr. Adams? Why are you here?"

"Come in, Kate." He stands back and lets Kate and Angel into Jackie's apartment.

"Alex, who is it?" Jackie asked as she wraps her hair up in a towel because she had just had a shower. Coming down the hall and stopping in midstride. "Oh, hi."

"Kate, this is my sister Jackie. Jackie, this is Emma's daughter, Kate, and her granddaughter, Angel."

"I'm pleased to meet you. Come in and sit down."

"I'm sorry, I must have gotten the address Mom sent me mixed up. I didn't mean to intrude on your family visit. I will get the address so I can find Mom. She is expecting us." Kate starts to dig in her purse.

Alex reaches over and puts his hand on top of hers. Stops her from digging. "You are in the right building, Kate."

"But Mom said she was staying with a friend."

"That would be me," Jackie said as she came over and takes Kate's hand.

"Well, you look like you must be feeling better. Mom must have been a very good nurse? Where is she?"

Alex takes her by the arm and says to her, "Kate, did Jake not come with you?" "Yes, he did, he was just answering a call and we were into big of a hurry to see Mom, so we left him behind. So where did you say Mom was?"

"Kate, sit down, I want to talk to you."

"Oh, this sounds serious."

"Yea, it is." Alex takes Kate into the living room and sits her down just as the doorbell rings again.

"I will get it, Alex."

"Thanks, Jackie."

Opening the door, thinking it was Jake and ready to be pleasant, Jackie instead got a box handed to her with the man saying, "We are returning Mrs. Blakely." Jackie didn't know what to do.

"Mom is here?" Kate gets up and heads for the door. Alex reaches for her but was too late to stop her. Stopping dead in her tracks when she saw Jackie standing there with the box in her hands. Kate's face was white as snow.

"Dr. Adams, what is going on? Where is Mom?"

He goes over and pulls Kate into his side and says, "There." He points to the box Jackie is still holding. Kate buckles and starts to scream, and that got Angel screaming, and Jake could hear them outside. He dropped the phone and took the stairs two at a time. He didn't have a door number; all he had to do was follow the screaming. The door was still open, and people were starting to gather around outside the door. When he entered it, he saw Dr. Adams trying to get Kate under control and Jackie trying to get Angel under control. No one seemed to be having any luck, and Jake couldn't make head or tails out of what the hell had happened. He goes to Kate first, and she threw herself into Jake, still hysterical. Then it hit him.

"It's Emma, isn't it?" he asked Dr. Adams as he held Kate close and hard.

Alex just nods his head and then stood and waited until Jake had gotten Kate settled down a little. Alex was standing there thinking, *Jake knew about Emma? She never told me she had told anyone. If Jake knew, why didn't Kate know?* Watching Jake get Kate under control was amazing. Alex was so glad that Jake was here. Before we knew it, he had both girls sitting on the sofa. They were both still sobbing but quieter now.

Jackie had remembered the door was open as we had drawn a crowd, so she politely went to shut it and apologized for the disturbances that they had caused.

"Kate, are you ready to let Dr. Adams explain this to us now?"

Kate just nods her head in between sobs and pulls Angel deeper into her side.

"Dr. Adams, please explain to us what happened?"

"All right." He goes and gets a kitchen chair so he could sit facing all of them. He wanted to make eye contact as much as possible. To him, this was important for Kate to know how sorry and sincere he was. Taking Kate's hand in his. "First off, Kate, Angel, Jake, I would like to say how sorry I am that this is how you had to find out. Second, I want you to know Kate that your mother and I have been friends for many years."

This had Kate looking up at him with the WHAT look.

"Yes, Kate, we have been friends for years. We felt it best to keep it to ourselves as we weren't ready to go public and didn't want to be the talk of the town. Your mother was a very respectable woman, and I would have done anything for her. Some of this we can talk about later. Your mother found out at the same time you had lost baby Ben that she had ovarian cancer."

Kate puts her hands over her face and shakes her head.

"It had already spread too far to be able to stop it, and she wouldn't take any treatments. Not that they would have helped. Maybe slow it down some. Emma was firm on her decisions, and I could not sway her to change her mind. That also goes for telling you. I tried many times over the time she had to get her to tell you, to let you come and be with her, but there was no way in hell she would let me go back on a promise I had made her. I tried to get her to talk to you about it when you went on the holiday. Every evening when she would call me, I would beg her to tell you."

"So that is why she was so tired and she had lost weight. It wasn't my imagination. I thought something was wrong, and when I asked her, she said it was just her age that she had been in and had her checkups and all was well."

"Yea, that's what she would say. Your mother was a very proud woman, and she didn't want you and Angel to watch her die. She said you had been through enough already and you were finally happy. She wasn't doing that to you. Emma was so happy, Jake, when you came into Kate and Angel's lives. She worry more about them and how they would be once she was gone."

"I tried to get her to talk to me. She told me to leave it alone, so I did."

Kate's head spun around so fast she almost snapped her neck. "You knew my mother was sick, and you didn't tell me, Jake. How could you?"

"I didn't know for sure, but she had the same signs as my wife did, and I didn't know for sure. So I didn't want to scare you. Emma already had her plans set, and she wouldn't talk to me."

"For Christ's sake, someone should have told me. My mother died alone, and she didn't have too. I never got to say good-bye. Angel never got to say good-bye."

"No, she didn't, Kate. That is why I brought her here to Jackie's. She did not want to be in the hospital, and Jackie was kind enough to offer her a room. She passed in my arms. I was with her always in the end. I came every week until I knew I had to be here all the time."

"This is where you were coming to when I would see you in town and you were always in a hurry. Going to see a friend, you would tell me."

"Yes, Kate, it is. I came to be with Emma."

"Don't any of you understand that I had a right to know? That I had a right to be here to be able to say good-bye?"

"Yes, Kate, we know that. Emma also had rights, and as her doctor as well as her friend, I also had rights. She had wishes, and she had asked me to carry them through for her the best I could. It was a hard call, Kate. I had come close so many times to calling you. The respect I had for your mother always stopped me. I know you're mad at me, and I understand. I can only hope that one day, you will find room in your heart to forgive me."

"Mad at you! Goddamn right, I'm mad at you. You took what time Angel and I had left with my mother and threw it away. Forgive you, probably not."

"Now, Kate, that isn't fair," Jackie snapped at her. "Alex is the one to arrange for you and Angel and your mother to get together and go on that long holiday together. Even though Alex knew it would wear her down fast. I think you are a little out of line here."

Alex reaches up and takes Jackie's hand as the tears rolled down her cheeks. Daughter or no daughter, she wasn't letting Kate jump all over Alex like that. After all, he loved Emma just as much as they did. She is the one who will have to watch him crawl to the top again.

"I'm sure Kate will see things different in a few days. This has been a big shock to them, and you will all have to give them time to adjust to the news."

"You're right, Jake, I will make some fresh coffee."

Alex gets up and follows Jackie out to the kitchen, leaving the three of them sitting there.

"Do you think they will stay the night, or will they take Emma's ashes and leave." "Emma's ashes, my god, where were they put with all the commotion?" "I set them in her room. Did you want me to go get them?"

"No, let's give them time to talk, and we will have to do whatever they wish."

"I will make some sandwiches to go with the coffee."

"Thank you, sis."

"You're welcome, Alex. What are you going to do?"

Getting up and hugging his sister, he says, "I'm going to go have a shower, maybe my head will feel better. I know my heart won't."

Jackie just crumbled inside for Alex as he turns around to go take his shower.

She was busy getting the sandwiches made and fresh coffee and some baking onto a platter. Standing there looking at it and trying to decide whether it would be a good time to take it to Kate, Jake, and Angel when she felt a hand lightly come down on her shoulder, and she jumped a little and went stiff not knowing what was coming next.

"I would like to thank you for taking care of my mom."

Jackie lets her breath out, and her shoulders relax as she turns around to face Kate.

"It was my pleasure. Just so you know, Kate, I am a registered nurse. I do this for a living, and we gave your mother the best care."

"I know you would have. Otherwise, Dr. Adams wouldn't have brought her here. Can I ask you some questions?"

"Yes, dear, you can. Come sit down."

We sit down at the table, and Kate sits staring at her hands.

"What is it that you would like to know?"

"Was Mom in lots of pain?"

"Off and on. But Alex made sure that there was as little as possible."

"Was she scared? I mean of dying?"

"In the beginning she was, then Alex talked to her about the unknown. That is what scared her the most. Not knowing what was going to happen and where she was going. Alex had told her to look at it the same as when you went on your holiday. None of you knew where you were going or what to expect, and you all had a very good trip. He told her to take this trip the same way. Then she seemed to calm right down and never spoke about being afraid again."

"That was a nice way of Dr. Adams to put it for her."

"If you think about it, Kate, he is right. It is a journey none of us know about, and it is the unknown that scares us."

"Did Mom ask for me?"

"Your texts kept her with you right to the end. She would pray for you and Angel every night."

"The last couple of days, there was no texting from her."

"That was my fault, I apologize. We wanted to keep the texting going so you wouldn't worry. When you text and said you were coming, there wasn't any need in texting anymore. We just sat and waited."

THIRTY-FIVE

"When did Mom pass away?"

"It was late yesterday afternoon. Alex was sitting and holding her in the love seat, and they both fell asleep. She passed on while sleeping."

"He was her best friend, wasn't he?"

"Yes, he was."

"I never knew my mother knew your brother that well or you?"

"I had met your mother a few times over the years when I went down to visit Alex. She knew what I done for work, and so when she found out how sick she was, and decided she wasn't putting you and Angel through the hell of watching her die. She had Alex ask me if I would consider taking care of her when she got back from your holidays."

"Mom had all this arranged already?"

"Yes, she did."

"Why didn't she say something? We wouldn't have gone on that trip? We sure wouldn't have stayed so long and wore her out like we did. She never got over the trip."

"That was exactly why she didn't say anything. She wanted you and Angel to remember her on your holiday. Not lying and dying in a bed. She was the most honest-to- goodness person I had met in years."

"Did she tell you what she wants done with her ashes? I don't know where my father's ashes were put. I was too young when it happened, and then we moved."

Just then Alex came into the kitchen. "Here, Kate, maybe this will help you." He hands over a brown envelope. "Jackie, we can take this into Jake and Angel and give Kate some time."

"Oh sure, we can do that, Jake probably needs a cup of coffee."

"Thank you, I will join you in a bit."

"Take all the time you need. We aren't going anywhere."

Kate opens up the envelope and unfolds the pages her mother had written to her. Her hands starts to shake when she sees her mother's handwriting and realizes this is the last she will hear from her mother.

To my darlings, Kate and Angel

I know right now you are mad as hell at me; maybe you even have the right to be. As your mother, I feel I have chosen the right thing to do.

I have watched you go through more hell and pain than any young person should have had to go through in such a short time. I could not bear to burden you with any more pain. Please, Kate, as a mother yourself, try to understand why I have chosen to do things this way. Remember, I was not alone; my best friend and doctor was with me every step of the way. Alex was with me right up until I took my last breath. He kept me comfortable, and I was able to face this journey that I'm about to take with such calm. It has been remarkable. Thanks to Alex. We are always afraid of the unknown, but Alex made sure I understood that this journey was going to be the same as going with you and Angel.

I'm grateful that he got you to take me on that holiday with you and Angel. He knew we needed the time together to make special memories. So please don't be upset with him. He has done nothing wrong. I will always be forever grateful that he managed to get you to take that holiday, and take me along. It gave you, me, and Angel the time we needed. It meant everything to me. You and Angel meant everything to me, and you have to know how much I loved you, and I only hope that I can continue to love you from the hereafter.

I can't tell you how happy I was when Jake came into your life. I knew then that the choice that I had made was the right one. Knowing Jake will be there to help my girls through this is making my passing a whole lot easier. I want you both to remember me as I was on our holiday. Not lying sick and dying in a bed in some hospital. I did not want that for Angel; she also has seen too much pain for someone her age. I pray to God that Jake will now put an end to all the sadness you two have had to bare. I see the sunshine he has restored in your lives, and I want you to promise to never let it go.

Alex's sister has taken very good care of me. I never wanted for anything. She was so kind to do this for us. Please don't be anything but grateful for what Jackie and Alex have done for me. Alex came on his days off and stayed with me until he felt the need to be with me all the time. I know you would approve of this as I could tell that you had this dream that he and I should be together. I know you had this idea that we should have been a couple. If we would have had more time, it would have happened. I do love Alex as much as I love you and Angel. The time was never right for us. So please, Kate, I'm asking you now to be there for Alex as he has been here for me. He may need someone to lean on after all I have put him through.

You and Angel have Jake, and Alex will have no one, so please don't be strangers to him. Remember, he has only done what I have asked of him. You were always first and foremost in my life. You were my life. As much as this is hurting you at this moment and knowing how angry you are at me right now, it will be easier to get over than having to watch me fade away to nothing and die in front of your eyes because there was nothing you could do to prevent it from happening. The guilt that you would have felt would have driven you mad. So please I ask you to know in your heart that this was right for me.

Kate, my darling, child, I love you with all my heart, and yes, I have missed you over these last days of my life, and I would have given anything to see your beautiful face and the face of that beautiful Angel. But I would not have been able to stand to see the pain in those eyes of yours as you looked on to me with pity.

Please tell Angel that her grandma loves her as big as the sky, also you my darling Kate. I know you are having a hard time with the fact that you think you never got to say good-bye. Remember your wedding night and our good-byes then. I'm saying good-bye now my angels, and I will be watching over you always.

The one thing I will ask of you, Kate, is to take me home and put me to rest with Ben and Benjamin.

Please, Kate, remember me always, and whenever you are heavy at heart or are lonely for my presence, please just look up to the heavens and know I will always be loving you and Angel from a distance.

xoxoxoxoxox forever and always, Mom.

THIRTY-SIX

"Kate, are you all right?" Jake asked as he puts his hands down on her shoulders and give her a bit of a rub.

"Hi, Jake." Blowing her nose and wiping her face, she looked at Jake. "Mom wants us to take her home and put her to rest with Ben and Benjamin."

"We can do that for her, Kate. No problem." He squeezes her shoulders. "I'm sorry, Kate, that I didn't talk to you about my feeling that I was getting from your mom. I had hoped she would come and talk to you. When she didn't, I thought maybe I was wrong, even though I had this feeling in the pit of my stomach. There were too many signs to miss I had seen them with Grace."

"It isn't your fault, Jake. Mom done what Mom wanted to do. I don't like it, and it will take some time to get over the fact that we didn't get to say good-bye. Jackie told me she wasn't in much pain and that she wasn't scared. This makes me feel a little better. The fact that she passed away being held by her best friend also brings some comfort. Oh, Jake, I will miss my mom." Kate breaks down and Jake pulls her up into his arms.

"I know you will, baby, but we have to move on. She would want you to, as much as we will miss her, we must remember Angel has had enough grief in her life and is just starting to come around. We will have to make this as painless as possible for her. Emma would want you to do that for Angel and you. That is why she chose to do what she did, and you have to love her for that."

"I will always love my mom, but right now, I'm very angry at her."

"I understand, babe. Now let's go talk to our daughter and see where we are staying tonight?"

"I just want to go home. So much for a honeymoon, hey."

"It's fine, Kate, we are getting a room, and we will go home tomorrow. We all have had a shock, and it won't do any of us any good to be on the road today."

"Of course you're right. I feel like I'm in a bad dream."

"Of course you do. Reality hasn't hit yet because you didn't see your mother sick. This really blindsided you, and I'm so sorry. Remember, Kate, I'm here for you and Angel. Please don't shut me out. You can talk anytime you need tonight or day."

"Thank you, Jake, I know that."

Taking her face in his hands and tipping it up to look into her eyes. "I mean it, Kate, promise me that no matter what it is, you will talk to me. I may not have all the answers, but maybe together, we will be able to get one."

"I love you, Jake, so much." She presses herself into his body where she finds comfort and feels safe.

Jake knew this was far from being over for them, and he only hoped that Kate will be open. She had told him how she had shut herself away from Angel and her mother when Ben had died, and he really hopes she won't go down that road again. It is not a healthy one for her or Angel. Angel will need them both; he knew he couldn't be her mommy.

Going back into the living room, they find Angel on Dr. Adams's lap, and he has her wrapped in a fairly good bear hug. Angel did have a smile on her face, and Jackie was teasing her about something that Angel was finding funny.

"Hey, what's going on in here?"

"Mommy, are we staying for a while?"

Kate goes and sits in the chair across from them, and taking Angel's hands in hers, she says, "We are staying overnight, Angel, then we must go home. Grandma wants us to lay her to rest with Daddy and baby Ben."

"She does, Mommy?"

"Yes, honey, is that okay with you?"

"I think Daddy and baby Ben will be happy that Grandma is with them."

"I think Grandma made a very good choice, and you're right, they will be so happy to see her."

"Mommy, I will miss Grandma, I hurt here." And she puts her small hand over her heart.

"Oh, sweetheart, of course you hurt. It is just like when Daddy died. Remember, it hurt then too. Time makes things better, and we just have to remember what Grandma would want us to do. She wouldn't want us to be sad all the time. But it is okay to be sad now, and once in a while, when you think of her, you will be sad. After a while, you will think of the fun things you and Grandma done together, and it won't make you sad anymore. It will make you happy."

"Like Daddy."

"Yes, sweetheart, just like Daddy."

Dr. Adams turns her around so she can see his face and says to her, "Angel, the times that you get to be sad and Mommy can't make you happy, you come see this doctor, and he will make you happy. Okay?"

"Okay, I will."

"Anytime you need me, you know where my office is. You just tell the girls you need to see me right away. They will get me. All right?"

"Yes, Dr. Adams."

"All right. Now I'm taking everyone out to supper in memory of your grandma, so why don't you take some time and get freshened up."

"Oh, you don't." *Kate, please remember Alex in this. He will need someone too.* "We will go get our room and call you when we're ready."

"That sounds good, Kate." Standing up, he gives her a bear hug and shakes Jake's hand. They leave in silence and go find a room. Having their showers were more to refreshen their minds than anything. Angel was happy to lie on the bed and watch TV. Whether she was really comprehending anything she was watching was anyone's guess. She seemed like she was relaxed, and so I didn't want to ask any questions if all I would do was upset her. Yes, it was a cop out on my part because if she were to start crying, so would I. I wanted to hold myself together; there was going to be a lot of time for crying. Like days. Taking a deep breath and asking Angel if she were about ready to go.

"No, Mommy, I want to lay here for a while."

"Oh, all right then." I look at Jake, and he's looking at me as if to say, now what? So we go to the other bed and lie down together and watch the show she was watching in silence. I fell asleep.

"Kate, Kate, wake up, Angel is ready to go for supper."

"Okay." I could tell by how hard it was to open my eyes. I had just gotten into the deep sleep. Moving slowly and not wanting to get up wasn't a good combination.

"Come on, Mommy, we are going to be late."

"Late?"

"Yes, Mommy, Daddy called and told Dr. Adams that we would be there shortly."

What is she talking about, Daddy, Doctor? I pulled the pillow over my head. I just wanted to sleep just a little longer.

"Kate, sweetheart, you have to get up. You are going to spoil your night's sleep if you don't."

"Yea." Why were my eyes so heavy? I rolled over and looked at Jake, and he had the biggest smile. It made waking up worth it. He was so easy to look at whether I had heavy eyes or not. I did get up, and we went to meet Dr. Adams and his sister, Jackie. Supper was very good, and we chatted about a lot of things. Everyone had stories to tell about Mom, and I knew this was going to be the last time we gathered around a table to chat with Mom. I did not know about the rest, but I could feel Mom's presence and smell her perfume. It was almost like she was sitting between Angel and me. I had to keep glancing to see if I could catch just a glimpse of her. I know my imagination is good but not this good; the hair on my neck stood up. She was with us, and I knew she was. I wasn't scared, but I long to see her face and to have her hold me just one more time.

"Kate, you all right?"

"Yes, Jake, I'm fine, thank you." The rest of the supper went by quickly, and Dr. Adams said he would call us when he got home. He was staying a few more days with his sister.

I knew he was having a hard time with Mom's passing. He just wasn't himself. I was surprised to find out they were friends for so many years. I thought they had just met around the time Ben had died. Mom had kept it a very well hidden secret. Guess what they say about everyone having ghost in their closets is true.

Saying good-bye to Dr. Adams was hard this time. It involved him personally, and I felt for him. I wish he had been my dad, then I would know how to help him. We would have so much more in common and in memories together to share. I felt like I was leaving him stranded.

Sleep did not come easy to me although I was tired. I tossed and turned most of the night waking Jake up many times doing so. That made me feel bad because he was going to be so tired for the drive home tomorrow. I won't be in any shape to drive.

So as it was, the drive home was long and tiring for everyone. Angel slept now and again and didn't say much. We would talk to her, but her answers were short and to the point. I figured she was in deep thought about Grandma. I could see her wheels turning as she rode along, looking out the window to the sky. I hope the questions will come soon. I will give her a couple of days, then I will ask the questions. I know Jake will be good at helping me with Angel. He just has that way with him. I'm so glad we have him in our lives now.

"Jake, how did you handle losing your parents so close together?"

"I think I was still numb from Grace, and so I walked through it and I can't tell you much about it. Things come to me now, and I have to really think about how it got to be. My mind was not mine then. People would talk to me, and I wouldn't hear a thing they were saying. After a year or so, it got better."

"Did you get to say good-bye to them?"

"Yes, Kate, I was there holding their hands, and it wasn't easy knowing they were dying and there was nothing I could do. I had wished many times that they would have been killed in a car accident. It might have been a shock, but every time I think of them now, I see the last days as I sat at their bedsides and they weren't even my parents anymore. The beds had bodies in them that didn't even resemble my parents. Cancer is a horrible sickness, Kate. It takes people and changes them so much within a month you almost don't recognize them. You might not like to hear this, but I'm going to say it anyways. I'm glad your mom did what she did. I know you and you would agonize over her death for a very long time if you had seen the cancer take her like I have seen it take people. Trust me, it would not have been easy for Angel to see her grandmother waste away.

"I know you all think she done the right thing. I want to believe you and believe in her. Why didn't she at least tell me she was sick and tell me what she was going to do? I could have said good-bye and waited for Dr. Adams to call me."

"Like hell you would have, Kate. You would have ended up fighting with your sick mother and trying to change her mind on what her last wishes were. Not because you were being cruel but because you loved her so. You would not have wanted her to go so far away knowing that she was dying. Kate, she knew you better than you know yourself."

"I don't ever want not to be able to say good-bye to my daughter. Or not having my daughter being able to say good-bye to me. It just isn't right in my books."

"Each to their own, dear. I hope you never have to watch someone die of cancer." "So if I get sick with cancer, you just going to disappear on me, Jake?"

"No, Kate, I would not do that to you. I love you, and I'm in it for the long haul, good or bad."

"Thank you. That's how I felt about Mom, Jake. I wanted to be there. I loved my Mom more than words can say, and I never got to tell her that." The tears came now, and I wasn't worrying about stopping them. Jake reaches over and takes my hand and says, "It's okay to cry, Kate. Let it go, you will feel better after."

I did just that it sure didn't take much convincing from Jake. It was a good long hard cry I had for my mom. I don't know where we were when I started. But we were pulling into home when I started to easy off. Wiping my face and blowing my nose had seem to become habit forming.

"I'm sorry, Jake."

"No need to be, Kate, you are human after all."

We got our things into the house even though Jake wanted to do it himself. But I was wanting to keep busy as well. The help was surprised to see us back already. I know by the uncertainty on their faces they thought it was because something was wrong between Jake and me. Angel had run right up to her room.

Jake had the staff all come around to the sitting room, and he went ahead and explained to them all that my mother had passed away and they were to help me with whatever I needed. I tried to tell him not to bother anyone with this. I could do it on my own. I had been down this road twice already. He wouldn't hear of it. I wasn't alone anymore, and there would be no need for me to carry all the stress alone. The driver was to take me everywhere until I had come to terms with my mother's death. Jake figured I wouldn't have my mind on safe driving. He was so right, and Angel would be with me most of the time. The next few days, I spent my time making arrangement for Mom to be put to rest with Ben. We were going to do a morning service the following Saturday. I had to get our local minster, for Dr. Adams was not back, and there was no way I would ask him to do this for me. Not knowing how close he was to my mother.

I picked out a small casket that matched both Ben's and Benjamin's. Mom thought theirs were beautiful, and she also deserved one that was beautiful.

It was raining lightly Saturday morning. I told Angel it was raining because all the angels in heaven were crying because they were so happy that Grandma had gone up to heaven to be with them.

"I'm not happy, Mommy."

Holding her close, I say to her, "I know you're not, Angel. Our tears are because we are sad that Grandma has left us."

The minster begins reading to us.

"Kate, Angel, Jake, it is important to know when you're troubled and worried and sick at heart and your plans are upset and your world falls apart, someone is ready and waiting to share the burden you find too heavy to bear. So with faith, let it go and let God lead the way into a brighter and less troubled day.

"Let you face the trouble that is yours this present minute and count on God to help you and put his mercy in it. And forget the past and the future and dwell wholly on today. For God controls the future and he will direct our way.

"Emma! God be with you and your family. May you rest in peace."

THIRTY-SEVEN

Turning to leave, I saw Dr. Adams standing off by a large tree, and when he saw me, he turned and walk away. That was strange. I wonder what was up with that? I must remember to go see him this week.

"I hope I don't have to come to this place for a very long time, Jake."

"Won't we come and visit Daddy and Grandma anymore, Mommy?"

"Oh yes, we will do that, Angel. Mommy doesn't want to come here and say good-bye to anyone else for many, many years."

"Me too, Mommy."

We went and had lunch and going home to where life was going to change for all of us again. There would be that empty feeling for a few years and always the feeling that we are forgetting someone whenever Christmas comes around. Every holiday is a tough one for a while, but Christmas has to be the worst.

Angel grew up fast and gave us very little trouble in school. She loved to go to school, so that was never an issue. Getting her the help she needed in school was an issue. Jake ended up hiring a retired teacher to come to the house and work with Angel so she could get her marks that she would need to graduate. Angel had problems with her kidneys in grade 10 but was able to do schoolwork from the hospital, so she did just fine.

Angel and Jake had grown very close, and she had told him over the years that she was so happy that he was her daddy.

"You know, Mom, you couldn't have picked a better daddy for me even if you were shopping through the catalogue."

"Well, thank you, Angel," Jake said as he kisses her on top of the head. But remember, your mom didn't pick me. I found you and her at the park."

"Oh, Dad, we weren't lost."

"Oh, but you were! I was meant to find you."

"I'm glad you did." Hugging Jake around the waist, Angel heads for the door; she decides to tell us she has a date. This has become a little bit of a problem. Angel likes all these older guys. Of course when the time came to put down my foot, she just politely told me if I didn't like it, she would just pack her bags and move out. She was fifteen at the time. I let it go because I had seen too many parents try to stop them from doing things and their child would just leave anyways. The parents then would have the police bring them home, and they would go through it all over again until the child finally just left once they were old enough or the child came and went for however long it took for them to finally move out on their own. This is becoming more of the ways today. It seems like they never leave but want to live off Mom and Dad. It becomes a big stress causer in most marriages.

I thought we kept a pretty good handle on Angel until the day she came home to tell us she was moving away with this older man. She was barely out of school. Didn't know what she wanted to do with her life yet and had so much living to do. I tried to talk her out of the move. I had told her if she wanted to move to do it on her own, not with this guy. I was thinking. What is wrong with this guy, he is over half her age. Taking advantage of young girls and taking their virginity away was putting a notch in his belt. So it was obvious that she no longer was a virgin. When that happened, I could not say and it made me sick to know that my daughter no longer talked to me. This guy she was with knew I didn't like anything about him. I read him like a book, and he was getting her out as fast as he could.

He played the "Boo-hoo, poor me. Your mom didn't talk to me a couple of times," and she fell for it hook, line, and sinker. So here I am today trying to figure out what I really have done that has been so horrible that my daughter won't talk to me or see me. The holidays that were always so special to us come and go, and I hear nothing from her. Christmas Eve I sit on my chair in front of the window, and I watch all the lights that come and go. Hoping that one of them was going to be her. When I wake up in the morning, still sitting in my chair, and she hasn't come, then I wait all Christmas Day to hear from her, and again there is nothing but horrible silence.

Jake tries to make it okay, and he knows he doesn't dare say anything because I will blow up at him. To me, it is not Christmas without my Angel; she has always been my Christmas spirit. When I was down at Christmas, she was always the one to pick me up. So Christmas without Angel is like having Christmas without a tree and gifts or the turkey.

The lights of the city come into view, and my cell phone ringing brings me back to the ache in my chest. I'm feeling tired, and checking my phone, I see it is Jake calling. He always knows about what time I will arrive anywhere I go. He knows my driving habits too well. I will get a room for the night and call him to let him know I have arrived safely. Tomorrow I will take a trip down Main Street to where I knew Angel was working to see what I can find out. The butterflies in my stomach made me not want to eat. I didn't think much would stay down and right now. Just being in the same town as Angel has my heart racing. I must remember to take my heart pills as soon as I'm settled in. Going out to eat somewhere was going to be taking a risk of running into her, and I wasn't quite ready for that to happen.

Sometimes the element of surprise is good and will work in your favor. If it doesn't, I have driven a long way just to turn around. Tonight I will lie low and get my bearings, and tomorrow I will make my move. Good God, I sound like I'm getting ready to pounce on my prey. What has become of me thinking like an animal?

There was a small cafe in the hotel, so I ordered a sandwich and some milk just in case I could eat a little later. I needed food to take my heart pills with, so I ordered double. While I waited for my food to be delivered, I called Jake. "Hi, hon."

"So you arrived safely."

"Yes, I did, I got in half hour ago. It feels like a very long trip."

"You know, you and driving don't get along anymore."

"I know, Jake, but you know this is something I have to do on my own."

"So you say. Doesn't mean I have to agree with you."

"No, guess you don't. Please try to understand."

"I am trying, Kate. I feel like you are shutting me out, and there is nothing I can do about it."

"I don't mean to make you feel that way. I have to try to fix whatever is wrong. I don't know what it is, so I don't know how or what I'm looking to do."

"I don't like you there alone. I'm coming to see you this weekend."

"All right, Jake."

"I don't mind saying I'm scared. It has been a long time since I've seen her, and I don't know if I will be able to hold it together when I do."

"Just remember you have waited a long time to do this, so make sure everything you do or say is what you really want."

"I just want to hold my baby girl again. I want to be able to tell her how much I love her and I miss her."

"I know you do, Kate. You have to remember that you are the one who is stepping up, and if she isn't ready to receive you, it could be ugly and painful. Not to mention embarrassing for you. You have no idea what this guy has said or done."

"I know, and that is what worries me the most. I'm hoping to get her alone. It isn't going to happen overnight, I know that, and I'm prepared to do the waiting game."

"Are you really, Kate? I don't think you are. You have always been strong- minded, and you go for whatever you think is right full force."

"Jake, I know I can't turn back, and I know I have to take it slow and easy."

"I hope for your sake, Kate, you can do just that."

"You know, Jake, I have a hard time seeing her face. I used to be able to close my eyes, and she would come so plainly into view. That doesn't happen anymore, and I carry a picture around in my purse as well as in my car so I can see her face. When I'm thinking of her, I pull out my picture. This worries me. What mother forgets her daughter's face?"

"A mother that has gone through hell for her daughter."

"No, a poor mother."

"Kate, you are not nor have you ever been a poor mother. You gave Angel everything you could give her and then some. She is so totally loved by you, and if she can't see that, it is her mistake, not yours. So don't you dare put yourself down to justify what she has done. Angel has chosen this road."

"You mean that guy she is with has."

"Yes, he is a big part in it, but she is a big girl and could have come home at any time. Angel knows I would have gone anytime day or night to pick her up from where she was. That has never been a problem."

"You're right, Jake. You have never given her a reason not to call for a ride. I thank you for that. You always went the extra mile just so Angel could do what Angel wanted to do."

"I'm in the dark about the reason she won't come home or talk to you as much as you are. I'm sorry, I can't help you."

"Just being there so I can talk to you is a big help. Knowing you understand why I'm here instead of there is a big help."

Jake wasn't going to push that any further because he knows Kate will get her back up and that will be the end of their talk. Since this has all happened with Angel, Kate has more than once made me feel that Angel is her daughter and not mine. I know Kate feels bad because of all I have given and done for Angel, she has turned on us this way. But that is just the point. She has turned on both of us, not just her mother. I feel the pain I'm sure as deeply as Kate. Angel has been my daughter now for twenty-four years in every way a daughter could be. So for Kate to think that this is only tearing her heart out, she is sadly mistaken. I miss Angel as much as Kate does. I don't know how she can't see that.

To come home and have no Angel greeting me as I come through the door or to be pulling my leg about something at our supper table. Not having my little girl asking me for advice or just coming over because she needs a hug has had me turn inside out. I kept myself together for Kate. I needed to be Kate's rock as I had promise Emma I would take good care of them. *Well, Emma, I'm sorry to have let you down. In both cases.*

"You know I'm here for you, Kate, whatever time of day or night, please call."

"I will, Jake, thank you and good night."

"Good night, Kate, I love you."

"I love you too, Jake, take care." Once I hung up from talking to Jake, I put my things away and thought I should try and eat. Then I will have my bath, and then I will try to get some sleep. I can't see that happening but maybe. I made the decision to be here; I am here now. I will take it one day at a time; after all, I have nothing but time.

Eating and bathing took up some of my evening but found I had a lot more hours to kill than I wanted to. I kept replaying the scenario over and over in my head. If we were to meet up unexpectedly. More so for Angel than me. After all, I am the one here looking to see my daughter.

Angel is not looking for me, so she wouldn't be expecting to run into me anywhere.

Some of the scenarios I had in my head were not very good. I tried to see it on the positive side, but seeing how she hasn't talked to me in three years, I can't see there being any good scenarios. I only hope that if the time comes and we are to run into each other and Angel were to recognize me, she will be so shocked and perhaps surprised enough to take it as we had always told her. Things happen for a reason. Of course this reason being because her mother has made it happen. Angel will be too surprised, I hope, to get too pissed off right away.

Not being able to take her into a loving hug would be hard for me. I'm also afraid that time might have made us strangers. She is older now and I would hope wiser. But obviously not wise enough, but maybe that will come in time.

What does a mother say to her daughter that she hasn't been able to talk to or have any communication with for this long? I have had friends that I haven't seen for so long, and when you do, it's like "hi, how are you," "that's nice," and "good-bye." This isn't what I want with my daughter. I know she is the second part of this equation and him the third, so I don't hold all the cards. I hope to be able to play with my cards close to my chest and know how to play blind man's bluff if the need arises.

I have also wondered if I should have booked a room at the mental hospital before coming this far. Being afraid they might think I'm already unstable and book me before I'm ready, so I chose to wait that one out. Her rejection could be more than I'm able to bear. It has taken me two years to be able to feel like I have wanted to live since she left. Nothing was worth getting up for. I have done nothing but put in time. Long lonely hours, day after day, waiting to hear from her or being able to see my daughter.

My daughter has no idea how her leaving has killed a big part of me. I'm looking to be reborn, and she holds the key.

It was a very restless sleep and a very long night. Tossing and turning had me awake most of the night, so if I were to see Angel today, it would be a fright for her. The suitcases that I now carry that hang below my eyes were something I have become accustomed to. Of course I have cried a lot and for long periods of time, so cucumbers and I have become the best of friends. They do take the puffiness down as well as ice packs except the ice is too cold for me. I had actually called Jake four times during the night, each time with him offering to come to my rescue. Telling me that I didn't have to go through this alone. Each time I found it hard to turn him down, knowing within my heart this is something only I can do.

The eerie quiet of the room and not having him within walking distance made me feel like I was in a dream and on this planet alone. All I needed was the mist to be coming up around me and having everything become distorted with horrible sounds, and there would have been the making of a movie in it somewhere.

THIRTY-EIGHT

I got up and had something light to eat so I could take my medication. Letting them know at the front desk that I would be staying for a couple more days for sure. I knew that I wanted to get downtown before the shops opened up to be able to sit and do a surveillance of people who will be going into the shop where Angel used to work. Did I say surveillance? Hell, I don't know anything about that. I will stick out like a sore thumb I'm thinking with my big hat and newspaper. Isn't that how it's done? Oh yea, I must remember to get a coffee. I think these things all go hand in hand.

My stomach is doing some flip-flops as I pull into the space just a block down from the shop. Now I sit and wait, and wait some more. Coffee is gone, and newspaper is read. Damn, I can't remember what they do after this. It has been too long since I've watched anything like this on TV. Anything like this is right. I could be hauled away to a loony bin if people only knew what I was doing. Getting restless and wondering if I should go get another coffee, seeing how I don't have a partner riding with me, I didn't really want to leave my post in case Angel were to show up after I left. I know they have different shifts, so I will have to wait out the day. If I haven't seen anything of her toward the end of the day, then I will go in and see what I can find out.

At lunchtime I felt it was safe to go get coffee and a sandwich. This time I was smart enough to buy a thermos and fill it up too. Wish I could have bought a potty. Good thing the restaurant was at the end of the block. I just hated getting in and out of the car. That would have people watching I'm sure, so I waited to go pee until I was bursting. At one point, I thought I would pee myself. Once there I couldn't go at first I had held it too long. Damn, I hate when that happens.

I was almost ready to doze off when a young lady pushing a stroller came around the corner. This had me sitting up and taking notice. I was sure that was Angel. My heart was racing so fast I was thinking of taking another metoprolol tartrate; these are the pills I take to keep my heart from racing. As she came up to the door, she had to go around the stroller to open the door, and I had to stop myself from jumping out of the car and calling out to her. My daughter was pregnant. Now the child in the stroller didn't look to be that old. Was she babysitting or was that child hers too? Oh my god, I'm going to be a grandmother and I didn't even know. How could Angel do this to me? To the baby? How do you raise a child and not have them know their grandparents? I wonder if his side will get to know the baby. I wonder if she is even with the same guy. Surely she would have called me. OH god, Angel, why won't you call? Why won't you come home?

I sat and shed tears for my daughter, which I have done so many times, but today I also shed tears for a grandchild that I may never see. Oh, Jake, I wish you were here now, my love. I'm so shaken I don't know what to do next. For Christ's sake, what would they do on TV?

Maybe I will be wishing I hadn't started this. The saying "what you don't know won't hurt you" really applies right now. Oh god, Angel, what has happened that you and I are strangers? How can a person just walk out of another person's life the way you have and not seem to have it bother you? Angel, you are loved so much and missed so much. Your baby would be loved so much and will be missed horribly. You both are missing out on more than you realize.

The door of the shop opens, and Angel comes back out. She stops and is looking around. Aww shit, does she see me as I put the paper back up to my face? Angel pulls her sunglasses down now that she will be walking into the sun. Bending over and saying something to the little one in the stroller before she leaves.

Now do I follow her? Should I wait? My daughter is walking away with not a bit of knowledge that her mother is within a block of her. Holding my hand over my chest, the tears come, and I can't stop them. This is like having her walk out of my life twice. No mother should have to feel this pain. Taking a deep breath and talking to myself. If someone sees me sitting here crying, that is really going to bring on suspicion.

Okay, okay. What to do now? I would like to know about the second child. So I will go in and browse and see what I hear. I hadn't realized I was shaking until I got out of my car, and my legs were shaking so bad I hardly could stand up. Okay, Kate, take some breaths and take your time. I decided I would walk up and down this side of the street and look in the windows until I had my wits back before entering the shop where Angel used to work. As I made my way down the corner, I saw a park, and there was Angel and the wee one. She had it out on the swing. It looked to be a little girl. Being this far away, I couldn't tell for sure. I just step back a bit and watched until all of a sudden, like she knew she was being watched, she put the little one back in the stroller and walked off. She was walking with such vigor that she was almost running. Why? What was up? Perhaps she is just late to be somewhere else. Maybe he is going to be home, and she will be in trouble if she isn't. He seemed to be very controlling from what we had known of him. Could it be that she is babysitting and the child's parents will be picking it up soon?

Surely she doesn't know I'm here, or does she? Can Angel feel my presence as I know I would feel hers. After all this time, is my daughter still tuned in to me? Is she getting an uncomfortable feeling? Not too sure why, can't really put her finger on it maybe. I really do hope so. Although I don't want her running scared and locking herself away. She knows I handle the unknown just fine, but it used to scare her. I would always tell her to face it with interest and learn from it, don't be scared of your sixth sense. We all have it; it's just that some are able to use it more than others. I being one of them and that used to freak her out.

Going into the shop and finding them busy was a good thing. It gave me time to just look and eavesdrop if possible. I was in there for about twenty minutes when the young girl working came over to see if I needed any help.

"May I help you?"

"Not really sure what I'm looking for. I would like to get something nice for my husband. He has been away awhile, and I wanted to surprise him."

"I'm new at this, but maybe I can help. I don't know much about the clothing yet, and my trainer is off on sick leave."

"Oh, sorry to hear that." Now is the time, you fool. "Hope it's not that terrible flu that is going around."

"No, madam, she is expecting and is having troubles with her kidneys. They say the pregnancy is causing stress or something."

I'm finding it hard to breathe with the news that my daughter is not well. I think I must look it 'cause the young girl was asking, "Are you all right?"

"Oh yes, just a bit of a head rush. I will be fine." I start to push some shirts aside like I'm looking but not seeing a thing. "How long has she been having that problem?"

"I guess she had some trouble with her first one. The little girl had to be delivered by caesarean to save them both."

Now before I do faint with this, I had better find out who she is talking about for sure.

"This young girl work here long?"

"Oh yes, three years now or more."

"Wish her well next time you see her."

"Too bad you wouldn't have been earlier. She was here with her little girl but had to take her to a sitter. Because Angel had a doctor's appointment."

Now I needed to sit down.

"You don't look so well, can I get you a chair?"

"Please."

She leaves to get me a chair. My god, Angel, what are you doing? Is what was going through my head when the girl came back with the chair.

"Here, madam, you best sit a bit."

"Thank you."

"Should I be calling for help or something?"

"No, thank you. You've heard of menopause well. I have it bad, and sometimes it really hits. I will be fine here shortly. It passes about as fast as it hits."

"If you are sure, I will get you a glass of water."

"Thank you, that would be very thoughtful of you." I couldn't help but think about Angel. What the hell would she be thinking? The first baby was hard on her; why would she have another?

"Here you go, madam."

"Thank you. Does that young girl have a good doctor here in town? I sure hope so.

"She has a doctor here, and there is a specialist that comes to see her every month. Next month he will start coming to see her twice a month until it is time to deliver the baby. If she has any problems, she just has to call him."

"Well, that is good to know. Where is the clinic from here?"

"It is two streets over and down about the middle. It is a big blue building, you can't miss it. Are you thinking of maybe seeing a doctor yourself."

"I might later."

"I think that might be a good idea. You're really not looking well."

"If it doesn't pass, I will, but for now, I would like to get my husband that black and white shirt."

"All right, I will get it packaged up for you then."

"Thank you." Taking my package and the news I was just told, I headed to my car. I wanted to throw up so bad, and I wanted so much to talk to Angel. Oh god, what is she doing? What is that idiot that she is with doing to my daughter? Why in hell would you take that kind of a chance, and for God's sake, why didn't he call me? I felt he didn't have much upstairs, but good God, any man would know when to call a mother. OH, Angel. I pull out and go back to my hotel room. I needed to talk to Jake; he would tell me what I should do. I could probably figure it out myself if I calm down and think about it. Right at this moment, I needed a fresh strong cup of coffee and a headache pill. Maybe a few pills. I went into the cafe and got both coffee and pills and just sat there. I will give my head a little time before calling Jake. I hate bothering him at work with personal problems. He can't do anything, and many times he is sitting with other men, so I would sooner wait until I know he should be at home. Calling the house number, I left him a message for him to call me when he got home. I tried to sound cool and calm so he wouldn't panic. It was a very hard thing to do, but I managed, I think.

Once my coffee was down, I went back to my room and took a bath. I knew Jake wouldn't be home for about an hour yet. Lying back in the tub, I got to thinking about what I wanted to do. First of all, I want to find out who her doctor is and then find out what it is that is happening with her. Why is the pregnancy being so hard on her kidneys?

Angel had some problems in school, but no one ever said pregnancy would cause a problem. I also wanted to know how far long she was with this pregnancy and what kind of danger she was in. Were they going to do another caesarean before she went full-term or got into trouble? Will the problem she have be passed on to her children, especially her daughter?

I have a granddaughter, and she doesn't even know me. I could be standing right beside her, and she wouldn't know I was her grandmother. Does she know what a grandmother is? I have been cheated out of two years plus of enjoying my granddaughter. How can Angel do this? Does she not remember all the time she spent with my mother her grandmother? She and my mother were so close, and I would not have dreamed of doing that to Angel or my mom. What a waste of time and no memories being made.

Angel, I'm so angry with you and so hurt. How could you do that to that precious child and to me? Or herself. How will she explain where Grandma has been all this time? My cell phone starts to ring, and I struggled to get out of the tub. How silly it was of me to leave it in the other room. Just wrapping in a towel and running to grab my phone. I see it was Jake calling. I knew he would call right back; he always does when he misses me the first time. When it started to ring this time, I was able to get it on the first ring.

"Hi, Kate."

"Hi, Jake, how are you?"

"Better yet, how are you?"

"Oh, Jake." I break down.

"Come on, Kate, what is it? Did you see Angel?"

"Humm hum" was all I could say.

"And what happened, Kate?"

"I'm a grandma, Jake, I didn't even know it."

"Oh, sweetheart, I'm sorry, but that's great, isn't it?"

"How can being a grandma be great when you can't hold or talk to them?"

"Oh, it didn't go well than I take it?"

"I only saw her, I didn't talk to her. I saw her with her daughter, and, Jake, she is pregnant again and has kidney trouble. Guess it was a pretty bad last time. She had to have a caesarean to save both her and the baby."

"Oh, Kate, I'm sorry to hear that. How did you find all this out already?"

"After she left the store, I went in, and the young girl who is taking her places was very talkative. Didn't take much bating to get her to talk."

"Lucky you. Now what are you going to do?"

"I'm hoping to find out who her doctor is and get some questions answered."

"You think anyone is going to talk to you, Kate? She probably hasn't told anyone about you. Seeing how bad it was last time. I would have thought your daughter would have wanted you there."

"I don't understand, Jake, what have I done that is so terrible that my daughter's life is in danger and no one lets me know. I cannot fathom why. I never mistreated her. I was always there for her and love her more than life itself. I would give her my heart if she needed it."

"No! Kate, I would put my foot down to that. You are my life, and I would not let you end yours for her. I'm sorry, but some things I can deal with. Losing you isn't one of them."

"Jake, she will have two babies to take care of, my life is almost over. So if that is what it took to see that she could continue to raise her babies, then that is just what I would do. I wouldn't ask any questions nor would I ask your permission. I'm sorry, Jake, but it would not be open for discussion."

"Are you serious, Kate? You would do something like that to me, and I wouldn't have a say in the matter?"

"Jake, she is so young, and her babies, they would need their mother."

"Kate, she has shown you that isn't true."

"How can you say that?"

"Where has she been for the last three years or so, Kate, while you have gone through hell waiting for her? She has shown you just how much she has needed her mother even though she has had a rough time with her pregnancies. I, on the other hand, do need you, Kate, and would miss you terribly, so please before you do anything stupid, you talk to me."

"I'm just saying I love my daughter and I would do anything for her."

"Oh, baby, I know you would, and I'm sorry she has been too selfish to know what kind of love her mother has for her."

"Now what are your plans for tomorrow?"

"I know where the clinic is, so I'm going to go see if I can find her doctor and maybe get a chance to talk to him. Until I do that, I don't know what else to do."

"That's sounds like a good start. Just go slow, Kate, and keep your cool. You will catch more with honey than with vinegar."

"I know, Jake, thank you. I love you."

"I love you too."

"Can I come and see you this weekend?"

"I will let you know tomorrow, okay? If I'm staying in this hotel, it will probably be safe 'cause she lives close to downtown. So the chances of her running into me here are slim. Unless they like the food in this restaurant, which I can't see why it would be better than the ones downtown."

"All right, I will wait for you to call tomorrow then. Good night, Kate, I love you."

"Good night, Jake. I love you too."

The evening was very uneventful. I could not get my mind off the fact that I was a grandma. I should be out shopping for that little girl. I should have been able to share all her firsts with my daughter. I should have been there while she was in trouble, and I should be there now. I close my eyes and pray, "Good God, can you not find a way to get Angel and I back together? She is in need of a loving mother, and I am in need of my daughter, my grandchildren. Please open her eyes and make her see that I'm here for her, for them. Is there not away that you can rejoin us in any way at all? I pray in your son's name, Jesus Christ. Amen."

THIRTY-NINE

First thing in the morning, I headed for the clinic. Sitting and waiting for it to open, I wondered what Angel and her daughter were doing today. Wouldn't it be great if I could have just driven over there to see them, have coffee with my daughter like I used to? Like my mom did with us. There weren't too many mornings Mom missed having coffee with us on her way to wherever she was going. She always made a point of stopping in to see us. I knew it was more to see Angel than me, but I loved her for it anyways. I would give anything to have those days back. My phone called me back into the present taking me from the past.

"Hi."

"Good morning, Kate, how are you today?"

"Good morning, Jake, I'm okay, and you?"

"I'm as good as I can be with you so far away."

"I know I miss you too."

"What are you doing today?"

"At the present, I'm sitting outside the clinic."

"Oh, the case of the early bird gets the worm."

"Something like that."

"Good luck today, Kate, call me later, let me know how you made out. Please."

"I will, Jake, hope you have a good day. I love you."

"I love you too, Kate, bye." He was gone. Here I sit waiting. Looking at my watch, it said nine fifteen. Well, it should be open. Why haven't I seen anyone going in? Going up to the door, I find out that today it is closed. Oh, for Pete's sake, now what? Taking time to think, I chose to go back to the shop to see if I can get an address of where Angel lives. This wasn't as easy as it seems, although the young girl remembered me from yesterday. I told her I would like to send Angel some flowers and wish her well. Because of the damn privacy act, she was hesitant in giving me her address. She had pulled out her card, and just then someone came in, and she excused herself to go help. So I just turn the card around, and pulling out a pen, I wrote down the address on my hand. I left while she had her back turn to me. I wasn't worried. I got all I needed from there. I wasn't going to have to go back and face the young girl again. I probably will never be back in that store now that I have Angel's address. I was smiling to myself as I climbed into my car. Sitting, I finally let out my breath. I thought that just maybe, she would come calling after me. I didn't know what I would have done. Maybe pretend I didn't hear her. This gave me a great feeling. I haven't had Angel's address for over three years now. So if nothing else, I have accomplished that much. If I don't get to see her, I can send her and the children gifts anytime I want to now. I could write to Angel and actually send this one instead of putting them in a shoe box for her to get whenever. Maybe now I could start sending those shoe boxes to her that I have collected up for her. Each month she has been gone, there is a shoe box with different things in it. Special little things that I saw that I know Angel would like along with a card letting her know how much I love her and how much I miss her.

Driving around until I saw the cutest little house for rent. I would like to see the inside of that house. I pulled over to the sidewalk and was going to get out when movement caught my eye. It was Angel, and she was letting her dog out. Well, I'll be damned, she still has Minnie. Her house was just up the street four houses from this one on the other side. I slowly went up to the little house and looked in the window. Yes, that is my kind of house, all right. Hardwood floors and clean. I take the number off the door and go back to my car to call it. Closing my eyes and saying, "Thank you, God." My mother's saying of "Everything happens for a reason" came back to me loud and clear. A woman answered right away. She seemed pleasant enough and said she would come down right away when she found out I was at the house already. It took her fifteen minutes to get there. While I waited, I looked over the yard. It had been well kept, and the trees were huge. Not like the ones we had at home, but around this little house, they looked huge.

Mary Ann was her name, and she was very easy to talk to. I told her I didn't know how long I would be there, but there was a good possibility of me looking to buy. She said I could have first choice of the house to buy if I wanted it. She doesn't have it up for sale, but if the right buyer came along, she would sell. The house belonged to her mother, and she was now in the nursing home and wouldn't be needing the house any longer. It came with some furniture. Her mother took what she wanted and had room for. What was there was all I needed. A bed and a table, love seat, and chair. I would go and pick up the things that I needed. I was feeling great. I paid for three months so she would be happy knowing I wasn't pulling out anytime soon or overnight sort of thing. Mary Ann gave me the keys, and she left. There I stood looking out my window at the house where my daughter and her daughter were living; I was in heaven. Wait till I tell Jake. He will be so happy for me. Walking on cloud nine, I decided to go and get a few things, and I would stop and get my clothes and check out of the hotel. "Yes, thank you, Lord." The rest of the day went by so fast. It didn't take me long to put my clothes away. I polished up the house and got rid of the closed-up smell. This was great, life was great, I almost have my daughter back, I can just feel it. This feels so right. It had a nice drive in the back, so that is where I parked just so Angel didn't see me coming and going. I didn't want her to see too much of me just in case she recognizes me. Not sure how she would, but I didn't want to take that chance. Not yet any ways. Once I was settled, I made myself a cup of tea and sat in the big chair that was by the window and watched Angel outside with her daughter. The window had sheers on them, so she wouldn't know I was watching them. I wonder what she called her daughter; guess that was one of the questions I overlooked asking the young girl in the store. In time I will find out.

Angel put the little one on a tricycle and had her peddling around. They were coming right past the house, my breath caught, and I stood very still, so Angel wouldn't see me in the window. Oh, what a beautiful little girl. Blond curly hair and big blue eyes. Angel walked like she was in pain. Oh, how I wanted to go to her. Was it her size in pregnancy that made her walk that way, or was it the pain from her kidneys that made her walk like that? Once again she glanced around as though she could feel me watching her. "That's right, sweetheart, Mommy is here. Please feel my love for you and know I mean you no harm." I could tell something was making her uncomfortable, and they headed back to the house. They stayed outside but in their yard. Angel was a very protective mom, I could tell.

I decided to call Jake. I couldn't wait to tell him the good news.

"Hi, hon, guess what?"

"You talked to Angel?"

"How I wish, but no. It is almost as good."

"Lay it on me then."

"I'm renting a house, four houses down from where Angel and her daughter are living."

"You're renting?"

"Yes, I'm in it now, isn't that great?"

"I guess so, Kate."

"You don't sound so happy for me."

"I didn't know you would be getting a house."

"I didn't know either, but this is perfect for me and will be cheaper than the hotel was."

"Okay, so what does this mean for us?"

"Oh, Jake, you can come down. You just have to come in the back way and make sure she doesn't see you. We have a house, and you will also be able to see our granddaughter."

"That is the first time you have said that, Kate."

"Said what, Jake?"

"That I have a granddaughter."

"I'm sorry, Jake, I didn't mean to hurt you like that. I guess I was just so wrapped up in all of this. I didn't think about how I was saying things. Of course you have a granddaughter. Will you come this weekend then?"

"When have I ever said no to you, Kate?"

"All right then, I will cook you a supper that you will really like, and we will sit and watch her play with a glass of wine. She maybe twosomething, but we can still celebrate her birth."

"Okay, Kate, we will do that. I'm glad you're happy, Kate. It is nice to hear that smile back in your voice."

"This isn't over, Jake, by a long shot, but it is a start."

"You're right, Kate, we have to start somewhere. I hope it all plans out for you." "For us, Jake, for us."

"Sorry, for us, Kate. I love you."

"I love you too, Jake, talk to you tomorrow. Good night."

"Good night, Kate, and I love you too." Oh, Kate, I hope you're not headed for a big fall. Jake worries about what will happen if Angel rejects Kate. He knows Kate was close to the breaking point at one time after Angel had left. Would Angel's rejection break Kate this time and especially now that she knows she has a grandchild and another one on the way. Would it be too much for Kate to accept the fact that Angel isn't ready to want her back in their lives. Children or no children. What is he supposed to do? Drag her home and say she has to wait until Angel makes the move. That isn't going to happen. The best he can do is be prepared to grab Kate if she falters and be ready to try and put her back together like Humpty Dumpty and pray he has more luck than they did doing so. It was a long night for Jake. He got up early and was done work early; there were a few things he wanted to do before heading out to see Kate. Stopping at the drugstore was a must. The next two days went by slow for Jake as he was excited about the week coming up. Kate didn't know he took a week off work to be with her. He wasn't going to tell her until the weekend was over, and she would be expecting him to leave.

He only hoped that Kate would receive it well and not think of him as he were intruding on her plans. He felt he had to make her understand how much she meant to him. Without her, his life means nothing. She and Angel had given him reason to go on living.

The last three years have been hell watching Kate go through this. She wouldn't talk to Jake anymore about her feeling, and he knew he had shut her down. He had totally thought that Angel would be back before the week was up. When that didn't happen, Jake was just as stumped as Kate as to why. There was nothing so horrible that should have kept Angel away. The guy in her life was the problem and until she grew up and was able to see him for who he really was. He is a horrible man, and we use the term *man* loosely. The little bit of texting that Kate tried to do with Angel didn't go so well because he always got involved. I wanted Kate to change her number, but she wouldn't hear of it because someday Angel would need her and she had already told Angel that she wouldn't ever change her number so she could call whenever she needed to. I had asked Kate why she would do this to herself. Her reply was "I am her mother, and I always will be. I can't just turn that off. Once a mother always a mother. She will have children someday, and she will understand then." All I could do was shake my head and take Kate into my arms and hold her while she cried.

Kate has shut me out a lot, and I have to find a way back in. I know she still loves me, but the strain that this has caused between us is almost more than I can handle. I know I need this week with Kate. Maybe now that she is able to visually see her daughter and granddaughter, perhaps we will be able to talk like we used to. Maybe I can get my Kate back.

Getting everything done that he wanted to. Heading out a day earlier than planned to find Kate. He would call her later when he got into town for the house number. He wasn't going to let her know he was even there until she opens her door. He was going in the front door. He wasn't hiding from Angel, and he was ready to have a few choice words with the guy she was with. Jake is thinking it is time to show Angel just what kind of man she has. Maybe if he talks to us in person as he has while texting, it may shake her up enough to make her see him for what he really is.

He had texted Kate once and said that he had her right where he wants her. What the hell did that mean? Kate never replied, but I do know that Kate went for counseling over all of this. She had no idea how to handle this, and it had been happening for some time before she finally told me about it. I know if I have my way, that loser is going to know it was my wife he was talking to. Angel can be mad at me a little longer. But she will see what a real man does when someone mistreats his wife. I really hope their little one won't be around to see Grandpa lose his cool.

A memory like "Yea, the first time I met my grandpa, he decked my dad." I don't think Kate would approve of this.

This trip gave Jake lots of time to go back over their years together and remembering the good times that they had with Angel all the time she was growing up and becoming that beautiful woman she had turned into. All these memories still outweighed the bad. In his books anyway. He was feeling like he had let Kate down because he was more a laid-back kind of person. Didn't let any of this really get to him. By the time he saw what it was doing to Kate, she was on the way out of their door and maybe their marriage. How could he have been so blind? He has always known how Angel was Kate's life and to Kate life isn't worth living without her. He knew Kate loved him; there was never any doubt about that. But being the mother that she is, her child would always come first when push comes to shove. Jake didn't hold that against Kate; he was proud to know that no matter what, Kate would be there for her child. He knew that if they had ever been able to have a child, he would have considered himself a lucky man to have such a woman as Kate being the mother of his child. Kate is one of these women who should have had many children. She was like a mother hen and had always took Angel's friends in under her wing. Kate was known as Mom to many of the young girls and boys in town. Many would stop over and see her whenever they came back to town once they were finished school. A few had quit coming once Angel wasn't around anymore.

The lights of the city came into view, so he calls Kate.

"Hi, Kate, how's things today?"

"Hi, Jake, good, what about you?"

"Good. Just finishing up my trip."

"Did you start early today?"

"Yes, I did, I wanted an early evening. Kate, I should get your house number so when I get there on the weekend, I will know where I'm going."

"Okay, I'm at 2211 Evergreen Street. It is in the older neighborhood. Easy to find.

"Oh, I think I will be able to find you. I have worked the bush long enough to find street addresses." He talks to her all the way up to her door, hangs up in time to ring her doorbell. She tells him to hang on, someone is at her door. Her mouth drops.

"Jake! Jake, is that you?"

FORTY

Stepping inside and taking Kate into his arms. "Yes, Kate, it's me."

"I love what you did with your hair, but can't say I'm too fond of the missing mustache."

"Really, now why is that?"

"You look so young."

"What did I say about you?"

"What? You getting even?"

"No, silly, I'm joining a good cause." He kisses me like I've been missing for a year.

"Wow."

"Do you have coffee in this little teahouse?"

"I will have. You should have told me you were coming. I would have had it ready."

"No, I liked the look on your face when you open the door. It's nice to know I can still put a smile to this pretty face of yours."

"Oh, all right, but you have to let go of me if you want coffee." While Kate went to make coffee, Jake checked out the little house, and it was all Kate said it was. He could see them living in this house and loving it. Our mansion has outgrown us since Angel left. If she and her children were ever to come back, then it would be great and the children would learn to love it there. With all the wide-open space.

"Kate, don't you think having this love seat sitting in front of the window is a little too conspicuous?"

"With the shears closed, you can't see it from outside. I already went for a walk to see if that was possible."

"Glad you thought about it and checked it out."

"Now, Jake, really."

"Well, I could see you not thinking that far ahead. With everything on your mind." "Guess you're right, sorry."

"No need to be sorry."

"Just be careful." He kisses her check as she hands him his coffee, and they sit down in the love seat together.

"Jake, do you think this is how it was for Mom and Dr. Adams when they were sitting in the love seat?"

"Somehow, I don't think so, Kate."

"Why do you say that?"

"Well, first off, he didn't love her as I love you, and secondly, they weren't spying on their neighbors."

"You don't think he loved Mom?"

"I don't know, Kate. I have no idea how they felt about each other. You would know more about that than me."

"No, I don't. I had always wished he and Mom would get together. It never seemed like either one of them were interested in the other. I always felt it was a waste. They were both lonely people and free to be with whoever they wanted to be with."

"Guess it doesn't really matter, now does it?"

"No, guess not." The rest of the evening, they just sat in their love seat and chatted about whatever would come up. With it being nighttime, they couldn't see anything of next door, so Kate just pulled her heavy drapes as well.

Finally, at four in the morning, they decided to go to bed. All Kate had was a double. This made it cozy like it used to be. The big king-size bed back home always made her feel lost and small. This double was for a loving couple; there was no room to be mad. So Jake and I made good use of our time.

Waking to the sun shining in on our faces. It was so warm and inviting. I got up first and put on the coffee. We had to wait for twenty minutes or so as I didn't have a fast coffee maker. Jake was able to have his shower, and I was in my bath when he brought the coffee in. He hadn't sat on the toilet with his coffee for a long time. It had become the one time he said he could talk to me without chasing me around. I never sat and drank a full cup of coffee. I always had something I felt I had to do.

Then we got busier, and he quit the coffee on the toilet thing. Thinking back, I can't even remember when that happened. That is so strange as to how that happens. You start out doing all these little things with each other. Now you sit back a few years later and look at how things are now. You wonder when did it all change. Why did it all change? And do you like where your relationship is at now? Aww no, I don't, and I hope to change it soon.

We get dressed, and we go out for a walk around the area. Of course we were watching to see Angel and her little one. We were early and were back home sitting on the veranda with our coffee. I had on my big brim hat and large white sunglasses. Jake had on his cap and sunglasses. We thought we look like a retired couple.

Jake and I were in awe of the little girl when we saw her go by on her tricycle later. Jake said she reminded him of Angel even though Angel was older than what this little one is now when he had first met her. Especially with Minnie at her side.

When they went by the second time, we heard Angel say to her daughter, "Be careful, Elisabeth, you can tip over if you go too fast." This brought a lump to my throat remembering how Ben used to say that to her. Jake knew it was hitting home, and he reached over and took a hold of my hand and squeezing it lightly so I would look at him and not them.

Jake saw lots of Angel's ways in her actions. As Angel brought her by, we had our newspapers up pretending to be reading. We must have looked like a pair of fools. Something out of a comic magazine, I'm sure. Just so we didn't stick out, Jake got up and turned his back to them and poured us some more coffee. Then bending over as if he were looking at something that I was showing him in the paper that I had.

"Just look at me, Kate, they will be gone soon."

Elisabeth was having troubles trying to stay on the sidewalk, and Angel was having trouble bending over to keep her on the sidewalk. I wanted to go and help so badly, and Jake knew it. He just put his hand on mine and put enough pressure to keep me in my seat.

They might have been there all of three minutes, but it felt like half an hour. God, to be so close and not being able to say hi was killing me. I wanted to pick that little girl up and say, "Hi, I'm your grandma, and I love you as big as the sky." They got back to the other side, and there wasn't much more than Elisabeth playing outside with Minnie. Angel watched over her but mainly from the house.

We had moved in and sat in the love seat.

"You know, Jake, I want to go over there and just lay it on the line, and force Angel to tell her daughter who we are."

"In her condition, I don't think that would be wise, Kate. She will be having the baby soon. Maybe then if you are still here, you can go over one day."

"Still here. You damn right, I will still be here. I'm not going home until I have talked to my daughter and have met her children. I didn't come here to play hide-and- seek and go home empty."

"If you didn't come to play hide-and-seek, why are you hiding behind sunglasses and shear drapes?"

"Because I don't know what to do without making things worse. I know she isn't well, and I don't want to cause her any more stress. When I came here with my plans, I didn't know she was a mom and that she was pregnant and sick. These things change everything."

"Yes, it does. So maybe you should get a phone number and try talking to her first. See how that goes, then you will know more of what you should do."

"You think calling her is the answer?"

"I don't think it would be as bad as just showing up on her doorstep or asking her in for coffee as they walk by."

"Getting her phone number won't be easy. I don't think they will trust be back at the shop where she worked."

"There is always a way. Maybe I will be able to sweet-talk her into giving it to me."

"You? How will you do that?"

"I don't know, I will think of something. Why don't you take me to the shop, and we will see what I can do?"

Are you for real? You really want to do this?"

You think you are the only one who can play private detective?" We laugh as we go get into the car and head downtown. I pulled up in front of the shop, and Jake goes in and wasn't more than five minutes and comes out with a big grin on his face. Waving a piece of paper in my face as he climbs into the car.

"Now how and the hell did you do that with all this privacy act that is out there?"

"Wouldn't you like to know?"

"Did you pay like they do on TV?"

"Kate, do I look like that big a fool. Those guys always pay way more than they should for what little they get told."

"I think so too. So what did you say?"

"I told them I was Angel's uncle and heard she was working there. That I was passing through town and I had hoped to see her."

"That's all you said?"

"Yep. She told me she was off sick and was going to give me her address. I said a phone number would be better, then I could see if she was up to company."

"She fell for that right away and wrote it out for me, simple as pie."

"How would you know? You have never made a pie."

"Oh, you're right. It was simple though."

"So I see now we best get going." Kate hung the number on her fridge and looked at it many times. Picking up the phone and dialing the number but never pushing the Send button. These cell phones are very good for people who second-guess themselves as I was doing. This went on for the rest of the weekend. We never saw no man coming around, and so we tried to think up reasons. I knew what I wished for, but by the shape she was in, he was still around.

When it came later Sunday afternoon and Jake wasn't in any hurry to leave, I asked, "Are you not going home, Jake?"

"I am home, Kate."

"What?"

"My home is wherever you are."

"But your work?"

"It will wait, I took another week off, there is nothing to worry about. Remember, I don't even need to work, it was just a time killer for me."

"Yea, I know. I'm glad you decided to come."

"Me too, and don't you try to talk me into leaving early. We can do this together. You and I. We took the vows about partners, remember?" As he wraps his arms around me. "Kate, together we can do anything if we do it together."

"I know you're right, except I feel this is my problem. I don't know what went wrong or how it went wrong or even when it went wrong. So fixing it is going to be hard."

"You cannot do it alone, and you don't have to."

"You don't understand, Jake." Going over and sitting in the big chair.

"Then make me understand."

I couldn't bring myself to say anything for a few minutes. Can't he see. I sit with my head hung and my hands folded together.

"Come on, Kate, talk to me."

"I'm embarrassed of Angel."

"Embarrassed of Angel, why?"

"After all you did for us, for her. All you have given to her, and she treats you like this. I'm sorry, Jake. I don't know what else to say."

"Kate, you don't need to be sorry. You have done nothing wrong."

I become very emotional, and Jake just lifts me out of the chair and takes me over to the love seat; we sit down, and I fall asleep with him holding me.

Jake never went back to work; he took a leave of absence. He told them he had family matters to deal with it. He would check in with them on a daily basis but wouldn't be coming in because he would be out of town for a while. We just sat around in the sun and watched and read. Angel did not know we were in the house across the road from her. Jake and I kept up our disguises, and we weren't overly careful anymore. She didn't seem to notice us. The man from hell was back for a while and then gone again, so we took it he must be working out of town. Angel would have more time to herself, and I didn't think she was liking it. Angel never liked to be alone at night. During the day, no problem. Nighttime she would always spook herself somehow. Thinking she heard something outside or by watching a spooky show.

I knew that they were going to be doing a caesarean on her shortly, so I didn't want to cause her any stress. Like Jake had pointed out, we weren't going anywhere. So we just sat and watched her daughter, our granddaughter, play with her dog Minnie. Learning to love your grandchild from a distance wasn't easy. That brought back the note Mom had left for me, so looking up into the bright blue sky, I say, "Boy, Mom, I hope you're right, and I hope you know I need you right now. I need your arms around me telling me everything is going to be all right. I don't know if I can do this loving-from-a- distance thing very good." Closing my eyes, wrapping my arms around myself, and trying to draw the strength that I know my mom would be sending my way. At midnight, my cell phone beeps. Who would be texting me at this time? Rolling over and picking up my phone, I read, "Hey." I don't recognize the number.

I answer, "Hey yourself."

The reply comes back as "I miss you, my friend."

I reply, "Me too."

The reply was "I miss you, my best friend."

Now this has me sitting up and taking notice. Thinking this is this my daughter? So I reply, "I don't have a best friend anymore."

The reply was "What about B. C. Lady?"

I reply, "Where in B. C." I have a friend in B. C., and if she says the right name, then I will know it is her.

But the reply was "I miss you, my best friend."

My reply, "So you keep saying."

"I need you now, my best friend." This has me a little panicky.

Thinking it is Angel and maybe she needs help over there, I jumped the gun and say, "Please tell me this is my daughter who I love and miss so much."

No reply comes back. I waited for over an hour. I had gotten up and made a hot chocolate and sat and waited some more. I couldn't take it anymore, so I texted back, saying, "I'm sorry, I didn't mean to scare you off. My ears are still on, so if you need to chat, go ahead." I fell asleep with my head on the table. I got up around three and went back to bed, leaving my phone on the table. When I got up in the morning, my phone beeped to let me know that I had a message.

FORTY-ONE

Picking up the phone, I read, "Best friend" My reply, "So you have said." Half an hour goes by and I get, "Where are you?" My reply, "At home." There is silence and I had finally decided to go on with my day. Then I decided to try again.

"What are you doing today?" I asked my caller.

"Spending time with my daughter." Thought I would get brave, my heart is racing again.

"How old is your daughter?" Silence again.

"She will be two here shortly." This was a really dragged-out conversation, and I was getting a little annoyed with the whole beating-around-the-bush thing. When my phone came to life again, "Thought maybe you and I could meet for coffee." All right, now we are getting somewhere.

"Yes, maybe one of these days we can do that. Let me know when you want to meet." I wasn't going to let her know how excited I was to be doing this. She has no idea how long I have waited to see her, and now I will get to meet my granddaughter. I sat looking at the phone when Jake came out.

"You haven't spent much time in bed, Kate. What's up?"

"Sit down and I will get you a coffee and tell you. You're not going to believe this."

"That good, is it?"

"Angel is texting and asking me to meet her for coffee." Jake chokes on his coffee and says, "What? When did that happen?"

"She started texting just after midnight. Guess she must be getting lonely with him gone."

"Really, how do you know it's her?"

"Just by the texts, and she has a daughter that is around the same age as Elisabeth. She sounds like she is really stressed out and is needing a friend."

"Be careful, Kate, and you make sure you meet her in public. In fact, I want to be in the same place as you, so you better let me know when and where that is going to take place.

"Jake, it's just Angel."

"Then why doesn't she just come home?"

"Maybe he won't let her."

"Maybe. Hope he isn't going to be there."

"Didn't sound like it."

"Well, either way, you are not going alone."

"That's fine with me. I'm a little nervous about this. which is stupid. How can a mother be nervous about meeting up with her daughter and granddaughter?"

"I think I would be too, so I don't think there is anything wrong with being nervous. I just hope it will be what you want and the two of you can go on from there."

"The three of us, you mean."

"Yes, Kate, the three of you." My phone starts beeping. Jake and I look at each other and let it go on. When it finished, it just went on to tell me I had a message.

"Are you going to check it out, Kate?"

"I'm scared to."

"Okay, I will." Jake takes the phone and reads, "Will meet you at cafe on outskirts of town at noon tomorrow."

"Kate, what do you want to say?" After ten minutes, I tell Jake to tell her. "That will be fine. See you then."

"What will you be wearing?"

"What will I be wearing? Oh, Jake, what should I wear?"

"I don't know what grandmas are supposed to wear."

"Come on, Jake, help me out here."

"Wear whatever you will feel comfortable in, Kate. What you wear isn't going to change anything."

"You're right. So tell her I will have on a black-and-white-striped dress."

"Done."

"This is stupid, when I could just walk across the street and knock on her door."

"Do it her way, Kate. You have waited long enough and have come this far."

"I know, I know." Needless to say, there wasn't much sleep happening in our house. It was like having Christmas in May instead of December. My nerves were on edge, and I worried about things I should say and things I shouldn't say. Went over and over things I knew I had to say after all this time. I knew some of it would upset her, but I knew it was something that if I didn't say, I would regret if I didn't get another chance. I had questions that I wanted answers to, and Angel was the only one who had them. The one that bothered me the most is the one she threw at me on the way out of the door that day.

"I'm sorry you are my mother." This has played and replayed in my head all this time. What did I do that was so horrible it would make a daughter say that to her mother?

Pacing the floor and noon not coming soon enough, I had a bath and redid my makeup. I don't know how many times I was going to change my mind on the dress except I had already told her what I would be wearing. Then it hit me. Why would she need to know what I was wearing? Won't she know her own mother? I stood looking in the mirror and thought, *No, you fool, look at yourself. How is she supposed to know who you are? You don't even know who you are*, running the brush through my hair one more time before leaving the house. Jake and I left early. He took his truck. I took my car. Not sure why we did, but that's how we left the house.

We didn't park beside each other, nor did we go in together or sit together. We sat and looked at each other for five minutes; then Jake pulled out his phone and texted me. So for the next half hour, we chatted back and forth on our cell phones. It was kinda fun. Didn't talk, nothing serious, Jake pretended he was trying to make a date with me. Every now and then I would glance through the cafe and see if I could see Angel. I had worried that just maybe she would change her mind. I had ordered a coffee and told the girl I had two more joining me. I would wait to order lunch when they arrived.

Jake and I had gotten into a funny chat, and then I heard, "Excuse me." I looked up and said, "Yes, how may I help you?" This young girl acted so nervous she made me scared. I couldn't see her face behind the big sun hat and sunglasses that she wore.

"I'm Barb. May I sit down?"

"Well, I'm waiting for someone to join me."

"I know," she said as she slipped into the seat across me.

"You know?"

"Yes."

"How do you know? Is Angel not coming now?"

"I'm sorry. Angel never was coming."

"What? How do you know? And who the hell are you?" Jake could see I was getting upset, and he stared my way. I was starting to get up as well.

"I'm sorry. Please don't leave. Let me explain." The girl sounded so sad I had to think twice before just walking out on her. I sat slowly back down, and Jake stopped and waited for my cue. She reminded me of me sitting out on the deck with my hat and glasses, watching Angel. I had to chuckle to myself.

"I'm sorry. Is something funny?" Barb asked me as the waitress came over to see what she would want. She looked at me and waited to see what I would say.

"Go ahead and order."

"Thank you. I will just have a coffee, please."

"Coffee it will be." And off she goes.

"Okay, Barb, you have my attention. Please tell me what you want from me."

"I'm sorry. I don't want anything from you."

"Then I don't understand."

"I called your number by mistake. I really needed someone to talk to, so when you answered and you sounded so concerned, I didn't want to say good-bye. When you asked if it was your daughter, I knew I would break your heart as I am now if I would have said I wasn't. But I really need someone to talk to."

"Why is that?" She took her sunglasses down, and I almost dumped my coffee. One eye she could not see out of, and her face was swollen and black and blue.

"Oh my god, what the hell happened to you?"

"My boyfriend beat me up three days ago."

"Where is he now?" I ask as I scan the cafe.

"At work. I have to be back in an hour, or he will think I'm with another man."

"Is there another man? Is that why he did this to you?"

"No, there isn't. He has it in his head that every time I go out of the house, it is to meet a man."

"Why do you stay?"

"'Cause he says he would find me wherever I go and he said he would kill me and my daughter. No one would ever find us."

"You believe him?"

"Yes, I do."

"How did you meet such a jerk?"

"Waiting on tables. He was one of my steady customers, and then he asked me out."

"Your daughter, is she his?"

"No, she was only one when I started to go out with him."

"You don't think you should leave him?"

"I know I should, but he always comes back and tells me how sorry he is and that he won't do it again. He is a very nice person."

"Oh, I can see that. You don't have to tell me. Has he ever beaten your daughter?"

"No. She did see him do it this time, and she is so scared. When he comes home, she hides in her closet. That, of course, makes him angry."

"I would be hiding too. I would also be running away. Where are your family? Can't they help?"

"My family is not from here. I cannot get help. The shelters only offer help for a few days. So then we have to go back to him." I could tell from her accent that she was maybe Polish or from somewhere over there.

"Can't your family send you money so you can go home with your daughter?" "They do not have money. No. I came here to work so I could send them money, but I'm not able to do that now.

"Where is your daughter now?"

"I have her hiding in safe place outside."

"What? You are hiding your daughter outside."

"Yes, madam, I just wanted to say I was sorry I'm not your daughter. And explain to you why I talked to you."

"Is your daughter close by?"

"Yes, I have her behind all the garbage cans. No one can see her."

"Please go get her and bring her in." When she left, Jake texted.

"What's up?"

"A long story. She is coming back. Will talk after." Barb came in then, and she had the sweetest little girl in her arms. Curly blond hair and big blue eyes. How anyone could be cruel to this, I cannot fathom.

"Hello, sweetie, can I buy you a pop?" She looks at her mommy, As Angel used to do to me. Looking for permission. Barb nods her head, and the little girl says, "Thank you."

"You're welcome." I call the waitress over and get her an orange pop and french fries.

"Now, Barb, if you could arrange to get home, would you go back?"

"Oh yes, madam. My little girl would be safe then."

"So would you."

"Yes."

We talked for another half hour. She told me where she was from, gave me a phone number of some relative abroad. I told her I would talk to my husband and for her to call me tomorrow when it would be safe for her to chat. We would see what we could do to get her home.

"Thank you, madam, but I cannot pay you. I will have no money."

"I don't want your damn money. I just want you and your daughter safe and living a better life than what you are now. Call me, and you be ready to go fast."

"Yes, we do not have much, just little bit of clothes."

"Will he be working the next few days?"

"Yes, he has three more days, then he is off for six."

"We will have to move fast. So please let me talk to my husband. Call me in the morning."

"Yes, madam, I will."

"Please, my name is Kate. Call me Kate."

"No, madam, you're are an angel sent to us from above." She hugs me with tears rolling down her cheeks. My tears are rolling too, some for her happiness and some because it wasn't my daughter I had come to meet.

She leaves, and Jake slides in beside me and takes me into his arms.

"I'm sorry, Kate. Did Angel send her?"

"No, Jake, she did not." I went on to tell him what had happened and what I had promised her we would try to do. He just shook his head.

"I hope if our daughter is ever in this kind of trouble, she will also have an angel sent to her."

"Oh, Jake, this is terrible. How does a man do that to a woman and a child and think it is all right? I do not understand."

"It is called power tripping, and who better than a woman and a child to take it out on? She is going to be one of the lucky ones."

"Why is that?"

"Because we are going to send her home, where hopefully, she and her daughter can carry on and have a normal happy life." I snuggle into his shoulder and sigh.

"So let's go see what we can do for her."

"Are you really okay with this, Jake?"

"Yes. Kate, I don't have a problem with helping someone who needs it."

"Thank you, Jake."

"No thanks necessary." They leave and go to the airport and make all the arrangements needed to see Barb and her daughter get home safe.

That night, Barb texted and said that he had to work late but would be home in the morning. She wouldn't be able to be in contact with her. Jake and Kate thought about it and figured that if he got any idea that she was leaving, he could kill her and his daughter, judging by what he had already done to Barb. So they had her get their things together, and they went and picked them up and took them home with them until it was time to take the plane. Barb kept looking over her shoulder, thinking he would be following them. The plane left half an hour before the jerk was to be home. He never knew what hit him.

FORTY-TWO

We got Barb and her daughter off safely and went back to our little house. Sitting in silence and thinking about how disappointing yesterday had been, I tried not to show it to Barb. I felt very good that we were able to help her out of a bad situation. The only thing was, it did nothing for my broken heart. Bedtime came early, and sleep didn't take the heavy feeling in my heart away. At one point, I was so pissed at Barb I could have slapped her.

At the end of the month, I decided I would take the bull by the horns and try to send a simple text to Angel. I hoped she still had her old number. So I texted.

"I pray for you every day and hope you are well." There was nothing for half the day. When I saw Angel's name come up on my phone, I had to sit down. My heart was doing double flips. I slowly checked to see what she had to say.

"I don't need a mother like you praying for me. Pray for yourself." This had my head spinning. After all this time, that was all she could say. I just let it go. I wasn't up to any of this. What is wrong with her?

I continued to stay in my little house, and Jake went back and forth. It was working out okay. I had so much time on my hands and was sitting out here on the veranda when the weather was nice. With my notepad in my hand, I had decided to work on the story that I have been working on for years, and I started to rewrite it so many times over the years. It had been lost once. It had been burned up once and had just so many times of starting over. So now it was time to put all my energy into my writing. I was going to make something of all this mess. My writing came along great, and before I knew, it two months had gone by and I had my first novel done. Of course, the one person I wanted to share it with wasn't here. So I decided again to send my daughter a text.

"I finished that novel you help me start. I just wanted to share it with my daughter." I wasn't ready for what came back as her reply.

"You're not my mother. Can't you get that through your head? Leave me alone. Any mother who would treat her daughter the way you treated me has to be sick." I wanted to throw up. I must have had the wrong number. No way does Angel think that I have mistreated her.

"I have never done anything but love you with all my heart." When my phone beeped, I jumped.

"Don't use the word *love* to me. You don't know what love is. Now leave me alone. Got it?" Now I'm getting a little angry.

"What have I done that is so terrible that you would talk to me like this? Love, Mom." I figured if me using the word *love* is getting to her, then I will use it as much as possible. Then I get a nasty one.

"You are dead to me, got it? I want nothing from you. Don't call me. Don't text me, and don't say I'm your daughter because I'm not. I don't want to hear from you or anything about you."

"What is wrong with you?" is what I wanted to scream at her.

"Well, my dear girl, you are my daughter from the day they put you in my arms. I have done nothing but love you with all my heart, and I have always been here for you. So when you grow up, you do have my number and we can talk then. I miss you and love you as big as the sky, Angel. Good-bye."

There was no more texting between us. I just let it go. People are known to say terrible things that hurt deeply, and you can't take them back no matter how hard you try. The wound is deep, and some just don't heal.

I went on doing my daily work and getting things set up with my novel, and now it just didn't mean as much to me as it had in the beginning. Jake tried to make it sound so exciting, and I had invites to attend book signings. I didn't want to do any of this without my daughter. We had always shared so many things. I would say she is the only person who really knows me, so what this is all about, I just don't know.

You cannot fix what you don't know is broken. Why wasn't I given a second chance?

I watched, and of course I continued to love them from a distance, and Jake had asked me to go home. He figured I had taken enough abuse and that I should just let her go. She will come back someday soon, he would tell me. He said, "You know the saying, Kate, about turning something free and if it comes back to you, it was yours and if it doesn't, it never was? Well, I think this applies here."

I told him, when Angel has the baby and I know she is okay, I will go home.

It happened to be 2:00 a.m. when there were lights and sirens going off all over, and I had just gotten to bed, so I was still awake enough to realize that it was right here where all the noise was. Jumping out of bed and running to my window, I saw that all the commotion was at Angel's.

Oh my god, what has happened? Grabbing my house coat, I ran outside and over to their house to watch like all the other neighbors did. The fool himself was home and he was holding Victoria and she was crying. My daughter was on the stretcher with hoses up her nose and bands around her arms, and the paramedics were moving so fast I stood in shock. This was my baby, and I couldn't be there for her. There was nothing I could do. As they pulled away, I heard him ask the next-door lady if she would keep Elizabeth so he could go to the hospital. God, I wish it were me he was asking. But then I wouldn't be able to go to the hospital.

Hospital, yes, I must go get dressed and go to the hospital. Running back to the house and throwing on some clothes, I didn't care what I looked like; and if he recognized me, I really don't give a damn.

I was walking around inside the hospital like I was lost, and of course I was. I was wasting time, but I didn't really know where to look for Angel.

"Excuse me, may I help you?"

"Aww, yes, the young lady that was just brought in. She's pregnant. Where did they take her?"

"To surgery. She needs to have a C-section right away. Just go down there. To the left is a waiting room. Someone will come and tell you when the baby is delivered."

"Thank you." I sat for no more than three quarters of an hour when a nurse came and said that she had a boy, that Angel wasn't doing very good. Her kidneys were not functioning well. They were waiting for a specialist to come in. That was all she could tell me.

I sat down hard on the sofa and cried for the joy of my grandson and the fear I had for my daughter.

"Hi, Jake."

"What is wrong, Kate?" Jake asks as he's getting out of bed and pulling on his pants. He knows when Kate is calling at this hour, there are problems somewhere.

"Angel has had to have a C-section, and they say she not doing too well. Her kidneys are not working properly. Jake, I'm scared to death, and what do I do?"

"Please, Kate, just stay calm and stay put. I'm on my way." He was running around getting dresses while talking to Kate. When he hung up the phone, he was ready to hit the road.

"Okay, Jake, I need you."

"I know you do, and I will be there as soon as I can."

"Drive safe." Staying put was easy; staying calm was not. Jake got there at 7:00 a.m., and I was dog tired.

"I'm sorry, Kate. I was going to come last night after work, but thought I would get an early start today."

"Looks like you did that, all right."

"Let's go down to the cafeteria and get a coffee and then see what we can find out about Angel."

"I could sure use one."

"Me too, Kate, was a long drive or at least it seemed like it. Guess it always does when you are in a hurry." They got their coffee and went back upstairs to check in at the nurses' station to see what they could find out. Of course, they didn't want to tell us anything. "Who were we?" is what we got asked. I finally had enough and blurted out, "I'm her mother, damn it, and I have the right to know."

"Okay, okay," the nurse said. "Stay calm and I will have her doctor talk to you. Just have a seat over there. He shouldn't be too long." Taking a seat and waiting seem to be all I have done for too long. I pulled out my phone and started to dial.

"Who you calling, Kate?"

"I'm calling Dr. Adams. He will help us figure out what to do."

"We don't know anything yet."

"Enough to know Angel is in deep trouble. Hi, Dr. Adams, I'm sorry to call you so early."

"That's fine, Kate. How are you?"

"I'm fine, but Angel isn't. Could you come and help us, please?"

"Tell me what's up." So Kate told him all she knew, and he said he would be there as soon as he could. Kate felt better knowing he was going to be there on their side in case Angel fought the fact that they were there. In the meantime, they went down to the nursery to see their grandson. He was a little early, but not enough that it should cause any problems. He was pink, bright, and he looked small. His lungs seemed to be working just fine as well.

"I think he will be one to speak his mind."

"You think so, Grandma?" Jake says as he wraps his arms around me.

"One thing about it, Jake. I was here, and I seen our grandson right after he was born. She can't take that away from me. Looking at him now, this picture will always be etched in my heart. It may be the only one I ever have of him."

"No, sweetheart, use your phone."

"What?"

"The camera on your phone. Take his picture now."

"Oh, Jake, yes! I forgot about this." Pulling out my phone, I got close enough to get really good shots. The nurse was in there washing him, so she made sure I had a good view.

"Oh, Jake, thank you."

"You're welcome." Once Dr. Adams got there, everything went so fast. We were told that Angel needed a kidney transplant and it had to be soon. She still didn't know that we were there. After a lot of discussions with the doctors and with Jake, I asked if Dr. Adams and I could go in together to see her. Her doctor didn't see a problem with it.

When we went into her room, she was facing the wall. I thought she was sleeping. Dr. Adams went over and took her hand. She turned to face him, and then I could see she was crying, and my heart broke.

"Angel, your mom is here to see you."

"No! I don't want to see her."

"Please, Angel, you have to talk to your mom."

"No! I don't have to talk to her now or ever."

"Angel, I love you," Kate says as she steps around Dr. Adams.

"I told you never to use that word with me. You don't know anything about love. Now get out." She turns her face back to the window.

I go over and I take a hold of her hand. I bend over and kiss her wet cheek. "I love you as big as the sky, Angel." She just pulls her hand away and turns completely over. I back up and wipe the tears from my face. I didn't need everyone outside that door to know my daughter hates me. For the love of God, I don't know why.

We go back to the doctors' lounge, and Jake knew as soon as he saw me that it wasn't a good visit.

The doctor was telling us how Angel was put at the top of the list for a kidney, due to her age and that fact that she had two little children. They have a very difficult decision to make when an organ finally comes available. Some of their patients die waiting. One of the other problems is that Angel has a standard blood type. So there are so many with the same type that there are just not enough organs to go around. They're talking weeks, months, maybe even years; and all this time, Angel will have to be on a machine to keep what she has got working. Just one kidney would give Angel her life back, the specialist had said. I was sitting in such a dream-type daze after being in with Angel that this is just all too much and it was going over my head. Then it hit me.

"You said Angel only needs one kidney?"

"Yes, I did." The look on my face must have told it all.

"No! Kate, you're not."

"I want to give my daughter one of mine." The specialist looked shocked, and he looked over at Jake.

"Please, Kate, no. Don't do this."

"Jake, that is my daughter lying in there and her life is in danger. She has two little children who need their mommy. How can I not do this if I'm a match? For the love of God, Jake, I love my daughter, and I will if I can. Give her life again." Jake sat down and put his head into his hands, and Kate saw the tears that fell to the floor.

Going over and squatting down in front of him and taking his hands down so she could see his face, she pleads with him, "Please, Jake, understand. She is my only daughter."

"Kate, you are all I have."

"If Angel only needs one kidney, then all I need is one kidney. It's one kidney, Jake, to save her life. The mother of our grandchildren. If we ever hope to see them or have a life of any kind with them, I have to give them their mother. Please, Jake, Angel will know just how much I love her. Let me do this with your blessing."

"Dr. Anderson."

"Yes, Jake."

"Can my wife do this and live a normal life with one kidney?"

"Yes, she can if she has no health problems."

"All right, Kate, I love you and I know how much you love Angel, and that girl had better come to understand just what she means to you. I'm agreeing with you, Kate, against my better judgment." Kate throws her arms around his neck.

"Thank you for understanding, Jake."

"Get this straight, Kate. I'm not understanding at all. I told you I'm agreeing against my better judgment. And my love for you. Don't get me wrong. I love Angel, and she has been like a daughter to me. But you have always been and always will be first in my heart."

"So if it is all right, I will make the arrangements for you to be tested, Kate, for a match." Holding Jake's hand and looking at Dr. Anderson, I say, "Yes, I'm ready."

"All right then, I will go get it set up."

"Thank you, Kate. Not every parent would do this. There are risks to this surgery, you understand."

FORTY-THREE

"Yes, I understand there are risks. I'm okay with that. What you all have to understand is that is my daughter lying out there. What kind of mother would I be if I just walked away and waited for a donor to do my job knowing my daughter could die. Leaving her two children motherless and I could have prevented it. Then and only then my daughter would have had the right to say I don't know what love is."

"Kate, I'm not saying it is wrong. I'm scared for you, for us."

"I know you are, Jake, and so we should be scared. This isn't a simple tooth extraction. I have no choice. Angel has no one else."

"I know, Kate, and I'm proud of you, and I love you so much." He takes me in his arms, and we cry together. Then we sit and wait for Dr. Anderson to come and get me. It wasn't a long wait because they move fast when there is a donor right on sight.

The testing was a match, and it was just after lunch when Dr. Anderson came and found us in the cafeteria.

"Kate, you are a perfect match for Angel. When do you want to be available by?" Jake and I look at each other and back at the doctor.

"Anytime. I'm free. Anytime."

"All right, I will go see what room there is in the OR and talk to Angel and let her know." He reaches the door, and Kate jumps up calling to the doctor.

"Dr. Anderson, just a minute please." Jake thought, *Thank God, she has changed her mind.*

"I don't want you to tell Angel I'm her donor."

Closing the door and frowning, he says, "Why not?" "She won't take it if she knows it's me. Please, do you have to tell her?"

"No, Kate, we don't. In most cases the patient have no idea."

"Good, and I would like it kept that way."

"Is that all, no changing your mind?"

"Thank you, that is all. No, I will not change my mind."

Jake and I sit, and we drink our coffee in silence. I knew he was madder at me than he was proud. I didn't know how to approach it because he knew how I felt and I knew how he felt. I was going to ask him if Angel had been still Angel and in our lives like she used to be, would he be okay with it then? This was a critical situation, and it was my only daughter, my only child. I couldn't and I wouldn't just sit by and watch her suffer and perhaps die. I was thinking back to the times when Angel was small and happy and I was everything to her.

"Kate." A hand gets put on my shoulder. Turning, I see it is Dr. Anderson.

"Yes, is something wrong with Angel?"

"No, not at all, in fact she is so happy that we got a donor this fast. The OR has room tomorrow morning. Is that good for you and Jake?" I catch Jake's eyes, and he looks down at our hands that we had been holding and not being aware of it.

"Yes, that is fine. The sooner you do this, the sooner Angel can go home to her children."

"All right then, I will let my associates know that it is a go and to be ready for six a.m."

"Six a.m. That early."

"Yes, Angel and you are first on the list. So you will be checked in here by two this afternoon. All right?"

"Yes, that is just fine. Thank you for moving so fast on this."

"No," he takes my hand and says, "thank you for donating an organ. I know it is your daughter and all. But, Kate, this is a big step when you are a live donor. There are not many of you out there, and it is a shame. We have watched parents sit in here and watch their child die waiting, and neither one would even consider this. So thank you." He kisses my check, and away he goes.

Jake stands up and says, "Should we go look at our grandson one more time before Grandma can't get out of bed."

"I think that is a very good idea, Let's go." We get up there just to find the baby crying his heart out, and no one is around. I saw the gowns there, so I slip one on and go in and pick up my grandson. There is a rocking chair in the room, so I sit down and start to rock the baby. He quiets right down and snuggles into Grandma. Jake took my phone, and he's busy taking pictures.

"Oh, you sweet little man. Bet you are going to give Mommy a run for her money." Kissing him and saying. "Please remember Grandma loves you as big as the sky, little man." I will treasure this moment always. There is no telling when Angel will let me see him or them. I might want to keep the little house just so we can see him grow up too.

The nurse comes along and starts to get a little huffy 'cause I have gone into the nursery. Jake takes her by the arm and takes her back out into the hall. I could see they were having quite the conversation, but I didn't care. If this was going to be my only chance to hold my grandson, I didn't care whose toes I stepped on to do it.

"Is everything okay, Jake?"

"Yes, Kate, it is. They want you in your room in a half an hour."

"That's fine. I will just sit and hold this little man until I have to go." Jake pulls up the other rocker, and there they sat admiring their new grandson and dreaming of the days to come.

"I wish I would have been able to do this with Elisabeth."

"I know you do, Kate, and all we can do is hope that when Angel gets well and she realizes that she got the second chance at life. And when she finds out who gave her that second chance. She will be willing to give you the second chance that you so deserve."

"I guess all we can do is pray that this opens her eyes and she will know how much I love her."

"This is a very big chance you are taking to show her what kind of love you have for her."

"I know it is, Jake, but things have come a long way in the medical field when it comes to these operations. I will probably be out in a week's time. Gallbladder are done one day, and you're home the next. When I had mine out I was in for a week plus. Now people are back to work in a week. Good Lord, I wasn't even standing up straight at the end of the week. So please don't worry so much, everything will be fine. I will be somewhat lighter on one side and maybe walk funny because of it. But that is all. Jake, I am strong and healthy. If it were really risky, the doctor would tell us. All he said is that there are risk. So please just relax. I'm glad I can do this for Angel. If she won't understand how much I love her any other way, at least I know I have given to her all I can possibly give."

"I know that is how you feel. It doesn't mean I have to like it."

"No, it doesn't, and I love you for being honest." The nurse came back, and I now had to give up my grandson and go to my room so they could do whatever it was there needed to do to get me ready for surgery in the morning.

"Kate, what can I bring from home for you?"

"I guess everything, Jake, I didn't come prepared for this."

"So tell me what you want the most."

"Makeup bag from top draw of dresser. Comb and brush. Slippers and my housecoat. Please throw in some clean panties."

"Do I get to choose the panties?" He raises his eyebrow up and down in a teasing way that he does.

"I guess if you want all these doctor and interns seeing what I wear for you. Could be dangerous."

"Oh, maybe I better keep it to your old faithfuls."

"I think that might be wise. My book bag is still in the back of the car from when we went to see Mom, would you bring it in when you come back."

"Sure, did you need for me to pick a book out for you?"

"Oh no, I still have the books in there that I took then so now I can read them. Just bring in the bag please."

"All right. I will go and get your things so you will have what you need to get ready for bed. What about toothbrush?"

"Everything is in the makeup bag." Jake leaves, and I get to thinking about how Angel was the last time I tried to see her. I could tell she was hurting and she wasn't happy. Of course, some of that is because she knew she had to have a kidney transplant, with no donor in sight. But the birth of her son should have been something she should have shared with me. What was her son's name? I didn't even read on the card to see if she was married to the fool. Or how big the baby was. I will have to get Jake to check it out for me and see what she has done.

"Knock, knock. You up to company, Kate?"

"For your company, always." Dr. Adams pulls up a chair and takes my hand.

"You know, Kate, I'm proud of what you are doing."

"Thank you but I'm not looking for anyone to be proud of me. I'm just helping my daughter. I only wish she would at least talk to me before surgery."

"I have been to see her. I gather she doesn't know you are her donor?"

"No, if she knew she would refuse."

"You really think so, seeing how you are saving her life."

"Dr. Adams, I gave her life once already, and that hasn't been good enough." "Kate, do you have any idea what is going on with Angel?"

"Oh God, I wish I knew. Since she has been with this guy it has been a nightmare. I tried to text to her, and she just told me plain out I wasn't her mother and to leave her alone and that I knew nothing of love."

"Well, that is just stupid. Look at what you are doing out of love for her. I have a good mind to go back to see her and give her a piece of my mind."

"Please don't, not tonight. Don't get her all upset before surgery, that won't do her any good."

"All right, Kate, but after tomorrow she is getting a piece of my mind. You and her have been the closest people I have had to family, and I won't stand by and see it destroyed over a man or stupidity. I think it is high time that this man steps on her. She has been spoiled way too long. It is time she grew up."

"You know she has two children now?"

"Yes, she was telling me about them."

"What did she call the little boy, do you know?"

"Gregory."

"A very old name, like her daughter's."

"Yes, she has picked very strong and admirable name for her children."

"Yes, some people believe that your name will get you through life."

"Do you believe that?"

"I wouldn't want to be called by a silly name."

"Whose is silly?"

"Hi, Jake." Dr. Adams stands up and shakes Jakes hand. As Jake hands Kate the two bags that she was wanting. Jake and Dr. Adams get into the discussion of the surgery, and I decided to check out the books that I had put in my bag. I didn't want to hear about Jake's fears of tomorrow. I was giving Angel a kidney. End of story. Digging in the bag I pulled out papers that belonged to my mom that Jackie had given to me, and I just stuck them in here so I could go through them later. Well, I guess this is later, all right.

There were two envelopes, one addressed to me and one that read "My Dearest Alex." I look over to him, and he is still chatting away explaining surgery to Jake, so I just lay it aside and carry on going through the rest. I would read mine when I was alone. No doubt I will cry, and I want it to be just Mom and I when I do. This is like getting a gift from Mom after all these years of her being gone, and I was going to cherish it alone.

"Well, Kate, I will go now so you and Jake can have some time together. I'm going to stop in and see Angel one more time and take a look at your grandson as well. I will be here tomorrow so I can be with you." He kisses Kate good-bye; he shakes Jakes hand and is headed for the door when I remember.

"Oh, Dr. Adams, I have something for you." Holding up the white envelope.

"Oh, what is that, Kate?"

"A surprise." He takes it and sees the handwriting and goes white in the face like he had just seen a ghost.

"Think of it as a late Christmas present from Mom."

"Where did this come from?"

"It was in Mom's belongings that were stuck in my book bag. I just never looked at anything until now," I wave mine up in his face and smile, saying.

"I got one too. Will share mine with you tomorrow."

"All right, Kate, I will share mine with you."

"Deal, good night."

"Good night, you two."

"He looked a little disturbed when you gave him that envelope, Kate."

"Probably just a bit of a shock after all this time. I'm finding it to be exciting, not sad. To get something from Mom now is like heaven to me."

"Yea, well, I wish everyone was like you. You can see the good in so much."

"No, Jake, I can't see the good in that man Angel is with. He has rubbed me the wrong way from day one."

"Let's not go there. You have a big day tomorrow. Let's just think good things. Let's remember our fun times we have had and all the ones that lie ahead of us after tomorrow. It does you good to go into surgery with happy thoughts. Dr. Anderson told me that."

"Dr. Anderson is a smart man."

"Yes, he is." We talked until midnight then they asked Jake if he would mind leaving so I would sleep. He wasn't happy about it, but they told him I needed the strength. So he left without a hassle.

"I will be back bright and early, I love you, Kate, sleep well."

"I will, Jake, and I hope you sleep well too."

"I won't promise, but I will try." Kissing me good night and then I found myself alone with Mom's letter. I opened it as if it were made of glass. This was the last thing Mom wrote to me, and I wanted it to last.

My Darling Kate:

I hope by the time you get this letter you and Angel have healed and moved on with your lives. Life takes us down so many roads, and we never know where we are going to end up. Some for the good and some for the not so good.

I spent my time wanting and wishing and never had the strength in me to see my dreams come true. It is always said that if you want something bad enough you just have to go for it. Anyone can make their dreams come true if you want it bad enough. The only thing is. I don't believe in taking someone else's dream and destroying it to get yours.

This might be hard for you to understand, and I am sorry that it has taken my death for you to find out. I knew that if I didn't tell you now. You would never know. Be happy and enjoy this new life you are about to embark on with the understanding that moms do things always for a very good reason.

Kate continues to read, and it takes her a bit for everything her mother has written to sink in. She folds the envelope up and hugs it close to her chest. Looking up she could only say, "I LOVE YOU, MOM."

She falls asleep with the biggest smile on her face. Kate was sure that her mother could see her smiling and knowing that she was still loving her from whatever distance she was at.

FORTY-FOUR

Sitting off to the side of doctors' lounge, he pulls out his envelope from Emma and runs his finger back and forth along the edge.

"Oh, Emma, I have missed you so much, but I don't know if I can bring myself to read this and open the wound that isn't quite healed. But has become livable. You know you were my love, and every day that goes by, I think of you. There will never be another you, and I am not able to move on this time without you.

Your daughter and granddaughter are both going to have surgery tomorrow and are in need of me, and I have to be able to be in my right mind to help. If I were to read your letter, it would put me in such a state that I would be letting not just the girls down but you. So I know you are watching over us, and I know you understand what I'm saying, so if you don't mind, I will keep this until Kate and Angel are out of surgery and recuperating before I take time to wallow in self-pity."

"Dr. Adams, Angel was asking to see you."

Slipping his letter back into his pocket and getting up, he says, "Okay, I will be right there." He goes to see what is up with Angel. She should be sound asleep by now. He had requested that they both be given sedatives so they wouldn't worry all night. Pushing Angel's door open slowly so he wouldn't disturb her if she had fallen asleep. Finding her sitting up in bed.

"Hey, kiddo, why aren't you sleeping?"

"I can't sleep, Dr. Adams."

"Well, how about telling me what's on your mind." He climbs up and sits on the side of her bed.

"I don't know really."

"Are you scared about tomorrow? It's normal to be scared. This is a big thing that you will be going through."

"Yea, I am a little, but I know if I don't do this, I won't live to raise my babies."

"That is true. You have to remember your children and that they love you as much as you love them."

"I do love my children, very much."

"Of course you do. All mothers love their children, and there isn't anything you wouldn't do for them because you are their mother." He waited a bit, and Angel didn't say anything. She just sat with her head hung.

So he decided to go further. "You know, Angel, your mother loves you as much as you love your children."

"But Mom doesn't like Chris."

"That maybe true, but it doesn't mean she loves you any less. As a parent, we usually never like our children's choices in partners. It is only out of love, and it is because they have been responsible for you for so many years it is hard to see someone else take our place. You will see. You will have the same problems, and if you don't, I want to be the first to hear about it."

"I wasn't very nice to Mom."

"No, you weren't, and I understand you haven't been for quite some time. Do you think deep down you really have a justifiable reason to be treating your mother this way?"

"I thought so."

"Honestly now,,Angel what has she done that has been so horrible that you would go this long before talking to her?"

"I can't think of why I was mad at her. Then Chris just kept telling me that my mother wasn't nothing more than a tramp. That she didn't love me because she didn't love him. He said she couldn't have one without the other. At first, I got mad at him for saying those things about Mom, but then I guess I believed it, and I didn't know how to stop it all." She starts to cry, and I take her into my arms and rock her as if she were a baby. In some ways, she was just a baby, and the man she is with has forced her to grow up to his standards.

"You know, Angel, it is not too late to tell your mother that you love her. She would love to meet your little girl and help you with your son."

"Maybe after my surgery."

"Angel, don't wait too long. It has already been long enough."

"I know, and I really wanted to tell her that today, but I keep hearing him in my head."

"How about after you are well. I take you and your children to see your mom."

"Chris won't let me go home. He says I don't need my family."

"Well, I'm here to tell you that you do, and I will tell him where he can go and how to get there the fastest way."

Angel chuckles. "Dr. Adams, you wouldn't do that."

"I sure the hell will. Your mother needs you and your children in her life. She loves Jake, but you have always been her Angel, and she has been sad ever since you left. She almost quit living, Angel. She had me very worried for a very long time."

"Is Mom okay now?"

"She is trying to accept that fact that you don't want anything to do with her. She has loved you from a distance long enough, it is time you come home."

She nods her head in agreement. "Okay, young lady. I want you to get some sleep, and we will get this all straightened out after surgery."

"Do you think Mom will be here tomorrow?"

"I don't think a team of wild horse are going to keep her away." He kisses her forehead and says good night. Angel couldn't help but replay the last time her mom had come to see her and how terrible she had treated her. She couldn't get over the horrible feeling that she had caused her mother so much grief. She knew that her mother had seen a lot of grief in her lifetime, and she had just added more to it. How blind she had been and how selfish and self-centered. Why had she let this man come between her and her mother, they were always close and had always been there for each other? God, with Grandma gone and me gone, Mom has been left alone. We were all she had besides Jake, and I still knew in my heart that I was her number one. "Oh, Mommy, I wish I could see you now. I need you, and I need to be able to tell you. I love you as big as the sky, Mommy." Angel rolled over on her side and curled up into a ball. She thought about how it was going to be when Dr. Adams takes her and her children to see their grandma. Angel knows her mother will be ecstatic to see her and the children. It's what she is going to have to put up with at home that scares her. She feels she has let it go on long enough and she must try to fix what her and her mother used to have. The trust, the love, and the friendship that they had banked on all those years. It was what got them through the time when her dad died and baby Ben died and Grandma died. Mom has had it hard. With that thought in mind, she fell asleep.

Just to be woken up by the OR nurse. She was prepped and ready to go within a half hour. It was early, but Angel knew she was going right back to sleep. She was so tired that she didn't have time to get scared. When she woke up, she would have a new lease on life. Thanks to some poor soul who has lost their life. She had thought she should have asked the age of her donor. But she didn't want to know if it was a young person like herself or younger.

Kate had been prepped as well, and both ladies were in their own OR rooms. Their surgery was going to be hours, and both Jake and Dr. Adams waited in the halls of the hospital. They had asked Dr. Adams if he wanted to stand in and watch, and he decided that Jake would need someone, and so he chose to be with him. After all, both the girls had several working on them and didn't need another in the way. The two men walked the halls and went for coffee and walked the halls some more. They made a few trips to the nursery to see the baby; neither one had much to say. Of course their minds were on the same thing and were scared to mention it to each other.

Jake was sick at heart and knew that he couldn't have stopped Kate if he had tried and Angel didn't have a choice. In her case, it was do or die. Throwing them in the basket and picking one still wasn't giving her much of a choice.

"I'm taking Angel to see her mother when she has recovered from this," Dr. Adams tells Jake just out of the blue.

"You are?"

"Yes, I am. Enough is enough."

"Angel know about this?"

"Yes, she does, we talked it over last night. She was feeling bad about how she treated Kate when we went in to see her."

"So she should have. She has been doing that for a long time."

"That's what I said. Told her it was over. She was worried about Chris. I told her I would deal with him. But I was taking her to see her mother and the children to see their grandma."

"Good for you. Thank you. Did you tell Kate?"

"No, I think it will make for a good surprise when she wakes up. It will give her the motivation she will need to recover."

"Oh, for sure, I don't know how you did it, but thank you." They shook hands and patted each other on the back.

Hours had gone by, and they knew it was going to be a long day. The day was coming to an end, and still no one has come to tell them what was happening. Jake was starting to get antsy and didn't know what to do with himself. He thought he would try reading one of Kate's books that she had in her bag. When he took the first one out, it had the white envelope in it. Looked like Kate was using it for a book marker. So instead of messing with that book, he took the other, and it was also a James Patterson book. Kate had a lot of his books; she was a great fan of his. She said she could never write like him but loved his stories. Taking her book and finding a place to sit and read wasn't easy. This was a very busy place, and Jake liked it quiet when he read. He ended up outside under a tree. He found that Kate had very good taste in books, and he got right into the story. He forgot to tell Dr. Adams where he was going but had mentioned it to a nurse. She had told him she would find him when the doctors came out.

The recovery rooms were busy with them checking their vital signs every ten minutes and working on getting the women awake.

It took some longer than others to come around. Some almost took a whole day to really wake up.

"Can I have a drink please?" she says in a whisper.

"You sure can, Angel. How are you feeling? Is there much pain?"

"No, it's not too bad."

"The drugs they gave you for surgery will be wearing off, and you don't be afraid to ask for something. You also have to drink lots and lots. We want you to pee as soon as you can. That will tell us your kidneys are working on their own. For now, you have a bag, and we are measuring the fluid you are discharging. We are keeping track of how much you drink as well. It is very important to drink, Angel, so ask for whatever you want except milk."

"I will, thank you." And she dozes off again just as Dr. Adams comes through the door. He didn't know where Chris was, and he didn't care. He was going to sit with her for a while before going to see Kate. He knew that they would call Jake in to sit with her. Kate was still sleeping deeply, and so he thought he might as well come in here; they had told him Angel was awake off and on. He pulls up a chair and takes her hand in his. Angel has always been the closest person to a grandchild that he had ever had. He didn't miss many of her school functions or special occasions. He had watched her grow up from the beautiful brown-eyed baby to the beautiful woman she is today. It saddens his heart to know that she hasn't seen her mother in all these years nor spoken to her. He knew Kate had tried to text her but never got good responses from Angel. He had even thought about hiring a private detective to find her and check this guy out that had her so brainwashed that she walked out of her mother's life.

"Mr. Sanders, you may come see your wife now."

Jake scrambled to his feet, dropping the book and cursing. Turning all red in the face as the nurse stood by and watched him get his bearings.

"Are you going to be all right, Mr. Sanders?"

"Yes, sorry, I was startled by you and excited to hear I can see my wife. How is she doing? How are they doing?"

"Angel has been awake off and on, but your wife hasn't come around yet."

"Is that normal for Kate not to be awake yet?"

"It takes some people longer to come out of the anesthetic than others. Your wife is one of them."

Jake said no more and just followed the nurse into the room where they had Kate.

He goes over to her and takes her hand and starts to squeeze it. He is watching the nurse, and she is taking Kate's vitals, and they are calling her name and telling her it's time to wake up. Kate wasn't having anything to do with them.

"Mr. Sanders, please just keep talking to her. This will bring her around faster than if we leave her to come around on her own."

"All right, I can do that."

"We will be back in fifteen minutes unless you need me before that, please just ring that bell."

"Okay, I can do that too."

The nurse leaves, and Jake stands staring at his wife lying there so lifeless. It pulled at his heart.

"Okay, Kate, you heard them. It is time to wake up now. Angel is already awake, and you can't see her with your eyes closed."

Kate can faintly hear a voice. She can see Ben off in the distance, and she feels the pull toward him. Ben is calling her, and she finds she is drifting his way. Then she hears her name called again, but this time it's not Ben but Jake that is calling her. Her eyes are so heavy. In her mind, she says, *I hear you, Jake.*

"There's still nothing from your wife?" a nurse asked.

"No, nothing. I keep talking, but she just doesn't want to wake up yet."

"Dr. Anderson is coming back in to check her out. He should be in right away."

"All right, I will talk to her until then."

"Good man. That's what she needs." It was just a couple of minutes, and Dr. Anderson came in, and he went over Kate. Did all kinds of things and in the end says, "Jake, your wife has gone into a coma."

"What? Why? How long will this last?"

"Sorry, we have no way of knowing these things."

Jake drops his head into his hands, and Dr. Anderson saw the tears hit the floor.

"Jake, we have to keep talking to her, and the more we talk to her, the better the chance of her coming back to us faster are."

Jake just shook his head in agreement. This went on for days, and then Dr. Adams says to Jake, "We should bring Angel in to talk to Kate. I think it would do the trick."

"You really think so?"

"It did before."

"Angel doesn't know Kate did this for her. Kate didn't want her to know."

"You're right on both accounts, but I think this is one time you can override what Kate wanted and do what is best for Kate."

"All right, let's do it."

"I will go talk to Angel and come back as soon as I can."

"Okay"

Entering Angel's room, he saw the man that she was living with, and his blood boils right away. He continues to go over to Angel, not making eye contact with the guy at all. For one thing, he couldn't remember his name, and also he didn't give a damn. He was here to help Kate.

"Angel, I need to talk to you in private."

"Whatever you have to say to Angel, I can hear."

"I'm sorry, I'm her doctor, and no, you cannot. Now please leave."

"I will not."

"Then I will call security, you decide. Angel can talk to you later if she wishes, but for now, it is her and I."

"Go ahead, they won't remove me."

"All right then, have it your way." Dr. Adams picks up the phone, and before Chris knew it, he was being escorted out of the room before the next words were coming out of his mouth. Next step.

"Angel, I have to tell you something, and I want you to stay calm. You can't be getting all upset, but I need your help.

"Okay. But how can I help you?"

"Your kidney donor has gone into a coma, and we hoped you would come and talk to her."

"Wait a minute, my donor wasn't someone who had died?"

"No, Angel, you had a live donor."

"Who the hell would do that?"

"Your mother?"

Angel went pale, and I thought she was going to be sick, so grabbing the bedpan, I stuck it under her chin.

"Mom gave me one of her kidneys? Why would she do that?"

"Your mother knew it was a death threat to you if you didn't get one, and she was a perfect match. She loves you, Angel, can't you see that? There isn't anything. Anything at all she wouldn't do for you and your children. I think she has proven that to you. Don't you think? She has put her life on the line to save yours."

Angel's tears are rolling down her cheeks as she nods her head. "How can I help Mom?"

"You have to talk to her just like you did when you were little. We have to get her to wake up. I'm going to have the nurse wheel your bed down to your mom's so you can talk to her."

Angel cried all the way down to see her mom. When they entered the room, Jake was totally shocked to see them bring Angel in. Dr. Adams just holds up his hands to stop Jake from saying anything. They slid her bed in beside Kate's. Angel reached over and took Kate's hand.

"Oh, Mommy, why did you do this? Please, Mommy, wake up, I need you. I'm so sorry, Mommy, please wake up, don't sleep like you did last time."

Kate hears the voice of her sweet Angel, but Ben calling to her was stronger, and there was no way Kate's eyes would open, and she starts to drift again. This feels right to her, and she has no fears or worries. Ben is there, and she knows she will be safe and happy. She lets herself go.

"CODE BLUE. ICU. STAT "

"CODE BLUE. ICU. STAT "

Next thing Jake knew, the door was flying open, and he was being pushed aside.

Angel's bed was pulled away, and the three of them watched in horror.

"Clear," someone yells, and then he watches Kate's body jump up off the stretcher and then flops back down.

Again he hears, "Clear." He watches after they hit Kate with the paddles again and again. He finds he is leaning up against the wall, and the feeling of nausea came over him. Angel is now yelling for her mother. It seemed to take forever before he saw Dr. Anderson reach over and hold the hand of the one using the paddles. He saw him shaking his head, and they all turn and look at the straight line that was running on the machine. Then some of them looked down and others looked at Jake. Dr. Anderson came over, and he was talking, but Jake couldn't hear what he was saying. As he walked over to Kate's lifeless body, he knew what had just happened. He had just lost his best friend, his wife. Angel had just lost her mother and her best friend. The children just lost the grandmother that they will never know. Dr. Adams lost the one person he treated like the daughter he never had. Jake picks Kate up into his arms and pulls her in tight to his body and lets out a scream that was surly heard from one end of the hospital to the other. The cries that came from this man were one of a man whose heart had just been ripped from his chest. All the medical staff watch on until Dr. Anderson nodded for them to leave him so he could be alone with his wife. Dr. Adams holds Angel as she cries with regret.

"Please, I want to give Mom a hug and say good-bye."

Dr. Adams pushes her over as close as he could, and Jake picks up Kate and lays her beside Angel so she could give her mother the hug that Kate had dreamed of and wished for over the years that Angel had been away. Then Dr. Adams takes Angel back to her room, and they leave Jake alone with his beloved wife and friend.

"I killed my mom."

"No, Angel, you did not. This was Kate's choice. No one could change her mind."

"I don't understand. Mom never came out of surgeries well. Why would she put herself in such danger?"

"You know, Angel. There are none so blind as those who cannot see."

"I don't understand?"

"Unconditional love, Angel. Your mother gave that to you right to the end."

"My children will never know their grandma. Where will I go, and what will I do?" Wrapping Angel in his arms, he says, "You will have to live with your choices and learn to live with your regrets, Angel. You will also have to do the same as your mother did for all those years of loving you from a distance. Now you will have to learn how to love her from a distance."

Watch for the conclusion of this story by Darleen Turner called A Time to Run.

www.ingramcontent.com/pod-product-compliance
Lightning Source LLC
Chambersburg PA
CBHW021610120626
46545CB00001B/164